toni morrison

A *Modern Fiction Studies* Book

toni morrison
CRITICAL AND THEORETICAL APPROACHES

edited by ————————————————————
NANCY J. PETERSON

THE JOHNS HOPKINS UNIVERSITY PRESS
BALTIMORE AND LONDON

© 1997 The Johns Hopkins University Press
Previously published essays © Purdue Research Foundation, 1993, 1995,
1996, 1997
Nobel Prize Lecture copyright © 1993 by the Nobel Foundation & Knopf,
reprinted by permission of International Creative Management, Inc.
All rights reserved. Published 1997
Printed in the United States of America on acid-free paper
06 05 04 03 02 01 00 99 98 97   5 4 3 2 1

The Johns Hopkins University Press
2715 North Charles Street
Baltimore, Maryland 21218-4319
The Johns Hopkins Press, Ltd., London

Library of Congress Cataloging-in-Publication Data will be found at the end
of this book.
A catalog record for this book is available from the British Library.

ISBN 0-8018-5701-5
ISBN 0-8018-5702-3 (pbk.)

contents

acknowledgments———

I am grateful to the staff of *Modern Fiction Studies* for helping to produce the successful double issue on Toni Morrison that inspired this collection. In particular, I wish to thank Patrick O'Donnell for his enthusiasm and editorial advice, and Steve Merriam and Joseph Steinbach for countless hours of copyediting and proofreading. Deborah Mix deserves special recognition for compiling a comprehensive bibliography for the *MFS* issue on Morrison, which made it considerably less daunting to prepare the selected bibliography for this volume. My keen interest in Morrison would not have developed without the inspiration and influence of Susan Stanford Friedman and Nellie McKay. This volume is dedicated to Aparajita and Marcia, sisters in the struggle, without whom I would not have persevered.

INTRODUCTION: READING TONI MORRISON—FROM THE SEVENTIES TO THE NINETIES

Nancy J. Peterson

Toni Morrison: Critical and Theoretical Approaches builds upon the already substantial body of scholarship published over the past two decades on Toni Morrison's works. Close analyses of Morrison's novels abound, and other kinds of important investigations—comparisons between Morrison and other authors, especially black women writers; examinations of Morrison's place in African-American cultural traditions; analyses of the intertwining of race, class, and gender in her works; to name a few—have made a strong showing in recent years. The essays in this volume advance two lines of inquiry in particular: they situate Morrison's works within the age of contemporary theory, locating her novels and essays in relation to various theories of the post- that have come to proliferate at the end of the twentieth century in America, and they take the process of reading Morrison's works seriously, closely examining the dynamic effects of her language, her rhetorical and narrative choices.

Most of the essays included in this volume are drawn from those published in the past four years in *Modern Fiction Studies*, which devoted a special double issue to Morrison (volume 39, numbers 3–4) serendipitously at the very moment when she was awarded the Nobel Prize for literature in 1993. Eight of the twelve essays included here come from that special issue; two others (those by DeKoven and McKee) appeared in subsequent issues of *MFS*; one has never been published before; and Morrison's Nobel Lecture is included so that the author has a voice in theorizing appropriate perspectives for appreciating the world of her fiction and the richness of her use of language. These essays exemplify the kinds of issues being addressed in the nineties by scholars of Morrison's work and by the profession more broadly. The topics of the individual essays vary, but read together they offer valuable insights into why Morrison has become a much celebrated, widely taught author. Indeed, the volume as a whole demonstrates the ability of Morrison's novels and essays to spark illuminating discussions of the vexing and contradictory cultural conditions of late-twentieth-century America.

Of course, it would have come as quite a surprise to most readers and reviewers twenty-some years ago to think of Morrison's works in these terms. The dramatic shift in the reviewing establishment's view of Morrison as author is registered in the difference between the critical evaluation given to *Sula* in the *New York Times Book Review* in 1973 and the glowing commendation given to *Playing in the Dark* in the same venue in 1992. Reviewer Sara Blackburn in 1973 faulted Morrison for dwelling on black characters and their experiences, for not "transcend[ing] that early and unintentionally limiting classification 'black woman writer' and tak[ing] her place among the most serious, important and talented American novelists now working." Morrison, Blackburn concludes, "is far too talented to remain only a marvelous recorder of the black side of provincial American life."[1] Ironically, in 1992, reviewer Wendy Steiner began by praising the very quality that Blackburn had condemned Morrison for: "Toni Morrison is both a great novelist and the closest thing the country has to a national writer. The fact that she speaks as a woman and a black only enhances her ability to speak as an American" (1). What becomes clear by placing these comments side by side is that the rise of Morrison to national recognition has been motivated not only by the substantial, magnificent body of work she has produced but also by a consequential rethinking of what we mean by the term "American," a rethinking of the relationship between Anglo-American and African-American culture, of the relevance of race to all areas of culture and aesthetics, society and politics.

As an editor, college professor, lecturer, and author, Morrison worked hard—and continues to do so today—to bring about such a transformation. In the early seventies, while she was a senior editor at Random House, she helped some important black writers get published: among them were Gayl Jones, Toni Cade (Bambara), Lucille Clifton, Leon Forrest, and Henry Dumas (posthumously). She was instrumental in the design, editing, and production of *The Black Book*, published in 1974. She promoted black writers, black history, and black culture unceasingly in various essays and interviews. And she worried, with good reason, about black writers and their books

—including her own—receiving not only recognition but the kind of critical attention that would do them justice.

A look back at some of the earliest readings of Morrison's work demonstrates how crucial it was to raise this theoretical issue concerning critical approaches to black writing. The first scholarly article on Morrison did not appear until five years after the publication of *The Bluest Eye* and nearly two years after the publication of *Sula*. In the fall of 1975, a now-defunct publication, *Studies in Black Literature*, published an essay by Joan Bischoff titled "The Novels of Toni Morrison: Studies in Thwarted Sensitivity."[2] Even though her analysis of Morrison's first two novels is brief, Bischoff does call attention to the haunting divisions and moral tensions that contemporary scholars of Morrison's novels find so significant today. But Bischoff's method for reaching her conclusion is questionable. The essay begins with a move typical of several of the early critical articles on Morrison: Bischoff compares Morrison to a "great" canonical author, Henry James. This move is calculated; by comparing Morrison to James, Bischoff justifies her object of study as someone who, though currently unfamiliar to academics of the time, is deserving of their attention. But this comparison is also significant in terms of race. Morrison's work is made to resemble James's in order to suggest that her books speak to more than "just" a black audience. Indeed, Bischoff goes on to invoke the problematic language of universalism to promote Morrison: "Though her characters' problems are conditioned by the black milieu of which she writes, her concerns are broader, universal ones" (21). Hence, in her brief analyses of *The Bluest Eye* and *Sula*, Bischoff focuses on a universal theme—the "thwarted sensitivity" of Pecola and Sula.

Concerned that analogies made between herself and various (white, male) canonical authors were tantamount to imposing the wrong tradition on her novels, Morrison would remark in a 1983 interview to Nellie McKay, "I am not *like* James Joyce; I am not *like* Thomas Hardy; I am not *like* Faulkner" ("An Interview" 152). In this same interview, Morrison asks for the development of a criticism rooted in black culture to make profoundly intricate readings of her novels and those by other black women writers possible.[3]

In 1977, the roots of such a criticism had begun to emerge. The first extensive treatment of Morrison's work by black scholars appeared not in an academic journal, but in the winter 1977 issue of *First World*, a full-color, glossy-paper publication started by a group of black intellectuals who wanted to develop a forum for political and social analysis focused on the concerns of black Americans, and who wanted to emphasize coverage of black culture (music, theater, literature, the visual arts) to give attention to the strength, beauty, and "creative friction" of black Americans.[4] A telling editorial comment prefaces the close readings of Morrison's first two novels: "Although editor and former college professor Toni Morrison is among the most acclaimed of the newer writers, little scholarly or critical analysis of her work has appeared" (34).[5] This comment suggests the importance of having alternative publications in the mid-70's, like *First World*, to promote black authors such as Morrison. More important, though, was the way in which the writers for *First World* approached Morrison's first two novels: both Philip Royster, who analyzed *The Bluest Eye* (and who went on to write two more essays on Morrison's novels), and Odette C. Martin, who focused on *Sula*, compared Morrison's handling of certain issues to other black writers and intellectuals—William Wells Brown, W. E. B. Du Bois, Nella Larsen, Zora Neale Hurston, Gayl Jones, Wallace Thurman. In their methodology and in their nuanced readings of Morrison's novels, Royster and Martin carefully lay the groundwork for a criticism that locates Morrison specifically as an African-American writer—a critical approach that is so familiar to us today that it is perhaps difficult to recognize the struggle that took place to claim and articulate this methodology.

Royster's and Martin's analyses of Morrison's novels are also interesting to revisit because both critics felt compelled to comment on certain potentially troubling aspects of Morrison's novels: for Royster, it is the almost totally unalleviated pessimism he finds in *The Bluest Eye*; for Martin, it is the critical, negative depiction of the black community in *Sula* presented at a time when black activists and scholars were vigorously challenging the all-too-common negative stereotypes of black people circulating in the media and other cultural vehicles. Royster and Martin both convey a strong sense of admiration for Morrison's work, even while they make careful criticisms of her novels. They, in fact, adhere to Morrison's opinion in a 1974 interview that black critics must be unafraid to voice criticism of works by black writers: "I say you must always tell the truth. And I tell you that we are not weak people and we can stand it. I can take it," Morrison emphatically states, arguing that honest criticism is necessary to create significant black art ("Conversation" 6).

The attention Royster and Martin give to the troubling aspects of Morrison's works offers some insight into why her novels took so long to gain the recognition they deserve: they are designed to unsettle readers, sometimes dramatically, to provoke fresh and vital understanding. In another important essay of 1977, Barbara Smith claimed *Sula* as a text filled with such complexities that an entirely new mode of critical thought would have to be theorized in order to understand it, a mode that she called "black feminist criticism." Published in *Conditions*, a lesbian-feminist journal, "Toward a Black Feminist Criticism" set forth Smith's controversial analysis of *Sula* as a black lesbian text, a spirited reading which raised not only eyebrows but also consciousness of the inadequacies of current approaches, not just to *Sula* but to other texts by black women writers.

Smith's essay led to significant interrogations of black feminism as a distinctive perspective, including Deborah McDowell's "New Directions for Black Feminist Criticism," which appeared in *Black American Literature Forum* in 1980 and analyzed *Sula* to take issue with several points of Smith's definition of black feminist criticism.[6] The three years between the publication of Smith's and McDowell's essays witnessed a tremendous paradigm shift influencing not only the reception of Morrison's work but the work of all black women writers. While Smith in 1977 had to argue for recognition of the category of black feminist criticism by demonstrating the inadequacies of criticism written by white reviewers and black male commentators, McDowell in 1980 was able to assume the viability of the category and thus was able to devote the substance of her argument to defining the practice of black feminist criticism. By the end of 1980, complex analyses of Morrison's novels had begun to appear in a number of important black and ethnic studies venues— *UMOJA*, *Black American Literature Forum*, *CLA Journal*, *Black Scholar*, *Minority Voices*, *Obsidian*, *MELUS*—and in 1980, Barbara Christian published her benchmark study of black women writers, *Black Women Novelists: The Development of a Tradition, 1892–1976*, which included a considerable discussion of *The Bluest Eye* and *Sula*.

The evolution of a black feminist critical discourse meant that the inattention surrounding Morrison's first novels in the mid-70s had changed dramatically by the beginning of the next decade.[7] The glowing reception given to *Song of Solomon*, published in 1977, and to *Tar Baby*, published in 1981, fed these developments in criticism, leading to Morrison's emergence as a nationally known and acclaimed author.[8] Not surprisingly, then, Morrison's novels began to attract a variety of critical approaches, including Elizabeth Abel's 1981 influential feminist study of the dynamics of female friendships in texts written by women, Hortense Spillers's groundbreaking black feminist study of *Sula* in 1983, and Margaret Homans's 1983 feminist analysis of women's relation to language, "'Her Very Own Howl': The Ambiguities of Representation in Recent Women's Fiction," which took its primary title from *Sula*. As the decade unfolded, Morrison's works were discussed in book-length studies of African-American literature, most notably by Keith Byerman, Jane Campbell, and Melvin Dixon, and studies of black women writers specifically, such as Mari Evans's indispensable *Black Women Writers* (1984), Barbara Christian's highly acclaimed *Black Feminist Criticism* (1985), and Marjorie Pryse and Hortense Spillers's important collection, *Conjuring: Black Women, Fiction and Literary Tradition* (1985). Also, in 1985 the very first book devoted in its entirety to Morrison was published, Bessie W. Jones and Audrey L. Vinson's *The World of Toni Morrison: Explorations in Literary Criticism*. An obvious labor of love, Jones and Vinson's book (like several of the earliest black feminist collections) was printed using their own typescript. The book includes essays on various topics in Morrison's novels and study questions for teachers to use in the classroom, in addition to an important interview with Morrison.

From Jones and Vinson's book onward, scholarly work on Morrison has increased exponentially in terms of the sheer number of articles, book chapters, and books, as well as the variety of approaches taken—a diversity and abundance represented in the selected bibliography included at the end of this collection. Given the profusion of such scholarship by even the mid-80s, it is no wonder Morrison took the opportunity to comment upon the (in)appropriateness of some of these approaches. In "Rootedness: The Ancestor as Foundation" (1984), she writes, "My general disappointment in some of the criticism that my work has received has nothing to do with approval. It has something to do with the vocabulary used in order to describe these things. I don't like to find my books condemned as bad or praised as good, when that condemnation or that praise is based on criteria from other paradigms. I would much prefer that they were dismissed or embraced based on the success of their accomplishment within the culture out of which I write" (342). This comment might be taken to mean that Morrison claims only African-American culture as the relevant context for her work. But her continuing meditation on the question of cultural affiliation, on the relation of black and white America, would coalesce in a spectacular reading of Melville's *Moby Dick* and the ideology of whiteness in her Tanner Lecture of 1989, "Unspeakable Things Unspoken: The Afro-American Presence in American Literature," and in her analyses of Cather, Poe, Twain, and Hemingway in her Massey Lectures at Harvard University, published as *Playing in the Dark: Whiteness and the Literary Imagination* in 1992.[9]

Morrison's examination of the ways in which ideologies of whiteness are founded on "an American Africanism—a fabricated brew of
darkness, otherness, alarm, and desire that is uniquely American"
(*Playing* 38) suggests that blackness and whiteness are mutually
constitutive: thinking in terms of race is always already thinking in
terms of binary differentials, so that thinking about blackness *or*
whiteness in America automatically invokes the other racial-cultural
signifier. Indeed, the momentous recognition given to both *Beloved*
(1987) and *Jazz* (1992), two novels of the trilogy that Morrison is
currently completing, indicates that these historical novels speak
powerfully to reconsiderations of *both* African-American *and* American history. As the volume she edited on the Clarence Thomas–
Anita Hill confrontation and her recent volume on the O. J. Simpson
trial demonstrate, Morrison has become an increasingly important
voice of commentary on the absurdities and vicissitudes of American socio-political culture in the nineties. The essays collected in
this book give a full view of this extraordinary author, combining
theoretical, aesthetic, critical, historical, and political perspectives
to read the exquisite complexities of Morrison's novels and essays.

The essays that follow are arranged in four sections. The title of
the first group of essays, "Practicing Black Feminist Criticism in the
Nineties," pays tribute to the body of criticism most influential in
providing substantive readings of Morrison's novels and suggests
promising new directions for exploration. One of the most heated
discussions in the field concerns who practices black feminist criticism (only black—female—feminists?) and what kinds of analysis it
entails (the study of black women's writing only? the study of race,
gender, and class in any text?). To argue that black feminist critics
are the only ones attuned to the issues at hand in black women's
writing is to risk lapsing into a problematic biologism or essentialism. But to argue that the identity of the critic is totally irrelevant
would be to deny the particular insights that can come from the
experience of living as a black woman. The essays in this section
(two authored by black women, one by a white woman) follow the
middle ground Valerie Smith has identified for the field. In "Black
Feminist Theory and the Representation of the 'Other'," Smith defines "black feminist theory" inclusively as "theory written (or practiced) by black feminists" and as "a way of reading inscriptions of
race (particularly but not exclusively blackness), gender (particularly
but not exclusively womanhood), and class in modes of cultural expression" (39).

Barbara Christian's essay opens new directions for black feminist criticism by comparing Toni Morrison and Virginia Woolf, two authors who might be seen as having little to say to one another and who, in fact, have not been considered extensively side by side before. Christian's concept of "layered rhythms" allows her to read productively the striking similarities and contrasts of Woolf and Morrison as women writers. Despite being from different national cultures and historical moments, Morrison and Woolf faced similar obstacles and shared similar goals along the axis of gender. But differences in race and class matter, as Christian's remarkable analysis demonstrates. By bringing Morrison and Woolf together and examining the layers of contextual and material circumstances that distinguish them from one another, as well as the rhythms of fictional impulses that they share, Christian models a black feminist scholarship in which gender, race, and class are mutually illuminating.

Patricia McKee, like Christian, concentrates on the interdependent inscriptions of gender, race, and class in Morrison, but directs her attention specifically to *Sula*. McKee examines *Sula* the novel and Sula the character from a deconstructive perspective to bring into focus the powerful realization in Morrison's novel of "experiences of missing that are particular components of African-American life and, more particularly, of African-American women's lives." Like Christian, McKee is always careful to mark the discontinuities of her juxtaposition, as she distinguishes instances in her finely nuanced analysis of *Sula* where Morrison's project diverges from Derridean deconstruction.

Judylyn Ryan's essay on *Tar Baby* takes a critical angle similar to McKee's in looking at the missed experiences of Jadine, the central black female character of the novel. But rather than using French literary theory as her medium, Ryan turns to W. E. B. Du Bois's concept of double-consciousness to analyze the multifaceted conflicts between Jadine and Son that lie at the heart of Morrison's novel. Bringing Du Bois and Morrison into dialogue with one another also allows Ryan to extend Du Bois's theorizing in at least two significant ways: Ryan argues that Morrison's novel demonstrates the necessity of considering gender and class identifications along with Du Bois's emphasis on race; and she argues that Morrison's novel shows how Du Bois's concept of "double-consciousness," which describes a debilitating conflict between worldviews, can be transformed into an empowering "double-vision," in which competing visions are accompanied by a sense of choice and agency.

McKee's and Ryan's referencing of very different kinds of theory leads into the central issue of the second cluster of essays, "Morrison and Theories of the Post-." The essays in this section candidly probe the relation and relevance of current theoretical -isms—particularly postmodernism and poststructuralism—to Morrison's fiction and essays. In an often-cited essay, "The Race for Theory," Barbara Christian voices skepticism about the appropriateness of such theories for reading texts written by black women and by other radical or oppositional authors, because these theories have been constructed in almost every case without any reference to such texts. And because theory, by its very definition, is interested in abstractions, it tends toward the "monolithic" and the "monotheistic" (58) unless it is rooted in practice. As this qualification suggests, Christian's evaluation of theory in the essay is quite subtle: while the title of the essay critiques "the race for theory" among ambitious academics who want to get published, it also contains a marvelous pun on "race" to claim a particular connection of African Americans to theory.

The essays included here by Rafael Pérez-Torres, Marianne DeKoven, and Dwight A. McBride offer a productive interplay between theories drawn from the "outside" and theoretical positions generated from within Morrison's texts. Pérez-Torres examines the ways in which *Beloved* as a postmodern novel calls into question the excesses of postmodernism. While Morrison's text shares a pleasure in linguistic wordplay, pastiche, and metanarrative with quintessential postmodern novels written by Donald Barthelme, John Barth, and Thomas Pynchon, Pérez-Torres argues that, unlike these other texts, *Beloved* leads not to metafictional fantasy but brings us back into connection with the historical real. Grounding his analysis of *Beloved*'s postmodernism in the material conditions and historical specificities of African Americans, Pérez-Torres reads postmodern tropes such as "absence" literally; his approach to *Beloved* valuably outlines the terms on which our understanding of multiculturalism in relation to postmodernism must proceed.[10]

DeKoven, like Pérez-Torres, approaches *Beloved* in terms of postmodernism, but she focuses on postmodernity as the condition of living in a post-utopian America. Pairing Morrison's novel with E. L. Doctorow's *The Waterworks*—both set and written in the aftermath of utopian eras in America—DeKoven examines the visions of utopia in each novel and shows how those visions are destroyed by historical circumstances. These utopian moments, even though they are ultimately defeated or discredited, persist in postmodernity, DeKoven poignantly concludes, to register a desire for political change—an end to oppression and inequity—and for transcendence.

The difficulty of articulating a viable political stance within the contradictions of contemporary American society and culture is an issue that McBride's essay also addresses. Concerned about the implications of current theories of deconstruction and poststructuralism for the practices and claims of African-American scholars and writers, McBride turns to Morrison's renowned essay, "Unspeakable Things Unspoken: The Afro-American Presence in American Literature," to identify the ways in which her rhetoric negotiates between poststructuralism and essentialism. Studying Morrison's rhetorical and discursive strategies, McBride impressively argues, is crucial for understanding the complex and shifting grounds on which African-American intellectuals today must "authorize their critical voices."

McBride's emphasis on contemporary cultural concerns anticipates the focus of the essays in part three of this volume, grouped under the heading "Narratives as Cultural Interventions." Morrison's own work as a cultural critic sets a precedent for this approach to her novels; in the introduction she wrote for the collection she edited on Clarence Thomas and Anita Hill, for instance, Morrison shows how valuable it can be to read a political narrative alongside a literary narrative to examine contemporary cultural conditions. The title of her introduction, in fact, contains a critical double-meaning: "Friday on the Potomac" refers to Friday, October 11, 1991, when both Hill and Thomas spoke before the Senate Judiciary Committee; it also refers to Friday, the character in Daniel Defoe's *Robinson Crusoe* who is made to serve his master's interests and speak in his master's language for so long that he loses the ability to speak his own mother tongue or to act on behalf of his own people and culture. The essays in this section follow Morrison's method by reading the novels *Beloved* and *Jazz* as a means of intervening in the contentious debates and crises around issues of race, history, and canons in American and African-American culture today.

Richard C. Moreland productively sets Mark Twain's *The Adventures of Huckleberry Finn* next to Morrison's *Beloved*. Moreland argues that as Morrison's text reworks and reimagines Huck's story, particularly in Amy Denver's and Sethe's encounter, it "draws out and expands on conflicts and fears just at the limits of *Huckleberry Finn*'s reach." Reading Twain's novel next to Morrison's, Moreland ultimately concludes, enables us to recognize a particularly grievous American cultural crisis: the difficulty of narrating and making connections among our individual, isolated stories and identities.

Caroline M. Woidat's essay complements Moreland's approach

by examining *Beloved*'s relation to *The Scarlet Letter*. Woidat draws parallels between the antebellum racial politics that inform Hawthorne's novel and the contemporary debates about multiculturalism that surround Morrison's novel. Linking Hawthorne's emphasis on national consensus at the expense of racial difference to the efforts of Allan Bloom and E. D. Hirsch Jr. to define a monolithic, homogenous American canon, Woidat incisively locates the ways in which Morrison's novel resists these efforts to consolidate national "American" identity by suppressing racial, cultural, or gender difference.

While Moreland and Woidat focus on *Beloved*, my essay turns to *Jazz*, and reads Morrison's most recent novel as offering an intervention into the writing of African-American history. *Jazz* is a historical novel with an unconventional historicity and an unconventional form; my essay analyzes these aspects of Morrison's novel to argue that it works toward a model of African-American history aligned with jazz—a model that conceives of black history not as a fixed record of past events, but as a dynamic, collective, and improvised narrative.

The final paragraphs of *Jazz*, in which the book itself confesses "her" love for the reader, set the stage for part four of this collection, "Readerly and Writerly Perspectives." The essays included here come from readers of Morrison as well as from the writer herself, and they revel in the aesthetic and intellectual pleasures involved in reading works written in language that dazzles on every page. Over the years, Morrison has made comments that suggest that writing and reading must be linked to produce strong novels. To Jessica Harris for *Essence* magazine in 1976, Morrison admitted, "I didn't want to be a writer; I wanted to be a reader" ("I Will" 90). In her 1983 interview with Claudia Tate, Morrison elaborated, "I wrote *Sula* and *The Bluest Eye* because they were the books I had wanted to read. No one had written them yet, so I wrote them" ("Toni Morrison" 161). Elsewhere, Morrison has commented that one of her goals as a writer is "to have the reader work *with* the author in the construction of the book" ("Rootedness" 341). Intimacy emanates from the interrelationship of reading and writing: the writer is no longer an isolato but extends an invitation to readers to join with her in the text, and the reader is not merely a passive consumer of words on the page, but an active participant in the creation of the book.

The essays by James Phelan and Eusebio L. Rodrigues in this section testify to the pleasures and challenges of reading Morrison's fiction and her vibrant language. Phelan describes his own compelling experience of reading *Beloved* and trying to make sense of the various mysteries in the novel, especially the enigmatic phrases of the last two pages. This reading experience is so dynamic and profound that Phelan theorizes a new approach to literary analysis—"rhetorical reader-response criticism"—to do it justice. Like Phelan, Rodrigues finds the experience of reading Morrison so inspiring that he improvises a critical language worthy of the jazzy language and form of *Jazz*. Reading the novel as if it were a musical score, Rodrigues celebrates Morrison's ability to turn language into a musical instrument that trumpets the desires, disappointments, and triumphs of African Americans.

Morrison herself has the last word on relations between readers, writers, and language. In her Nobel Prize Lecture of 1993, Morrison emphasizes that language is a vital cultural and political resource. As she makes eloquently clear, language has the frightening potential to be misused, to censor, to oppress, but given the proper respect and devotion, language also has the power to inspire human beings toward love and liberation.

The essays collected in *Toni Morrison: Critical and Theoretical Approaches* bear witness to the powerful effects of Morrison's language, her fiction, her vision. They represent the most recent approaches to this remarkable author in order to inspire new appreciation of and future investigations into her writing—writing which is, as she once said the best work by black artists must be, "unquestionably political and irrevocably beautiful at the same time" ("Rootedness" 345).

NOTES

[1]Blackburn's review of *Sula* is so egregious that Barbara Smith used it as one of her examples to argue for the need to develop a distinct black feminist criticism.

[2]*Studies in Black Literature*, a publication of the Department of English at Mary Washington College in Fredericksburg, Virginia, began publishing in spring 1970 and ceased with volume 8, issue number 3, in 1977.

[3]The emphasis here should be on "black" *and* "culture." Morrison's comments from various interviews indicate her dissatisfaction with sociological readings of her novels, which tend to read blackness as pathology. By emphasizing culture in these interviews, she insists that critics look at her novels as artistic and imaginative works, and not as direct, unmediated reflections of black life in America. See Chikwenye Okonjo Ogunyemi's 1977 essay on *The Bluest Eye* for an example of an early sociological reading of Morrison.

[4]I have taken this description from the editors' statement on the inside cover of the inaugural issue: January/February 1977. The editors were Hoyt W. Fuller and Carole A. Parks, who had edited *Black World* until it folded in 1976. Among the

initial supporters, both editorially and financially, for *First World* were such luminaries as Maya Angelou, Houston A. Baker Jr., Toni Cade Bambara, Eugenia Collier, Ossie Davis and Ruby Dee, Mari Evans, Addison Gayle Jr., June Jordan, Eleanor Traylor, Darwin T. Turner, and Sherley Anne Williams. Despite their efforts, *First World*, which began as a bimonthly publication in January 1977, was publishing as a quarterly by the end of 1977, and ceased publishing altogether sometime in 1980–1981.

[5]Along with analyses of *The Bluest Eye* and *Sula*, this issue included a review of *Song of Solomon*, which had just been released.

[6]McDowell reprints a slightly revised version of this essay in her recent book, *"The Changing Same": Black Women's Literature, Criticism, and Theory*, and appends commentary in which she rethinks some of her assertions from that essay and suggests that she was too quick to criticize Smith's efforts; see 16–23.

[7]Morrison's dismissal of black feminist criticism in 1984 might suggest that my claim here is problematic, so I want to take a moment to set her comments in context. She writes in "Rootedness: The Ancestor as Foundation": "I don't have much to say about that [the necessity to develop a specific Black feminist model of critical inquiry] except that I think there is more danger in it than fruit, because any model of criticism or evaluation that excludes males from it is as hampered as any model of criticism of Black literature that excludes women from it" (344). It may be that Morrison was tired of the ways in which black women's writing was interpreted by some vociferous commentators as disparaging black men, and she simply did not want to participate in a battle of the genders among black men and women. She also has made it clear in many interviews that she adores black men, that she lavishes a considerable amount of attention on the male characters in her novels, so her dismissal of black feminist criticism in 1984 might be a way of insisting that readers of her fiction carefully attend to both black male and black female characters. But what is also clear from the many essays and interviews she has written and given over the years is Morrison's deep and abiding ties to black women as a distinct group; see, for instance, her article in *Essence*, "A Knowing So Deep," which includes a sisterly "letter" to all black women. Given Morrison's repeated claims of allegiance to black women's concerns, I would argue that despite her remarks in the 1984 essay, black feminist criticism provided (and continues to provide) extremely perceptive readings of Morrison's novels.

[8]This recognition even had a visual component: in 1981 Morrison became the first black woman since Zora Neale Hurston in 1943 to be featured on the cover of a major U.S. magazine when *Newsweek* put her on the cover of the March 30th issue, celebrating the publication of *Tar Baby*.

[9]The full titles of these lectures give some indication of Morrison's present stature in the academy and her prominence as a cultural commentator: Morrison delivered the Tanner Lecture on Human Values in 1989 at the University of Michigan; in 1990 she delivered the William E. Massey Sr. Lectures in the History of American Civilization at Harvard. Denise Heinze reports that Harvard University Press, mindful of Morrison's stature, decided on an initial print run for *Playing in the Dark* of 25,000 copies rather than the typical 1,500 copies (2).

[10]See his essay in *Cultural Critique* for an elaboration of the theoretical relation between multiculturalism and postmodernism.

WORKS CITED

Abel, Elizabeth. "(E)Merging Identities: The Dynamics of Female Friendship in Contemporary Fiction by Women." *Signs* 6 (1981): 413–435.

Bischoff, Joan. "The Novels of Toni Morrison: Studies in Thwarted Sensitivity." *Studies in Black Literature* 6.3 (1975): 21–23.

Blackburn, Sara. "You Still Can't Go Home Again." Rev. of *Sula*, by Toni Morrison. *New York Times Book Review* 30 Dec. 1973: 3.

Byerman, Keith E. *Fingering the Jagged Grain: Tradition and Form in Recent Black Fiction*. Athens: U of Georgia P, 1985.

Campbell, Jane. *Mythic Black Fiction: The Transformation of History*. Knoxville: U of Tennessee P, 1986.

Christian, Barbara. *Black Feminist Criticism*. New York: Pergamon, 1985.

——. *Black Women Novelists: The Development of a Tradition, 1892–1976*. Westport, CT: Greenwood, 1980.

——. "The Race for Theory." *Cultural Critique* 6 (1987): 51–63.

Dixon, Melvin. *Ride Out the Wilderness: Geography and Identity in Afro-American Literature*. Urbana: U of Illinois P, 1987.

Evans, Mari, ed. *Black Women Writers (1950–1980): A Critical Evaluation*. New York: Anchor-Doubleday, 1984.

Heinze, Denise. *The Dilemma of "Double-Consciousness": Toni Morrison's Novels*. Athens: U of Georgia P, 1993.

Homans, Margaret. " 'Her Very Own Howl': The Ambiguities of Representation in Recent Women's Fiction." *Signs* 9 (1983): 186–205.

Jones, Bessie W., and Audrey L. Vinson. *The World of Toni Morrison: Explorations in Literary Criticism*. Dubuque, IA: Kendall-Hunt, 1985.

McDowell, Deborah. *"The Changing Same": Black Women's Literature, Criticism, and Theory*. Bloomington: Indiana UP, 1995.

——. "New Directions for Black Feminist Criticism." *Black American Literature Forum* 14 (1980): 153–159.

Morrison, Toni. "Conversation with Alice Childress and Toni Morrison." 1974. Taylor-Guthrie 3–9.

——. "I Will Always Be a Writer." Interview with Jessica Harris. *Essence* Dec. 1976: 54, 56, 90–92.

——. "An Interview with Toni Morrison." With Nellie McKay. 1983. Taylor-Guthrie 138–155.

——. "Introduction: Friday on the Potomac." *Race-ing Justice, En-gendering Power: Essays on Anita Hill, Clarence Thomas, and the Construction of Social Reality*. Ed. Toni Morrison. New York: Pantheon, 1992. vii–xxx.

——. "A Knowing So Deep." *Essence* May 1985: 230.

——. *Playing in the Dark: Whiteness and the Literary Imagination*. Cambridge: Harvard UP, 1992.

——. "Rootedness: The Ancestor as Foundation." Evans 339–345.

——. "Toni Morrison." Interview with Claudia Tate. 1983. Taylor-Guthrie 156–170.

——. "Unspeakable Things Unspoken: The Afro-American Presence in American Literature." *Michigan Quarterly Review* 28 (1989): 1–34.

Ogunyemi, Chikwenye Okonjo. "Order and Disorder in Toni Morrison's *The Bluest Eye*." *Critique* 19 (1977): 112–120.

Pérez-Torres, Rafael. "Nomads and Migrants: Negotiating a Multicultural Postmodernism." *Cultural Critique* 26 (1993–94): 161–189.

Pryse, Marjorie, and Hortense J. Spillers, eds. *Conjuring: Black Women, Fiction and Literary Tradition*. Bloomington: Indiana UP, 1985.

Royster, Philip, and Odette C. Martin. "The Novels of Toni Morrison." *First World* 1.4 (1977): 34–44.

Smith, Barbara. "Toward a Black Feminist Criticism." *Conditions: Two* (1977): 25–44. Rpt. in *The New Feminist Criticism: Essays on Women, Literature, and Theory*. Ed. Elaine Showalter. New York: Pantheon, 1985. 168–185.

Smith, Valerie. "Black Feminist Theory and the Representation of the 'Other.'" *Changing Our Own Words: Essays on Criticism, Theory, and Writing by Black Women*. Ed. Cheryl A. Wall. New Brunswick: Rutgers UP, 1989. 38–57.

Spillers, Hortense. "A Hateful Passion, A Lost Love." *Feminist Studies* 9 (1983): 293–323.

Steiner, Wendy. "The Clearest Eye." Rev. of *Playing in the Dark*, by Toni Morrison. *New York Times Book Review* 5 April 1992: 1, 25, 29.

Taylor-Guthrie, Danille, ed. *Conversations with Toni Morrison*. Jackson: UP of Mississippi, 1984.

part one

PRACTICING BLACK FEMINIST CRITICISM IN THE NINETIES

LAYERED RHYTHMS: VIRGINIA WOOLF AND TONI MORRISON

Barbara T. Christian

> Writing and reading are not all that
> distinct for a writer. Both exercises
> require being alert and ready for un-
> accountable beauty, for the intricate-
> ness or simple elegance of the writer's
> imagination, for the world that imagi-
> nation evokes. Both require being
> mindful of the places where imagi-
> nation sabotages itself, locks its own
> gates, pollutes its vision. Writing and
> reading mean being aware of the wri-
> ter's notions of risk and safety, the
> serene achievement of, or sweaty fight
> for, meaning and response-ability.
> —Toni Morrison, *Playing in the Dark*

I SEE YOUR FACE, TONI MORRISON, possibly the best novelist in America today, when people ask, "What does it mean that you wrote your M.A. thesis in the early fifties on *suicide* in the works of William Faulkner and Virginia Woolf?"[1] Do such people want to inflict the "anxiety of influence" on you? Or perhaps is it that they want to be sure that your writing will be seen as a part of the Great Western tradition? What is the purpose of securing a link between you and William Faulkner, as Harold Bloom did in his introduction to an edition of collected essays on your work? Or between you and Virginia Woolf, as the program of the Third Annual Conference on Virginia Woolf suggests?[2] Why must you be studied in relation to such writers, icons of twentieth-century European and Anglo-American literature? Is it that as an African American woman writer, clearly a "genius," you must have a Western white literary father and mother? Not just any white father, but one such as Faulkner, who, as Ralph Ellison has put it in *Shadow and Act*, was one of the few Anglo-American writers to fight out "the moral problem [of Negroes in America] which was repressed after the nineteenth century" (43). Not just any white mother, but one such as Virginia Woolf, who is now clearly situated in the canon: as modernist, satisfying the twentieth-century Great Books requirement;[3] as feminist, satisfying the needs of twentieth-century women scholars.[4] You have commented on this tendency among critics. Your own words are a cautionary preface to our project:

My general disappointment in some of the criticism that my work has received has nothing to do with approval. It has something to do with the vocabulary used in order to describe these things. I don't like to find my books condemned or embraced as good, when that condemnation or that praise is based on criteria from other paradigms. I would much prefer that they were dismissed or embraced based on the success of their accomplishment within the culture out of which I write. ("Rootedness" 342)

I am an African American woman critic who wrote about your work before you were celebrated and who has, despite critical trends, maintained my sense of your writing as an African American woman. Please allow me to invent a fiction as you do in your novels—in this case, a fiction about you and Virginia Woolf—for fictions can be beneficial, imaginative, even transforming. Because I know this is an invention and I worry about "notions of risk and safety," I will rely primarily on your words and Virginia's in the charting of my invention. I am inspired by your and Virginia's different, yet related projects—layered rhythms I call them.

I see you in the early fifties, a colored graduate student when colored meant black, pacing yourself through Cornell, squinting your eye at that famous suicide point on the campus where too many students took their lives. I see you, a colored girl who, a few years before, had changed her name from Chloe (a name in America associated with blacks) to Toni (an androgynous name), because even folks at Howard University had trouble pronouncing it. I find that an instance of serendipity, for Virginia Woolf used the name Chloe in her fictional representation of Mary Carmichael's novel in *A Room of One's Own*—"Chloe liked Olivia," pointing to Shakespearean characters, even as she disrupted bourgeois heterosexuality (86).

Yes, yes, I do see you, assessing the wintry whiteness at Cornell. But you are used to whiteness. You are from Lorain, Ohio, where possibly your father, like Claudia's daddy in your first novel, *The Bluest Eye* (1970), became, in the winter, a "Wolf killer turned hawk fighter, [who] worked night and day to keep one from the door and the other from under the windowsills" (47). Yet how different this wintry whiteness is in this New England enclave of privilege. A graduate student, a black graduate student, a black female graduate student—what was there for you at Cornell? Years later, you would say about your stay there that "if [your] ancestors could go through slavery, you guessed you could get through that" ("Interview").

I understand what you mean. For I went to one of those graduate schools in English. But at least Columbia was in New York City, with its many colored folk, and I was there in the mid-sixties. Still I was one of a few blacks, possibly the only black woman (oh no, a black female West Indian, are you from Jamaica? No—from the Virgin Islands) graduate student. So I can see you pondering wintry Cornell. What do we want in these places to which we came, so far away from home—from Lorain Ohio, from St. Thomas Virgin Islands, from wherever, a black wherever.

Why are you, in 1953, majoring in English? I can see your parents asking you, "What are you going to do with that degree? To study English? At Cornell? You're so bright. Why don't you become a doctor, a lawyer, a Credit to Your Race?" But on some visceral level, you can't explain, you love language—the shapes of stories, the inheritance from your parents, who were great storytellers, but did not necessarily understand themselves as artists, nor what they bequeathed to you (*Toni Morrison*).

You want—what do you desire? Chaucer, Shakespeare certainly, but where do you dwell in their words? You'd certainly heard of African American writers. You'd taken a course at Howard during your undergraduate years with Alain Locke, that elder African American critic, who'd helped to make the Harlem Renaissance, who'd seen the beginnings of the Richard Wright era.[5] You would say, in one of your interviews, that reading much of the African American literature you encountered in classrooms had left you feeling bereft, for it did not seem to be directed to you, a black person, but seemed to be addressed to an other. You felt "bereft" (*Toni Morrison*). You "needed yourself" in language. How else to fulfill that need, and still be a Credit to The Race, except to go to graduate school in English?

Nineteen-fifty-three is New Criticism at its height: the text is all. No world lies outside the text. The text has nothing to do with race or even cultural specificity. You are reading not only Chaucer and Shakespeare, those ancient venerables from Europe, but also American writers—Hawthorne, Melville—for the American academy is finally admitting American writers into the canon. Even Faulkner, though he is still alive, might just have made it into the curriculum. Like so many of the few African Americans in literature, you will focus on Faulkner's works, a code even ten years later in the 1960s for those of us who wanted to study blacks in literature. There was no such thing as African American literature—studying Faulkner was what they call in the music business, a cover. Still, although blacks appeared to be absent from "American" literature, you sensed the ways in which the African presence in America erupted in the works of Hawthorne and Melville, a subject you would write about in 1992, in your book of literary criticism *Playing in the Dark*.

But what about Virginia Woolf? Not an American who was confronted with a black presence, whether she repressed it or not (although her antics in the Abyssinian Debacle so much discussed by Woolf scholars needs to be thought about from a black perspective).[6] Not a venerable British ancient, but an early twentieth-century British woman who, after all, had insisted in an essay that the reason why there was no female Shakespeare was because Shakespeare's sister did not have 500 pounds a year and a room of her own. Mrs. Woolf did not come to a writing career easily. As was true of her times, her so-educated father, Leslie Stephen, discriminated between her and her brothers. While they were allowed to go to Oxford, she had to stay at home. But you, Toni Morrison, in the tradition of black families, precisely because you were a daughter, were encouraged to go to college. How else might you survive, without the brawn of a black man, the sentiment that circumscribed white women?[7] Like so many black women, "[you] had nothing to fall back on; not maleness, not whiteness, not ladyhood, not anything. And out of the profound desolation of [your] reality [you] may well have invented [your]self" (Morrison, qtd. in Giddings 15).

Unlike Virginia, you would become a mother, and for much of your adult life a single mother, who would write, not in a room of your own, but with the interruptions of children and the jobs necessary for your and their survival, writing on scraps of paper at subway stops ("Interview"). You would see motherhood as "liberating," as your "best" self, for your children respected those parts of you that had little to do with society's demands, since they were fresh, not quite yet socialized. And through their eyes, you could see the world through an imagination not yet tainted by stereotypes ("Toni Morrison," Moyers 60). So different from the Virginia you would meet in 1953, who because of the incest she experienced in her childhood was concerned that having children would stifle her creativity and exacerbate her bouts of depression. One of the major themes of your work would be the complexities of motherhood, the liberation and restrictions of that role for African American women: how thick that mother love was, yet how complex, how beautiful, even monumental that role could be. So different from Virginia, who was living everyday with her fecund sister, Vanessa, a source of some sibling conflict.[8]

Although from different cultures and times, you and Virginia did face problems as women writers. While Virginia had to "kill the angel in the house" (Gilbert and Gubar 17), you, Toni, had to "kill the mammy in the Big House." Virginia was responding to the fact that women were not expected to write, and when they did write, their tone "admitted that [they] were only women or protesting that [they] were as good as any man" (Woolf, *Room* 80). When women wrote, they were still expected to write in specific ways about specific themes—that is, within the romance genre—about love, marriage, manners. Virginia did have some woman writers to whom she could refer: Jane Austen, for example, who had brought the comedy of manners to a peak of perfection. But you, Toni Morrison, could not in 1953, in spite of society's stereotype of the black woman as a mammy, know about any African American women writers of any substance. Before the 1970s few scholars, even of African American literature, saw women as writers or even knew that there existed a strong line of African American women. In fact, it is unlikely that you read inside or outside the classroom any African American women of the past except, perhaps, Gwendolyn Brooks, who won a Pulitzer in 1951. You had not read the domestic allegories, as Claudia Tate calls them, in the sentimental fiction of nineteenth-century African American writers like Frances Harper and Pauline Hopkins, or that great African American romance, Zora Neale Hurston's *Their Eyes Were Watching God* (1937). You could claim no maternal ancestors, although, of course, the stereotype of black women when they did appear would be as mammies in white fiction, "mammies" of a sort, in the black fiction of Du Bois, Wright or Ellison.[9]

What did Virginia mean when she used the term, "woman writer"? Was she speaking about you? No wonder, in order to write as a woman, you would focus so much on the subject of motherlove, while Virginia, because of her specific cultural inheritance, had to disrupt the European script of romance imposed on women.[10] Because of your folk's history, you did not have the same need as Virginia did to "kill the angel in the house." In contrast to Virginia's deconstruction of the nuclear family, your novels usually include a three-woman household recalling an older mythic familial structure. Thus, you would say in an interview that

> It seems to me that there's an enormous difference in the writing of black and white women. . . . Black women seem able to combine the nest and the adventure. They don't see conflicts in certain areas as do white women. They are both safe harbor and ship; they are both inn and trail. We, black women, do both. We don't find these places, these roles, mutually exclusive. That's one of the differences. ("Toni Morrison," Tate 122)

How to find a sentence for that difference in representing gender and race would become one of your abiding theoretical concerns.

But I've gone ahead of myself. What I want to know is how you got to know Virginia. Today everyone reads her. But this is 1994, 20 years after the Virginia Woolf fever of the 1970s. And you went to graduate school in the 1950s. Did someone just happen to mention her? Did you have one of those crazy teachers who insisted on exposing his students to odd writers? How would I know? I'm reaching across time from 1994 to you in 1953. Even in 1965, some 10 years later when I was a graduate student at Columbia, Virginia Woolf was still a suspect writer. Certainly her books were, mostly, out of print in the early fifties and were included in few college syllabi (Wilson 294). Yet, in 1955, you completed a thesis on an aspect of her work.

You are in graduate school at Cornell in 1953. That was the year that Eric Auerbach's classic *Mimesis* was translated into English. In it he included a long critique of an out-of-print book called *To the Lighthouse* by Virginia Woolf, an upper-class British woman who killed herself. Maybe one of your teachers' discussions of Auerbach's book in one of your classes led you to Virginia Woolf's book. After all, a twentieth-century woman writer was a relatively unusual item in your curriculum.

But what did you want with the work of a woman who killed herself? You know the way black people feel about suicide. As your narrator commented in your novel *Sula*, the black people of the Bottom feel that suicide is "beneath them" (9). Yet you were obviously intrigued by the idea of suicide, for that's what you focused on in your thesis. You'd clearly read *Mrs. Dalloway*, which was published in 1925 and in which Septimus Warren Smith kills himself, a victim of shell shock from World War I. So like, yet unlike, Shadrack in your novel *Sula*, published some 50 years later, who too is suffering from World War I shell shock. But your Shadrack does not kill himself. Rather "Blasted and permanently astonished by the events of 1917, he had returned to Medallion, handsome but ravaged" (7):

It was not death or dying that frightened him, but the unexpectedness of both. In sorting it all out, he hit on the notion that if one day a year were devoted to it, everybody could get it out of the way and the rest of the year would be safe and free. In this manner he instituted National Suicide Day. (14)

Shadrack turns shell shock and the possibility of suicide into a rite, which in turn is adopted by his community so that "they absorbed it into their thoughts, into their language, into their lives" (15). While the inhabitants of the Bottom might not understand Shadrack's experience in the war, ironically a misrecognition that will ultimately result in their extinction as community, they do understand the workings of rituals in staving off irrational catastrophic events like racism and war.

Like Virginia's works, your novels are bracketed by war—in your case the major wars in which America engaged—the Civil War in *Beloved*, World War I in *Sula* and *Jazz*, World War II in *The Bluest Eye* and *Sula*. Neither your works nor Virginia's are specifically about the action of war itself so much as they are about the effects of such tumult on the psyches of your respective communities. Virginia was an adult during World War I and experienced firsthand the devastating effects on her generation—on dazzling young men like Andrew Ramsey in *To the Lighthouse* (1927), whose death from an exploded shell she literally recorded in brackets (201). You were not born until 1931, but you must have known early on about the Civil War which changed the very status of your black being. Your childhood memories must have included stories you heard about World War I, the War to end all Wars, a war that ushered in a new period in African American history, the Jazz Age, when a flood of blacks migrated North to work at those jobs the soldiers had left. Your narrator in *Jazz* experiences the effects of the war quite differently from Virginia's characters, for that War is followed in America by the development of this whole new feeling among African Americans about themselves—that of experiencing the freedom and danger of the City, where one might be

Alone, yes, but top-notch and indestructible—like the City in 1926 when all the wars are over and there will never be another one. The people down there in the shadow are happy about that. At last, at last, everything's ahead. The smart ones say so and people listening to them and reading what they write agree: Here comes the new. Look out. There goes the sad stuff. The bad stuff. The things-nobody-could-help stuff. The way everybody was then and there. Forget that. History is over, you all, and everything's ahead at last. (*Jazz* 7)

How wrong your narrator is, as Virginia Woolf would come to know in 1941, when partially as a result of depression about the news of World War II she took her life.

But perhaps Virginia Woolf's works were not included in any of your classes. Maybe you, Toni, ran into her works in an avant-garde bookstore, and someone told you that her grandfather was a staunch abolitionist who married the sister of Wilberforce, the major speaker in the House of Commons against the slave trade (Bell 1: 3-4). Here your two apparently disparate cultures and histories cross, and you are not as distant from one another as it might seem. Or perhaps some crazy, too advanced graduate student who'd been to England talked incessantly about this innovative, what is the word, *experimental*, woman writer—check her out—not like those too old guys you're reading in class.

In an interview published in 1983, you made an observation: "My sense of the novel is that it has always functioned for the class or group that wrote it. The history of the novel as a form began when there was a new class, a middle class to read it, it was an art form that they needed" ("Rootedness" 340). You see your writing of novels as related to the needs of your group, African Americans. An English major, you knew the novel came out of an historical context, that as a form like any other that is not "natural," it was constructed in relation to the needs of a class. So you would state in that same interview that "the novel is needed by African Americans now in a way that it was not needed before," since "we don't live in places we can hear those stories anymore, parents don't sit around and tell their children those classical mythological archetypal stories that we heard years ago" (340). In order to create a novel that would accomplish these goals, that would be not only beautiful and powerful but would also "work," one needed to incorporate "unorthodox novelistic characteristics" ("Rootedness" 342). You did not "regard Black literature as simply books written *by* Black People, or simply as literature written *about* Black people, or simply as literature that uses a certain mode of language in which you just sort of drop *g*'s" (342). You saw your endeavor as the "struggle to *find* that elusive but identifiable style" that is Black art (342).

Virginia Woolf would seem to be coming from the other side of that problem. But she too had to define what she was doing—what it meant, assured as she was of the British tradition, to be a woman writer. She saw the British tradition of novel writing as being so fixed, so focused on the conventions of her ancestral class, the class which had created it for different purposes precisely because it was a different time, that the genre had not adapted to the catastrophic changes that her generation was experiencing in the early twentieth century. Freud's theory of the unconscious brought into question the nineteenth-century European idea of characters who had total control over their knowledge of themselves. The Great War had wiped away any sense of European cultural coherence. The Bolshevik Revolution had transformed world politics. Woolf would speak for a whole generation when she asserted, in her essay "How It Strikes A Contemporary," that in contrast to the novelists of the nineteenth century, contemporary writers are beset by the dilemma that they "cannot make a world," "cannot generalise": "They cannot tell stories because they do not believe the stories are true" (244). Yet as Ralph Freedman points out in his book *The Lyrical Novel*, Virginia Woolf saw that in order to write lasting, generally accessible works, the writer needed to find appropriate avenues of escape. "[Woolf's] attempt to translate the traditional forms of the novel into organized explorations of consciousness represents her contribution to this task" (187-188). But her concerns were not only and precisely with the traditional forms of novel, but with what these forms meant for a woman writer in that tradition. So Virginia saw that women writers, as she knew them in 1925, needed to "[break] the sentence . . . [break] the sequence" (*Room* 85).[11]

You, Toni, would also see the need for inventing "unorthodox novelistic characteristics." Your reasons, though related to Virginia's, were also different from hers, as indicated by your differing use of the concept of "stories," your inheritance from quite different cultures. For Woolf's contemporaries, it is novelists who tell stories; the novel as a genre developed out of a particular class in Europe as a means to creating a sense of coherence. For you, however, stories refer to a racial group who have maintained coherence by passing on stories, generally opposed to the dominant group. While Virginia's stories are print and class-based, your stories, Toni, are oral- and folk-based. Early twentieth-century British novelists were stifled by the novel of manners that Jane Austen had mastered, a construct of conventions that had been wiped away by the intellectual and social events of early twentieth-century European societies. But African American writers had been stifled by the necessity to write primarily to audiences other than themselves, restricted as they were by an American master narrative. So Virginia would question the existence of a coherent narrative, while you would feel "bereft" when you read literature that was supposedly about yourself.

As was true of Virginia's context in the 1920s, monumental social events in your time opened up a space for your development of "unorthodox novelistic characteristics" ("Rootedness" 342). As a result of the African American political movements of the 1960s, African American culture would begin to be conceptualized as a vital culture by intellectuals rather than a pathology of or a deviation from Euro-American culture, as it was characterized in the works of possibly the most visible of pre-1960s African American writer, Richard Wright. Increasingly African American writers would characterize their primary audience as that of African Americans. Oral storytelling, which had been one basis of the persistence of that culture, was increasingly recognized as having "legitimate" conventions capable of being refigured in literary genres such as the novel. So while Virginia could redefine the traditional concepts of British fiction in the 1920s, you could, in the 1970s, recuperate traditional concepts of African American linguistic expression, considered "unorthodox" in the Euro-American novel.

For while you saw the novel as valuable for its ability to carry on the tradition of African American oral storytelling, that it could be "both print and oral literature," that the novel could harken back to an older communal tradition even as it was very much of the modern world ("Rootedness" 341), Virginia doubted the "truthfulness" of stories. While your writing is clearly concerned with expressing the communal quality of African American life, its myths, beliefs, dreams, Virginia wondered about the idea of a communal narrative.

Yet, although your and Virginia's views of the novel might seem to be worlds apart, both of your writings are riveted on the relationship between the inner life of your characters and the world within which they find themselves, the object in fact of their consciousness. In this regard, I remember the talk you gave at Berkeley about your novel *Beloved* in 1987, when it had just been published. You stressed that one of your interests in writing it was that much of what had been written about American slavery ignored—repressed—the inner lives of slaves, sometimes for very good reasons, such as the fact that nineteenth-century African American writers had to be primarily concerned with the *institution* of slavery, with the abolishment of that institution, a concern which often precluded the exploration of their characters' psyches. Slave narratives used a formula based on the biblical story of the Fall and the Resurrection to engage the largely Christian white audience. Slave narrators had to hold back memories which might alienate their white readers.[12] But you were not so much interested in what happened: you already knew the Margaret Garner story. In fact, in every one of your novels, the reader knows what has happened or will happen on practically the first page. What you wanted to do was to fill those silences and to involve yourself and the reader in such a way as to feel the experience, both viscerally and as an idea.

As Virginia's works so amply demonstrate, memory is a central aspect of the inner life, one means by which we interpret the present as well as remember the past. How does one express that inner life without completely losing sense of the world in which characters in a novel must move, that is, losing the specificities of time and place? Virginia solved that tension between the inner and the outer life in the construction of her novels by using soliloquies, what Ralph Freedman calls "*dramatic* monologues in which psychological drama and common speech are replaced by lyrical drama and inner speech" (203). Unlike the stream of consciousness technique of writers such as Joyce, which Woolf criticized as being too "centered in a self which, in spite of its tremor of susceptibility, never embraces or creates what is outside itself or beyond" ("Modern Fiction" 156), her monologues were carefully crafted to reveal not only the quality of that particular character's mind, but also his or her ways of perceiving the world. In *Mrs. Dalloway*, we are in the minds of Clarissa Dalloway, Septimus Smith, Mr. Dalloway, Peter Walsh, during one day, a day framed by the tolling of Big Ben, clearly situating us in high society London. Even as the reader is experiencing reality in terms of the characters' inner lives, we are anchored in some time and place.

As a reader of Virginia Woolf, you, Toni, were clearly alert to the world evoked by her imagination. As a writer, you were confronted with some of the same issues of narrative technique with which she had to contend. In your first novel, *The Bluest Eye*, you would use soliloquies as she had, in order to capture the inner lives of your characters. However, you had to deal with an additional problem, for readers were not used to focusing on the inner lives of black characters. Racism, after all, affected the social lives of African Americans in such a way that the external social world had taken precedence over the inner lives of characters. How stunned I was when I first read Pauline Breedlove's soliloquy in *The Bluest Eye*, possibly the first evocation of a black domestic's inner voice. Although the omniscient narrator focuses on Pauline's social situation, her inner voice allows the reader to feel her specific dreams, her intense use of images of color, her individual way of perceiving the world in images of color even as it is rooted in her rural southern upbringing. You established for her a love of order, a sense of design which would have served her well, if she had had the opportunity to become an artist. It was from the African tradition of storytelling, where playing with images is as important as it is in a Woolf novel, that Pauline acquired her voice.

Perhaps your most characteristic transformation of the narrator is your different uses of a chorus, a community that includes the reader, in every one of your novels, since as you have said, "[your] audience is always the people in the book [you're] writing at the time" ("Toni Morrison," Tate 122). So there is the choral "I" narrator of *The Bluest Eye*; the town functioning as a character in *Sula*; the neighborhood and the community that responds in the two parts of town in *Song of Solomon*; all of nature thinking and feeling and watching and responding to the action going on in *Tar Baby*; the chorus of the community, living and dead, in *Beloved*; the City in *Jazz*. In your most recent novel, your unnamed narrator admits that she/he does not know everything about the characters in much the same way we do not know everything about someone by looking at a photograph, an aesthetic form that emerged in the 1920s, which seems to mimic life even as it freezes it: "When I see them now they are not sepia, still, losing their edges to the light of a future afternoon. Caught midway between was and must be. For me they are real. Sharply in focus and clicking" (*Jazz* 226). In her last novels, Virginia too began to use the concept of the chorus, especially in her last work, *Between the Acts*, in which she devises what Rachel Blau DuPlessis calls "a communal protagonist," "where no character in the plot stands above any other" (163-164). There are real differences between your respective uses of the chorus, however, for while both of you are insisting that there is a communal protagonist, your novels, Toni, still insist upon the tension between individuals, the experimental ones and their relationship to the community, to which, in your work, they return, as a means of testing out the extent to which difference is allowed and might even triumph.

Although you used soliloquy to express the inner voice, a choral note to express community, both social and mythic, you also needed an omniscient narrator in much of your work, for unlike Virginia, you were not usually writing about characters in the present. Part of your task had to be a remapping of the historical terrain for African Americans, a terrain that had been previously charted by a master narrative from the outside, rather than from the inside of their experiences, a history that even African American communities might have begun to forget, or might not want to remember. So, for example, although *The Bluest Eye* is set in 1941, so that the reader might understand Pauline and Cholly Breedlove, you had to move back in time to the 1920s of their southern youth. Even *Tar Baby*, your novel set primarily in the present, draws power from the mythic past of the island on which it is set. As critic Wahneema Lubiano has said about your work, because it "remaps the terrain of African American cultural and social history and allows for a community of the imagination, it interrupts the ideology that produces the kind of world we inhabit" (321).

But while your writing remaps American history, it is not historical in the usual sense of that word; linear progression is not its goal, for as you have so beautifully captured in your rendition of the inner voices of your characters, whatever we consider reality to be, we do not experience it either individually or communally as a march of years. Rather there is both inner time and outer time. Virginia expressed a similar sentiment, when in her essay "Modern Fiction" she critiqued the thirty-two perfectly balanced chapters of the Victorian novel which emphasized the material world as the real world, "Is life like this?" For "life is not a series of gig lamps symmetrically arranged; but a luminous halo, a semi-transparent envelope surrounding us from the beginning of consciousness to the end" ("Modern Fiction" 154). Virginia experimented with the formal monologue as a way of fusing inner and outer time, honing it from novel to novel until in *The Waves* (1931), no narrator intrudes, and the juxtaposition of the characters' inner voices produces its own design of the interrelatedness and separateness of the characters, the waves of lives being the intersections of the private inner voice, the continuity of the seasons with their mythic significance, the traditions and shifts of society. What Virginia wanted to do in *The Waves* was "to saturate every atom . . . to eliminate all waste, deadness, superfluity: to give the moment whole; whatever it includes. Say that the moment is a combination of thought; sensation; the voice of the sea" ("Nov. 28, 1928" 139). In *The Waves*, she eliminated the narrator, the external movement of the narrative being delineated by her juxtaposition of her characters' formal monologues. In contrast, Toni, you wanted

to make the story appear oral, meandering, effortless, spoken—to have the reader *feel* the narrator without *identifying* that narrator or hearing him or her knock about, and to have the reader work with the author in the construction of the book. . . . What is left out is as important as what is there. ("Rootedness" 341)

In your work, as in Virginia's, inner time is always transforming outer time through memory. But since memory is not only individual, but merges with others to create a communal memory, outer time also transforms inner time. It is that reciprocity between the individual inner and the communal outer which your work seeks. The folk's time, however, is not mechanical time, the march of years, which your chapter titles in *Sula* mock, but time as it marks an event in human society and in nature, which for you includes the folk as much as the seasons. The mythic quality of your worlds seems to be in opposition to many conceptions of human history, when in fact history and myth have always been related, myth being a central part of any people's history, history itself creating myth, time and timelessness in dialogue. In your work there is a deep relationship between your characters' belief system and their view of nature. Thus Baby Suggs preaches in "the Clearing"; in *Sula*, Eva can read the signs of nature. And in *Song of Solomon*, Milkman learns about "what there was before language. Before things were written down. Language in the time when men and animals did talk to one another . . ." (280).

Nature in its many aspects is central to your work, I believe, because nature is one constant, in time and space, for all human societies. So *The Bluest Eye* is structurally arranged in terms of the seasons; nature responds to the action in *Tar Baby*; Sethe has got a "chokecherry tree" inscribed upon her back in *Beloved*. Virginia too felt that deep connection with nature, that it is a crucial element of that "luminous halo" and is inside ourselves, even as it appears to be outside, thus her desire to fuse "thought, sensation, the sea."

But myth, Toni, in your work means not only a recognition of the power of primal natural forces, but also the presence of an ancestor. For African Americans, who were torn from their homeland and for whom migrations have been a constant, the ancestor female and male, rather than a particular homeland, is the ground of wisdom, the timeless presence. Art, for you, becomes one means by which that ancestor can be invoked. How does Virginia relate to an ancestor figure? Her evocation in *A Room of One's Own* of her father's favorite poet, Milton, not only critiques that male lineage, but also insists on creating a specifically female lineage. Thus she turns to the aunt who willed her money: "My aunt's legacy unveiled the sky to me, and substituted for the large and imposing figure of a gentleman, which Milton commended for my perpetual adoration, a view of the open sky" (39).[13]

Toni, you have described your own works in terms of rhythmic shapes: *Sula* as a spiral, for example, *Song of Solomon* as "a train picking up speed," for "every life to [you] has a rhythm, a shape," whose "contours" "you can't see . . . all at once" ("Toni Morrison," Tate 124). Virginia wanted to capture "the moment," which reveals that life; you want to revel in the rhythm of that life: related temperaments yet different in their approach to language and to the imagination. You see the need "to clean the language up and give words back their original meaning" ("Toni Morrison," Tate 126) so that "the language . . . [does] not sweat" ("Language" 24). In an interview, you set a new goal for yourself—to write novels in which you do not have to indicate that your characters are black or white by the use of modifiers—but that the reader knows because of the context, your use of language ("Toni Morrison," Moyers 56-57). What, you wondered, would that mean for you as a writer?

Like Virginia, writing novels for you is decidedly an experimental act, a creative one—so that you are always pushing against what you have already learned to do. Increasingly, as in the prose poems of *Beloved* and the painterly prose of the narrator's observations in *Jazz*, your language is symbolic, just as Virginia's language in her last works became more formal, more like poetic drama.

Novelists, you have said, are always influenced by the moral currents of their world. It is not surprising, then, that because you and Virginia come from different cultural cosmologies, the moral questions you pose in your work are somewhat different, even as women. While you both clearly acknowledge the imagination as central to your temperament, while you have used some similar narrative strategies, what strikes me as the major difference is your relationship to the idea of love in your novels. You have so many times said that love is your major theme: life is poor, uninteresting, without being able to love somebody; but love is also a dilemma for human beings because, like the elements of nature, it can run so quickly to excess. All of your novels deal with that dilemma. Virginia, on the other hand, was concerned that women were expected to write about love—love here meaning romantic love; she insisted that women also wanted poetry, dreams, imagination. Without question, so do you, though in a different context. You have said that you are "not interested in indulging [your]self in some private, closed exercise of [your] imagination that fulfills only the obligation of [your] personal dreams—which is to say yes, the work must be political" ("Rootedness" 344). Virginia, I believe, would have held to that same sentiment, while questioning whether the imagination can be anything but private.

Perhaps, Toni, because you are an African American woman writing in the latter part of the twentieth century, you can now write about expanded definitions of love, rooted in a tradition of a people who, from their beginnings in this country, had been denied the right to express love, and thus have invented their particular strategies to hold onto it. In your world, love is not so much romance as it is primal "risk" and freedom," incapable of being completely contained.

In keeping with the open endings of your novels, I hesitate to bring any resolution to my invention. For your work is not yet finished, while Virginia's is there for you to contemplate. In being aware of "her notions of risk and safety," you may well have expanded your own—creating layered rhythms in your fiction, that is both your own personal voice and that of the folk. I see you, Toni, continuing to write and read, read and write in layered rhythms.

NOTES

[1]Blake mentions this detail on page 189.

[2]This essay was first presented at the Third Annual Conference on Virginia Woolf, Lincoln University, Jefferson City, Missouri, 10-13 June 1993.

[3]For example, see Spender.

[4]See, for example, Marcus.

[5]A sister student of Toni Morrison who works at Sacramento State University told me this.

[6]For a discussion of the Dreadnaught Hoax, in which Virginia Woolf and friends darkened their faces and dressed as Abyssinian *men* in a protest against British policy in North Africa, see Wilson 297.

[7]See Lerner (especially 220-221) for a discussion of the reasons why African American families, in contrast to much of American society in the early part of the twentieth century, felt it necessary that their daughters, even more than their sons, needed higher education.

[8]Episodes of competition and rivalry recur in Virginia's and Vanessa's relationship. See, for example, Bell 1: 22-24, 88-90, 132-136, 164-169; 2: 89, 110, 147, 218-219.

[9]See Christian, "Shadows Uplifted."

[10]See DuPlessis, 47-65.

[11]This is the subject of DuPlessis' study.

[12]For a discussion of this point, see Christian, "'Somebody Forgot to Tell Somebody Something.'"

[13]I owe this insight to Stanford instructor Cheri Ross's lecture, "*A Room of One's Own* and the Revaluation of Space," 25 May 1993.

WORKS CITED

Bell, Quentin. *Virginia Woolf: A Biography*. 2 vols. New York: Harcourt, Brace, Jovanovich, 1972.

Blake, Susan. "Toni Morrison." *Dictionary of Literary Biography: African American Fiction Writers after 1955*. Vol. 33. Ed. Thadious Davis and Trudier Harris. Detroit: Gale, 1984.

Bloom, Harold. Introduction. *Toni Morrison*. Ed. Harold Bloom. New York: Chelsea House, 1990. 1-5.

Christian, Barbara. "Shadows Uplifted." *Black Women Novelists*. Westport: Greenwood, 1980. 3-34.

———. "'Somebody Forgot to Tell Somebody Something': African-American Women's Historical Novels." *Wild Women of the Whirlwind*. Ed. Joanne Braxton and André McLaughlin. New Brunswick: Rutgers UP, 1990. 326-341.

DuPlessis, Rachel Blau. *Writing Beyond the Ending: Narrative Strategies of Twentieth Century Women Writers*. Bloomington: Indiana UP, 1985.

Ellison, Ralph. *Shadow and Act*. New York: Random House, 1964.

Freedman, Ralph. *The Lyrical Novel: Studies in Hermann Hesse, André Gide, and Virginia Woolf*. Princeton: Princeton UP, 1963.

Giddings, Paula. *When and Where I Enter*. New York: Morrow, 1984.

Gilbert, Sandra M., and Susan Gubar. *Madwoman in the Attic: The Woman Writer and the Nineteenth-Century Literary Imagination*. New Haven: Yale UP, 1979.

Lerner, Gerda, ed. *Black Women in White America*. New York: Pantheon, 1972.

Lubiano, Wahneema. "Toni Morrison." *African American Writers*. Ed. Valerie Smith. New York: Scribner's, 1991. 321-333.

Marcus, Jane, ed. *New Feminist Essays on Virginia Woolf*. Lincoln: U of Nebraska P, 1981.

Morrison, Toni. *The Bluest Eye*. New York: Holt, Rinehart, Winston, 1970.

———. "Interview with Toni Morrison." With Ntozake Shange. *Steve Cannon's House of Magic*. WBAI, New York. Nov. 1977.

———. *Jazz*. New York: Knopf, 1992.

———. "The Language Must Not Sweat: A Conversation with Toni Morrison." With Thomas LeClair. *New Republic* 21 March 1981: 25-29.

_____. *Playing in the Dark: Whiteness and the Literary Imagination.* Cambridge: Harvard UP, 1992.

_____. "Rootedness: The Ancestor as Foundation." *Black Women Writers (1950-1980): A Critical Evaluation.* Ed. Mari Evans. Garden City, NY: Anchor-Doubleday, 1983. 339-345.

_____. *Song of Solomon.* New York: New American Library, 1977.

_____. *Sula.* New York: Knopf, 1974.

_____. "Toni Morrison." Interview with Bill Moyers. *A World of Ideas II.* Garden City: Doubleday, 1990. 54-63.

_____. "Toni Morrison." Interview with Claudia Tate. *Black Women Writers at Work.* Ed. Claudia Tate. New York: Continuum, 1983. 117-131.

Spender, Stephen. *The Struggle of the Modern.* Berkeley: U of California P, 1963.

Tate, Claudia. "Allegories of Black Female Desire; or Rereading Nineteenth-Century Sentimental Narratives of Black Female Authority." *Changing Our Own Words.* Ed. Cheryl Wall. New Brunswick: Rutgers UP, 1991. 98-126.

Toni Morrison. Videocassette. Part 3 of *In Black and White: Six Profiles of African American Writers.* Dir. Matteo Bellinelli. Prod. RTSI-Swiss Television. California Newsreel, 1992. 27 min.

Wilson, J. J. "Virginia Woolf." *Dictionary of Literary Biography: British Novelists, 1890-1929: Modernists.* Vol. 36. Ed. Thomas F. Staley. Detroit: Gale, 1985.

Woolf, Virginia. "How It Strikes A Contemporary." *The Common Reader, First Series.* 1925. New York: Harcourt, Brace, World, 1953. 236-246.

_____. "Modern Fiction." *The Common Reader, First Series.* 1925. New York: Harcourt, Brace, World, 1953. 150-158.

_____. "Nov. 28, 1928." *A Writer's Diary.* London: Hogarth, 1953. 138-139.

_____. *A Room of One's Own.* 1929. New York: Harcourt, Brace, Jovanovich, 1957.

_____. *To the Lighthouse.* 1927. New York: Harcourt, Brace, World, 1955.

SPACING AND PLACING EXPERIENCE IN TONI MORRISON'S *SULA*

Patricia McKee

In Toni Morrison's *Sula*, spacing—that is, closing down or opening up distances between things and persons—has extraordinary urgency. Houses and bodies are the sites of hyperactive mechanisms of containment and expulsion working to effect identity and distinction: of inside and outside, of self and other. Spacing, moreover, becomes crucial to issues of representation and meaning in the Bottom, the place in which most of the action of the novel occurs. Houston A. Baker, Jr., has called attention to the importance of place in the novel: "What Morrison ultimately seeks in her coding of Afro-American PLACE is a writing of intimate, systematizing, and ordering black village values," he suggests (237). Identifying this ordering with female domestic labor and rituals of cleaning, Baker argues that Morrison "places" African American experience by means of "manipulations of the symbolic," countering conventions of displacement by affording "a mirroring language . . . in which we can find ourselves" (258).

But although the manipulation of persons and things in space can effect a symbolic order, Morrison also uses other means of locating experience in *Sula*. In my discussion of the novel, I want to distinguish between systematic spacing arrangements, of the kind necessary to a symbolic order, and Morrison's placements of experience that orderly representation misses. Two places in the novel that indicate her concern to locate missing experience are "the place where Chicken Little sank" in the river (61) and the place Eva Peace's missing leg once occupied, "the empty place on her left side" (31). Neither of these is quite what one would expect a place to be, since neither is the present location of anything.

Like the empty spaces in a symbolic order, these places mark an absence. In *The Architecture of Deconstruction: Derrida's Haunt*, Mark Wigley emphasizes the spatial character of representation in Derridean deconstruction: "Spacing is the 'distance' of representation: both the spatial intervals between signifiers and the effect of substitution, the production of the sense that the material signifier 'stands in for' something detached from it, the sense that space is an exterior domain of representation detached from that of presence, which is to say, the sense of an exterior divided from an interior" (70). Derrida writes, *"[s]pacing* designates *nothing,* nothing that is, no presence at a distance; it is the index of an irreducible exterior, and at the same time of a *movement,* a displacement that indicates an irreducible alterity" (qtd. in Wigley 73). Given the dependence of presence on a spacing that produces presence as it produces absence, any system of representation, Wigley indicates, is haunted: indeed, "a house is a house only inasmuch as it is haunted" (168).

Unlike the haunted presences of deconstruction, the experience of missing in *Sula* is a particular historical experience. Missing itself takes place in the novel, as particular persons and things are missed from particular places. Although "the closed place in the middle" of the river (118) and the place where Eva's leg once was have nothing in them, they mark the absence of persons, or parts of persons, once present, rather than "an irreducible alterity." Morrison can be said to insist on the reducibility of alterity as she converts such unoccupied spaces into places on the basis of previous occupants. She locates missing persons, and parts of persons, in places they have formerly occupied. Locating such occupants is one kind of preoccupation in the novel.

There is a second kind of preoccupation, however, which rather than locating missing occupants who once were present locates missing occupations that never occurred at all. By this I mean that Morrison identifies both failed possessions of places and failed actions: various connections between occupants and their places that never took place. This second kind of preoccupation is a more absolute form of missing compounded by the prior as well as the present absence of what is missed. It is nonetheless a historical experience, given characters whose past is one in which the overwhelming "meaning" of experience was not positive but negative. Such a history is "missing," in the sense that it is not composed of positive facts known and recorded. But it is a missing history in another sense too: as a history of missing, a history *made* by people's knowledge of what they would never become, places they would never hold, things they would never do.[1] In the first kind of preoccupation, people are aware of something that once was present; in the second kind, people miss things that might have been but that never happened. Thus Morrison places both missed presences and missed absences in *Sula*.

The experience of missing what never was is clearest near the end of the novel, in 1941, when many people die at the construction site of the proposed tunnel. What the people of the Bottom see when they look at this place is not only what is there, but what might have been there and is not there: all the things denied or negated by the fact that black people were never hired to work there.

Their hooded eyes swept over the place where their hope had lain since 1927. There was the promise: leaf-dead. The teeth unrepaired, the coal credit cut off, the chest pains unattended, the school shoes unbought, the rush-stuffed mattresses, the broken toilets, the leaning porches, the slurred remarks and the staggering childish malevolence of their employers. . . .

Like antelopes they leaped over the little gate . . . and smashed the bricks they would never fire in yawning kilns, split the sacks of limestone they had not mixed or even been allowed to haul; tore the wire mesh, tipped over wheelbarrows and rolled forepoles down the bank. . . . (161)

The first "thing" located in this place is hope; the second is promise. Both these relations to things were once alive and are now dead. The construction site seems preoccupied by them, and with their deaths numerous other losses are remembered. The losses re-called are things that these people did not do, things that they lost, things that broke or fell apart; but things that might have been done, kept, and repaired for the better. What is missed here are hope and the promise of change in the things these non-events represent.

When people turn to look at the objects actually present, these too are seen in terms of failed relations to them. The bricks, limestone, and wheelbarrows have been denied to the people of the Bottom as objects of their labor. What these people see, therefore, are not only the objects but their own missing occupation with these objects: bricks not fired, limestone not mixed, wheelbarrows not used to haul. The collective realization of what is missed in this scene is not a recognition of lost objects but of missed relations to objects: the loss of hope, promise, repair, credit, attention, occupation.

The tunnel site, then, is preoccupied with absences. Missing absent attachments means a massive "displacement": people tear things apart, throw things around, and start a landslide that carries some of them to their deaths in the river and buries others in the tunnel. For most of their lives, therefore, these people do not allow themselves to recognize what they miss in this scene: meaningful relations to things. The role of Sula in the Bottom, I will argue, is to take the place of the absences that preoccupy these people at the tunnel in 1941. By identifying Sula as evil and rejecting her categorically, people in the Bottom are able to keep their distance from absences they cannot afford to acknowledge. In this case, keeping order depends not on emptying space of occupants but on filling in spaces whose emptiness is unbearable. Sula, occupied with loss, occupies the place of absences people cannot afford to miss. Morrison explained to Robert B. Stepto that she "wanted Sula to be missed by the reader. That's why she dies early" (" 'Intimate Things' " 218).[2] To miss Sula is to recognize her occupation in and of the Bottom: what she did there and how she was a necessary part of the place, not only as a presence but also because she took the place of absence.

In this essay, I will be concerned with space and place in *Sula* both as components of social and psychological order and as components of historical experience. Like deconstructionists, Morrison identifies spacing as a means of producing meaning; various symbolic, emotional, and communal orders in *Sula* depend on both emptying and filling in spaces. But Morrison complicates the deconstructive equivalence of empty and occupied spaces by identifying empty spaces as emptied spaces. Spaces emptied of contents for the sake of order are preoccupied with persons, things, and relations missing from orderly representations of experience. And spaces that are filled, forms whose containment of meaning provides order, are identified as places in which things are kept in order to hold them together. These spaces, too, are under pressure from preoccupation: a preoccupation with absences such as that which occurs at the tunnel site in 1941 and causes the place to come apart. Morrison activates the spacing of representation and realizes what is missing when representation occurs. Whereas many poststructuralist theories of representation assume absence or lack to be part of the structure of human experience, Morrison works against such a generalization, to realize experiences of missing that are particular components of African-American life and, more particularly, of African-American women's lives.[3]

PLACING EXPERIENCE

Before elaborating experiences of preoccupation in *Sula*, I want to consider some of the spacing practices that work to create order for characters in the novel who ignore, organize, or dissolve the confusions entailed in preoccupation. I will begin with the first personal perspective Morrison narrates, which is not the perspective of any character but instead an outsider's view of the Bottom. Not really even personal, this perspective belongs to a seemingly generic "valley man."

[I]f a valley man happened to have business up in those hills—collecting rent or insurance payments—he might see a dark woman in a flowered dress doing a bit of cakewalk, a bit of black bottom, a bit of "messing around" to the lively notes of a mouth organ. . . . The black people watching her would laugh and rub their knees, and it would be easy for the valley man to hear the laughter and not notice the adult pain that rested somewhere under the eyelids, somewhere under their head rags and soft felt hats, somewhere in the palm of the hand, somewhere behind the frayed lapels, somewhere in the sinew's curve. He'd have to stand in the back of Greater Saint Matthew's and let the tenor's voice dress him in silk, or touch the hands of the spoon carvers (who had not worked in eight years) and let the fingers that danced on wood kiss his skin. Otherwise the pain would escape him even though the laughter was part of the pain. (4)

A valley man is a European American, but he is identified in *Sula* not by race but by where he comes from: "white people lived on the rich valley floor in that little river town in Ohio, and the blacks populated the hills above it" (5). The identification of this man by his place begins a scene in which place seems the primary determinant of perception. The white man misses a lot when he looks at the black people because he does not see and does not go to certain places that are parts of their experience.

Seeing no sign of pain, the white man sees the people's laughter as excluding pain, whereas for them "the laughter was part of the pain." This difference in perception is located, as Morrison identifies places that pain resides, such as "somewhere under their head rags." Preoccupied by pain, the bodies of these people are locations of both laughter and pain, which the white man cannot recognize because he is ignorant of certain other places too. There are places he could go—to the back of Greater Saint Matthew's or up close enough to touch the hands of the carvers—where the pain of the black people's experience would not escape him.

The white man stands at a distance from the black people in this scene, excluded and exclusive. But he is separated from them by distances that Morrison fills in. Rather than being separated by an empty space of necessary detachment, a distance built into any knowledge or representation of other persons, the white man could move into places in which he could feel what he is missing. It is not only in the experience observed, then, that something is missed in this scene. Not only does the white man fail to recognize certain preoccupations in the people he watches, but he has never been in the places occupied by their pain. His distance from the people he watches depends on excluding certain occupations—and certain missed occupations such as spoon carving—from knowledge, and thereby converting places of occupation into empty spaces of separation.

PATTERNS OF CONTAINMENT

In the histories of the Bottom's inhabitants, Morrison goes on to redefine space as place. The occupants of the Bottom whose histories are first given in the novel are Shadrack, who was a soldier in the First World War, and Helene Wright, who came to the Bottom from New Orleans when she married. These are the first of the characters who practice strict containments and limitations of experience that keep things in their places.

Morrison charts the need for such constraints first in the story of Shadrack. Having seen a soldier's head blown off on a battlefield of the First World War, Shadrack reacts in terror to the displacement of objects:

Before him on a tray was a large tin plate divided into three triangles. In one triangle was rice, in another meat, and in the third stewed tomatoes. . . . Shadrack stared at the soft colors that filled these triangles. . . . All their repugnance was contained in the neat balance of the triangles—a balance that soothed him, transferred some of its equilibrium to him. Thus reassured that the white, the red and the brown would stay where they were— would not explode or burst forth from their restricted zones—he suddenly felt hungry and looked around for his hands. . . . Slowly he directed one hand toward the cup and, just as he was about to spread his fingers, they began to grow in higgledy-piggledy fashion like Jack's beanstalk all over the tray and the bed. (8–9)

Shadrack is able to put a limit on the size of his hands as well as the dimensions of death by "making a place for fear as a way of controlling it" (14). He finds a place in the Bottom, and he founds National Suicide Day, in 1920, as a place for death: "if one day a year were devoted to it, everybody could get it out of the way and the rest of the year would be safe and free" (14). Having focused his fears on this containment, Shadrack himself can be focused and contained: "Once the people understood the boundaries and nature of his madness, they could fit him, so to speak, into the scheme of things" (15).

Like Shadrack, Helene experiences psychic chaos once when

she leaves Medallion. With one slip, when she mistakenly gets into the "white" car on the train going south, she begins to lose control of her existence and slide back into an identity with her mother, "a Creole whore" (17), from whom Helene has spent her life trying to separate herself. Morrison traces this slide in a series of displacements:

"What you think you doin', gal?"
. . . So soon. She hadn't even begun the trip back. Back to her grandmother's house in the city where the red shutters glowed, and already she had been called "gal." All the old vulnerabilities, all the old fears of being somehow flawed gathered in her stomach and made her hands tremble. She had heard only that one word; it dangled above her wide-brimmed hat, which had slipped, in her exertion, from its carefully leveled placement and was now tilted in a bit of a jaunt over her eye. (20)

Watching Helene, two black soldiers observe her exchange with the conductor. Watching them all, Nel, Helene's daughter, sees Helene, "for no earthly reason," smile "dazzlingly and coquettishly at the salmon-colored face of the conductor" and then the soldiers look suddenly "stricken" (21): "She saw the muscles of their faces tighten, a movement under the skin from blood to marble" (21–22), and "she resolved to be on guard—always. She wanted to make certain that no man ever looked at her that way. That no midnight eyes or marbled flesh would ever accost her and turn her into jelly" (22). Like Shadrack glaring at his rice and tomatoes, Nel watches the "custard" and "jelly" of her mother (22), and she then resolves to resist their spread and slippage. Never again to leave Medallion, Nel returns home as her own self: " 'I'm me. I'm not their daughter. I'm not Nel. I'm me. Me' " (28).

The stories of Shadrack and of Helene and Nel's trip to New Orleans offer different experiences of a need for containment. Both characters set limits to preoccupations. These are memories that occupy their minds, but as memories of bodily disintegration they are, specifically, recollections of a loss of place. Shadrack, after seeing another body come apart, fears that his own body cannot be kept within bounds. Initiating National Suicide Day, he puts a limit to his fears, to death, and to bodily disintegration by limiting suicide to one day of the year and then "keeping" the holiday. Helene contains her fears by keeping house and keeping up standards of propriety, both in her house and in the Bottom.

But Helene's fears, and Nel's too, are apparently driven less by what they see than by what others, particularly men, see in Helene. Whereas Shadrack's body loses consistency in his own eyes,

Helene is watched by others who see her body as that of a "loose" woman, as "custard." Therefore Helene must contain not only her own slips but the way she spreads into someone else when men look at her. On the train south, she feels herself losing her place as Helene Wright and slipping into an identity with her mother, the whore. Then she sees herself losing her place in the men's eyes. They reflect not Helene Wright, nor her mother, but just another black woman in sexual complicity with a white man. Once she begins to "slip," she spreads into this generalized identity because of history, memory, and fears in the minds of the men: preoccupations over which she has no control.

Shadrack, in the hospital, is "relieved and grateful" when he is put into a straitjacket, "for his hands were at last hidden and confined to whatever size they had attained" (9). He is further relieved when he is able to see his reflection: "There in the toilet water he saw a grave black face. A black so definite, so unequivocal, it astonished him. He had been harboring a skittish apprehension that he was not real—that he didn't exist at all. But when the blackness greeted him with its indisputable presence, he wanted nothing more" (13). Helene, unable "to relieve herself" on the trip south because allowed no access to toilets (23), is perhaps also without access to the sense of presence that relieves Shadrack from his fears of nonexistence. As she sees herself reflected in men's eyes, she does not experience reflection as a means of bodily containment but as one other dimension in which she has difficulty keeping her place. Helene finds bodily relief in the grass but also in another "accomplishment": by the time she has reached Slidell, "she never felt a stir as she passed the muddy eyes of the men who stood like wrecked Dorics under the station roofs of those towns" (24). She is relieved here not by bodily containment but by getting rid of something in her body: not only the urine she expels but the feelings usually stirred by men watching her.[4]

PATTERNS OF EXPULSION

Other women in the novel enforce more violent expulsions from their houses and their bodies, intent on getting rid of things and keeping their distance rather than keeping order. Whereas Helene Wright maintains strict standards and an "oppressive neatness" in her home (29), the Peace women inhabit a "household of throbbing disorder constantly awry with things, people, voices and the slamming of doors" (52). Their messy existence may not result from an indifference to limits, however. It seems instead one effect of a history of ejections and rejections by means of which the Peace women find relief in discharging fears rather than containing them. Walking out, throwing out, cutting off, sending things flying, these women affirm boundaries and their power over boundaries by getting rid of things.

Sula will walk out of Medallion on the day of Nel's wedding, as her grandmother Eva once walked out on her three children, to return "[e]ighteen months later . . . with two crutches, a new black pocketbook, and one leg" (34). Eva's lost leg becomes the subject of various stories: "Somebody said Eva stuck it under a train and made them pay off" (31). But the stories Eva herself tells are of two kinds: "How the leg got up by itself one day and walked on off. How she hobbled after it but it ran too fast. Or how she had a corn on her toe and it just grew and grew and grew until her whole foot was a corn and then it traveled on up her leg and wouldn't stop growing until she put a red rag at the top but by that time it was already at her knee" (30–31). According to these two versions, Eva's body is subject to both excursions and incursions of parts. On her trip south, Helene Wright defends against the inconsistency of "custard" with "the best protection: her manner and her bearing, to which she would add a beautiful dress" (19). Eva Peace deals with the inconsistency of her body not by means of consistent and beautiful forms but by making visible, even decorative, the difference between her absent and her present parts: "Nor did she wear overlong dresses to disguise the empty place on her left side. Her dresses were midcalf so that her one glamorous leg was always in view as well as the long fall of space below her left thigh" (31). Rendering her inconsistency itself a consistent expression of her distinction, Eva in her refusals to standardize her identity nevertheless places it by securing the difference between self and other, opening to others' scrutiny the space of the missing leg.

Eva's interest in boundaries and spaces is evident in her house as in her body: "Sula Peace lived in a house of many rooms that had been built over a period of five years to the specifications of its owner, who kept on adding things: more stairways—there were three sets to the second floor—more rooms, doors and stoops. There were rooms that had three doors . . . others that you could get to only by going through somebody's bedroom" (30). This house does not seem primarily a container so much as an excrescence. Eva keeps building, repeatedly pushing out and throwing up forms in additions whose messiness lies in the irregularity of access to

them. Both over- and under-accessed, the parts of the house confirm Eva's control over ingress and egress. Spaces between are of
more concern here than spaces per se, with an unusual amount of
space given over to access. Even rooms are reduced to ways in and
out of other rooms, so that any space may become itself a spacing,
a distance between: not so much a room as room to get in and out.

It is not that Eva and her house are open and free, whereas
Helene Wright and her house are constrained and closed. In terms
of intent, the difference between the two is less than such oppositions suggest, since the primary concern of each woman seems to
be her capacity to control and manipulate boundaries. Helene tries
to preclude things slipping out of place; Eva lets things slip, even fly
out of places in what seems an equally obsessive insistence on the
permeability of boundaries. At one point hurling herself out a window of her bedroom to try to save her daughter Hannah, who has
caught fire in the yard, Eva at another time burns up her son in his
room because "[t]here wasn't space for him in my womb" and "he
wanted to crawl back in" (71).

Both women seem primarily occupied, then, with controlling, or
even patrolling, boundaries in order to control the definition of their
own selves. Both mark off the self through representations that rule
out certain parts of their experience. Helene with her good form—
her beautiful manner, bearing, and clothes—represents herself with
a consistency that she lacks in her body and in her history. Eva's
equally careful representation of her body presents an absence that
also sets limits to her bodily and historical inconsistency. One
woman places her past out of bounds to maintain consistency; the
other rules out history by maintaining inconsistency. By calling attention to the space once occupied by her leg, yet never providing
the history of its loss, Eva limits preoccupation to stories. Her past
"takes shape" only as something missing, a mysterious gap in her
existence.

SULA'S PERSPECTIVES

There are at least three distances at which characters in the novel
experience the representations that provide their identity. Two of
these I have indicated. Shadrack sees reflected back at him, in the
water in a toilet, his definite identity as a black man. As in Lacan's
"mirror stage," this experience of reflection defines the self as other:
"Alienation is the fact of giving up a part of oneself to another. The

alienated man lives outside himself, a prisoner of the signifier, a prisoner of his ego's image or of the image of the ideal" (Lemaire 176). If Shadrack sees his ideal self reflected in a toilet, that reflection is both ideal and abject. Yet nevertheless he is reassured that he is "real" by the reflected image (13).[5] Helene Wright and Eva Peace, I have argued, produce for themselves, by manipulations of things and bodies in space, definitive representations such as Shadrack finds in reflected images. For these women, definition is not provided by reflections. But they nevertheless, as they fill in and empty spaces, provide definite forms of and limits to meaning.

Eva's daughter and granddaughter both, like her, get rid of things or get out of things by increasing distances between one thing and another. As a child, Sula understands the defensive value of cutting off parts of her body; she scares away the white boys who chase her by chopping off the end of her finger (54–55). Later she lets fly a whole body when Chicken Little "slipped from her hands and sailed away out over the water" to his death (60–61). This is just after she herself has been "sent . . . flying up the stairs" by her mother's announcement that she doesn't like her (57). Sula, however, seems not to experience her manipulations of space as representative manipulations. Whereas Eva is represented in stories as having cut off her leg, Sula actually cuts off part of her finger. And whereas her mother sends her flying figuratively, she sends Chicken Little's body through the air and kills him. Yet Sula does not control such acts; she does not mean them, and they effect no meaningful forms of experience for her. It is as if Sula does not have the distance from such events necessary to experience control of them.

On the one hand, Sula, like her mother and grandmother, is identified with breaks and separations. On the other hand, she does not use breaks and separations to give form or consistency to her experience. Unlike Eva, Sula does not place or contain inconsistency so as to limit it. She simply allows a place for losses, breaks, separations that occur. She does not attempt to repair or reform or connect things that break or exercise any other control over them; she lets things go. Morrison says that Sula is "like any artist with no art form" (121), and Sula seems never to use form to control experience. But she nevertheless experiences definition, which occurs through her location of absence rather than any formal representation. Because she does not use form to provide definition, Sula realizes the capacity of absence to do so. It is her recognition of the definitive power of missing that makes Sula's perspective extraordinary.

DEAD LOSSES

The ways in which Sula breaks meaning apart are to some extent familial. The Peace women enforce emotional distances, for example, with their tendency to throw things around. Because of such distances Sula can be identified, as Hortense J. Spillers argues, as "a figure of the rejected and vain part of the self—ourselves—who in its thorough corruption and selfishness cannot utter, believe in, nor prepare for, love" ("Hateful Passion" 232). Sula's emotional detachment is evident in certain physical distances she maintains, for example by "standing on the back porch just looking" as her mother burns to death (78). With this perspective, Sula goes beyond the bounds even of her family's sense of proper distance. She repeatedly opens up what Spillers calls "sub-perspectives or *angles onto* a larger seeing" because she disconnects elements of meaning that other people connect.[6] Her capacity to "just look" depends on experiencing no emotions or intentions that connect her to objects, and no meaningful links either between one experience and another.

Not only, then, does Sula's looking break with conventionally gendered identities because she actively looks at others,[7] but Sula's perception also causes breaks with constructions of meaning at work as symbolic orders. As Mae Gwendolyn Henderson has argued, the effect of Sula's breaks with meaning is "to disrupt or subvert the 'symbolic function of the language'" ("Speaking in Tongues" 33). Yet I do not think Sula works as a deconstructive reader, as Henderson argues.[8] Although Sula certainly breaks apart meanings others assign to experience, she fails to produce the sense of contested meaning that deconstruction produces when a struggle for meaning is revealed within apparently masterful structures. Like Wigley's houses that are houses only insofar as they are haunted, the deconstructed structure is recognized as a presence inseparable from absence, a place constituted by displacements. In the eyes of others—within the community, and from the reader's perspective—Sula has a deconstructive effect, since she becomes a scapegoat, a necessary presence who is also outcast. But in Sula's personal experience there is little of the tension of deconstruction. She is capable of imagining anything as anything, it seems, and her "gift for metaphor" (121) suggests that she can imagine anything in the place of anything else. But her displacements lack the consistency necessary to both constructed and deconstructed meaning.

Whereas deconstruction contests the limits that hold meaning secure, Sula destroys meaning. One could say that she demeans experience, since she converts meaningful experience into sheer loss. Her losses are never recouped and her breaks never repaired, because they never assume a form that gives them consistency. As an "artist with no art form" (121), Sula lacks not only form but occupation, and her disengagement precludes meaning.

When Sula experiences consistency, it occurs only as an event in time, something that cannot be consistently maintained. There are several points in the novel when Sula attempts to hold herself together, or imagines doing so. But in each case her hold breaks, and she comes apart. Her experience of sexual intercourse is described in these terms; her body feels both pulled together and dispersed: "[P]articles of strength gathered in her like steel shavings drawn to a spacious magnetic center, forming a tight cluster that nothing, it seemed, could break. . . . But the cluster did break, fall apart, and in her panic to hold it together she leaped from the edge into soundlessness" (123). When she is making love to Ajax, she thinks about his face "in order to confine, for just a while longer, the drift of her flesh toward the high silence of orgasm" (130). But she only contains the slippage of her own body by imagining that she can split his apart.

> If I take a chamois and rub real hard on the bone, right on the ledge of your cheek bone, some of the black will disappear. It will flake away into the chamois and underneath there will be gold leaf. . . .
> And if I take a nail file or even Eva's old paring knife—that will do—and scrape away at the gold, it will fall away and there will be alabaster. . . .
> Then I can take a chisel and small tap hammer and tap away at the alabaster. It will crack then like ice under the pick, and through the breaks I will see the loam. . . . (130)

Breaking away his face in bits, Sula exercises no imaginative containment of her own body or his.

What might be parts of a struggle for representative order, then, occur as displacements with no meaning at all. Sula breaks apart bodies, in fact and in imagination, whose parts remain split apart. And as she claims to mean nothing by such actions, she also breaks apart the meaningful constructions that attach motive, intention, and logical causes to events. As she says of Ajax,

" 'It's just as well he left. Soon I would have torn the flesh from his face just to see if I was right about the gold and nobody would have understood that kind of curiosity. They would have believed that I wanted to hurt him just like the little boy who fell down the steps and broke his leg and the people think I pushed him just because I looked at it'" (136–137).

Attaching events to motives and feelings, others in the Bottom combine parts of experience that Sula separates. The neutrality of Sula's curiosity is seen by others as (im)moral intention, and events are made meaningful by being made to add up. But those who accumulate meaning by weaving persons, things, events together in this way become "spiders" in Sula's eyes, and she has contempt for them and their webs (120).

Neither weaving meaning together nor moving along the diverting paths of Derridean *différance*, Sula does not make the kinds of connections necessary to either process.[9] Perhaps, Morrison suggests, this is because Sula herself doesn't add up; her identity isn't the result of accumulation but instead is an experience of inconsistency:

As willing to feel pain as to give pain, to feel pleasure as to give pleasure, hers was an experimental life—ever since her mother's remarks sent her flying up those stairs, ever since her one major feeling of responsibility had been exorcised on the bank of a river with a closed place in the middle. The first experience taught her there was no other that you could count on; the second that there was no self to count on either. She had no center, no speck around which to grow. In the midst of a pleasant conversation with someone she might say, "Why do you chew with your mouth open?" not because the answer interested her but because she wanted to see the person's face change rapidly. She was completely free of ambition, with no affection for money, property or things, no greed, no desire to command attention or compliments—no ego. For that reason she felt no compulsion to verify herself—be consistent with herself. (118–119)

Morrison here suggests that an ego is some kind of accumulation that Sula cannot amass because of distances she keeps. On the one hand, Sula does not "accumulate" because she cannot feel love. But to use the more physical terms of Morrison's descriptions, Sula doesn't attach one thing to another. With no interest in acquisition, or accumulation, or drawing anything like others' attention towards herself, Sula simply doesn't function in terms of combination or collection or accretion.

She functions in terms of slippage. Sula's mother "slips" when she says she doesn't love her daughter within Sula's hearing. Sula's hand slips when she cuts off part of her finger, and Chicken Little slips out of her hold when he flies to his death. Giving her nothing "to count on," such slips give her no possibility of accumulation. Neither self nor other takes shape or acquires form in Sula's experience. Other characters in the novel can control slippage, with forms that set limits to things in time and space. But Sula has no form of keeping anything, and so every slip turns into a dead loss.

MISSING AJAX

How such experience might enable definition to occur is suggested most clearly when Ajax leaves Sula. Throughout the novel, Sula remains unable to hold onto anything: and this despite the fact that, with Ajax, she "began to discover what possession was. Not love, perhaps, but possession or at least the desire for it" (131). The first effect of this desire is to drive Ajax away. Once he is gone, moreover, Sula can find no "evidence of his having ever been there" (134).

The one thing of his that she finds is his driver's license, but that, bearing a different name, doesn't allow Sula to recover Ajax so much as it makes her feel she never knew him at all:

Albert Jacks? His name was Albert Jacks? A. Jacks. She had thought it was Ajax. All those years. Even from the time she walked by the pool hall and looked away from him sitting astride a wooden chair, looked away to keep from seeing the wide space of intolerable orderliness between his legs; the openness that held no sign, no sign at all, of the animal that lurked in his trousers; looked away from the insolent nostrils and the smile that kept slipping and falling, falling, falling so she wanted to reach out with her hand to catch it before it fell to the pavement. . . . (135)

As a representation of Ajax, the driver's license signals only absence. Not only does it give Sula nothing to hold onto, it generates memories of repeated slippages: open spaces that hold no sign, eyes that look away, open smiles that slip away too.

"In psychoanalytic terms," says Elisabeth Bronfen, "the healthy trajectory from mourning to remembrance or commemoration is marked by a freeing of libidinal energies from the first lost object that must be reinvested in a second surrogate object, who may be perceived in the image of the deceased" (327). Not only can Sula not attach herself to a substitute object, she cannot remember Ajax *as* an object. The images she recalls are not images of the deceased but images of decease, as she finds, in her house and in her memory, things already missed, or signs and images of him *as* missing, in part and whole.

Sula can't get hold of him, and she cannot "get hold" of herself. The forms in which she represents herself to herself are as inconsistent as the forms in which she remembers Ajax:

"When I was a little girl the heads of my paper dolls came off, and it was a long time before I discovered that my own head would not fall off if I bent my neck. I used to walk around holding it very stiff because I thought a strong wind or a heavy push would snap my neck. Nel was the one who told me the truth. But she was wrong. I did not hold my head stiff enough when I met him and so I lost it just like the dolls." (136)

Here Sula realizes two different forms, in the paper dolls and in the expression "I lost my head," which depict figuratively the human body or part of it. If her "gift for metaphor" is at work here, the attempt at representation nevertheless fails to produce any difference between the figures and the body. Sula might use the figure to distance herself from loss, by displacing loss from herself to the doll. But instead, Sula sees the figure's likeness as a mere *repetition* of her self; and as such, it is subject to the same slippage she is. Such representations provide no relief from her experience of loss because the initial displacement of loss, from her body to figures of the body, travels back to inhabit the same place as the body. One thing doesn't stand for another; both together fall apart.

Identifying, as usual, breakages rather than the attachments and combinations that would enable her to give her experience meaning, Sula experiences missing rather than mourning. Instead of recovering parts of the lost Ajax, she experiences his absolute absence:

[H]e had left nothing but his stunning absence. An absence so decorative, so ornate, it was difficult for her to understand how she had ever endured, without falling dead or being consumed, his magnificent presence.

. . . His absence was everywhere, stinging everything, giving the furnishings primary colors, sharp outlines to the corners of rooms and gold light to the dust collecting on table tops. When he was there he pulled everything toward himself. Not only her eyes and all her senses but also inanimate things seemed to exist because of him, backdrops to his presence. Now that he had gone, these things, so long subdued by his presence, were glamorized in his wake. (134–135)

What happens here is not traditional figuration, according to which forms contain meaning by the consistency and definiteness of their boundaries. Here, figuration depends not on internal consistency and presence but on an external suffusion of absence. Absence, that is, spreads around things, and as it does they become decorative and ornate; they begin to function as figures. In this passage, absence assumes the decorative and ornamental role taken by figures in traditional metaphysics. According to tradition, metaphysics, like architecture, composes meaning in layers of construction, from the ground up. Mark Wigley discusses the identification of philosophy with architecture in these terms: "Philosophy's traditional description of itself and its object as building invokes and sustains a particular image of architecture as a mechanism that precedes and controls the decorative images attached to it through its structural bond to the ground" (12). In Derrida's "displacements of the traditional architectural figure," Wigley clarifies, "structure is no longer simply grounding through a continuous vertical hierarchy from ground to ornament, but a discontinuous and convoluted line. . . . The sense of structure is actually produced by the supplementary layers of representation that appear least structural" (27). Morrison depicts an absence functioning as "ground" in terms that resemble Derrida's deconstructive analysis, insofar as the ground against which figures take form is not solid. But the crucial fact about the "background" that glamorizes Sula's things is that it is occupied by an absence. Not solid but not empty either, the ground for figuration is a missing person.

Given the absence of Ajax, every thing in the room acquires sharp edges as separate forms. What is missing is any relation between these objects, which were seen in Ajax's presence relative to him, as "backdrops to his presence." Sula does not now see things relative to each other; there is no center or standard to which she can relate the things she sees. This is a crucial characteristic of Sula's vision. She does not merely break forms apart; she perceives things without the connections between them afforded by relations. And this means that Sula has a strange experience of things and people that does not, perhaps, produce meaning but that does produce definition.

At one other point in the novel, Sula's capacity to do so is described. This is when she returns to the Bottom after years of absence and Nel realizes how Sula changes things:

Was there anyone else before whom she could never be foolish? In whose view inadequacy was mere idiosyncrasy, a character trait rather than a deficiency? . . . Sula never competed; she simply helped others define themselves. Other people seemed to turn their volume on and up when Sula was in the room. More than any other thing, humor returned. She could listen to the crunch of sugar underfoot that the children had spilled without reaching for the switch; and she forgot the tear in the living-room window shade. . . .

Sula would come by of an afternoon, walking along with her fluid stride, wearing a plain yellow dress the same way her mother, Hannah, had worn those too-big house dresses—with a distance, an absence of a relationship to clothes which emphasized everything the fabric covered. When she . . . stepped inside, the dishes piled in the sink looked as though they belonged there; the dust on the lamps sparkled; the hair brush lying on the "good" sofa in the living room did not have to be apologetically retrieved, and Nel's grimy intractable children looked like three wild things happily insouciant in the May shine. (95–96)

For Nel at least, Sula's presence has a glamorizing effect similar to the effect of Ajax's absence for Sula. Here, too, this effect seems due to an absence of relations. Sula sees things without relating them to anything else. Most strikingly, she does not recognize inadequacies, deficiencies, or anything wrong with things that are broken, dirty, or out of place. In order to do so, she would have to see things relative to what they should be, holding in her mind an image of how they would look if they were "right." But Sula's mind, not preoccupied by those forms or relations, does not reproduce them. She looks at things in an absence of relation. Thus it is that she dresses "with a distance, an absence of a relationship to clothes." Clothing might represent or reform the body, making it look different; this is the case with Helene Wright's clothing, for example. But for Sula there is no relation between her body and her clothes, which therefore do not seem to contain or alter her body at all.

Sula does not see things and think of what they might be or have been. She sees with an absence of the relations that would connect what is to what is not or to other things present. Things like the dirty dishes and the dust on the lamps seem to belong, therefore, where and as they are. This sense of belonging is different from a sense of place, because there is no relation between things and because there is no occupation with things. Sula emphasizes instead the absence between things and between things and persons; and in this she may be a sign of things to come. In 1965, when Nel misses the Bottom, she also misses places: "Maybe it hadn't been a community, but it had been a place. Now there weren't any places left, just separate houses with separate televisions and separate telephones and less and less dropping by" (166).

SULA'S PLACE

Finally, I want to consider one other pattern of spacing in the novel, which is the pattern used when most people in the Bottom deal with Sula. I discussed earlier ways in which Helene Wright and Eva Peace maintain consistency in their lives, by way of forms that set limits to experience. These women either rule out of bounds or carefully contain within bounds their histories of bodily loss of control, experienced when Helene turned to "custard" and Eva lost her leg. One holds herself together and the other displays her broken body, but both work to define and limit identity. When the people of the Bottom band together against Sula, yet another pattern of containment is practiced. Eventually, Sula becomes a "pariah" (122), but people do not throw her out: "The presence of evil was something to be first recognized, then dealt with, survived, outwitted, triumphed over" (118). Confusing and dangerous as she is, Sula becomes a means of limiting evil, of keeping others good, safe and secure.

These uses depend on recognizing Sula as a consistent phenomenon. In the eyes of others, she amasses weight and accumulates consistency, as evidence of her evil is collected together. The past is one source of evidence: "Everybody remembered the plague of robins that announced her return, and the tale about her watching Hannah burn was stirred up again" (112). The present is another source: Sula "came to their church suppers without underwear" (114); Shadrack "tips his hat" to her (116); and "Sula did not look her age" (115). Things that have not appeared evil before are suddenly recognized as such; thus the meaning of Sula's birthmark is suddenly "cleared up" (114). On the other hand, evil acts that have not before been attributed to her are suddenly reported as fact. In this collecting process, with "the weighty evidence piling up" (115), Sula is given "the final label." The men

said she was guilty of the unforgivable thing—the thing for which there was no understanding, no excuse, no compassion. . . . They said that Sula slept with white men. . . . [A]ll minds were closed to her when that word was passed around. . . .

Every one of them imagined the scene, each according to his own predilections—Sula underneath some white man—and it filled them with choking disgust. (112–113)

As the minds of others close to her, they also keep thinking about her. The choking disgust they can reiterate each time they imagine such scenes provides a constant replay of their distance from Sula. In these replays, they both contain evil within her and distance themselves from the forms she takes in their imaginations.

For all the disgust and separation produced in this process of placing Sula, she is not placed outside the group, which in fact comes to depend on her for their own sense of place. Once she is identified as a total evil, she becomes necessary to the Bottom as something like a moral standard, a limit marking off right from wrong.

Perceived as a generalized evil, Sula serves to make other people appear relatively good. Teapot's Mamma, called this "because being his mamma was precisely her major failure" (113–114), suddenly becomes a devoted mother when she can blame Sula for hurting her son. When Teapot falls down, Teapot's Mamma "told everybody that Sula had pushed him" and then "immersed herself in a role she had shown no inclination for: motherhood. The very idea of a grown woman hurting her boy kept her teeth on edge. She became the most devoted mother: sober, clean and industrious" (114). Once an "indifferent mother" (113), Teapot's Mamma becomes a good mother in order to be different from Sula. Sula becomes what Teapot's Mamma was formerly—"a grown woman hurting her boy"—and Teapot's Mamma, displacing her own evil onto Sula, becomes perfectly good. The space of difference here is occupied by Sula, who is used by others to realize and define the difference between good and evil.

Identifying Sula as a personification of evil relieves these people of the burden of their own evil and displaces it onto her. She then becomes what they are not, and others are seen in relief against her and distinguished by their difference from her. They can become good because, in their minds, she has become evil. "Once the source of their personal misfortune was identified, they had leave to protect and love one another. They began to cherish their husbands and wives, protect their children, repair their homes and in general band together against the devil in their midst" (117–118). Not only does Sula inhabit the space that provides moral distinction, but she is also both a means of distinguishing others and a means of bonding others together, since she is used to externalize difference and keep it beyond the bounds of those whose security lies in their consistency. They hold together insofar as they can use Sula to contain the differences that would otherwise divide them.

Sula becomes a means of relating people in the Bottom both because she is an excuse for them to band together and because she is a standard in relation to which they acquire relative value. She functions as she remembers Ajax functioning for her: as a presence who "pulled everything toward himself" (134) and gave things a center. But she remains an "absence of relationship," in that what collects around her are negations: what others are not and do not want to be. Sula is the figure constructed by others in patterns of collection and containment, a figure upon which their gossip and their imaginations can focus their own negation. She is a center, a mass, of negation. For this reason, when she dies people are glad to be rid of her.

Sula's place in the Bottom, then, is a place of absence: she is identified as evil, she is identified as what others are not, she is seen as having no place there. Sula places absence in another sense too. As the location of evil and the reference point for others' negation, Sula takes the place of evils that are absent from the Bottom, specifically the evils of racism practiced by white people. Identifying Sula as evil allows them to contain both good and evil within their midst and to thereby avoid making any reference to the white people outside the Bottom. Insofar as they can contain evil within Sula, people can use her to contain their anger at those evils they are powerless to remedy.

When Sula dies, nobody misses her. People feel "that either *because* Sula was dead or just *after* she was dead a brighter day was dawning" (150–151). But instead, without Sula the Bottom begins to come apart: "mothers who had defended their children from Sula's malevolence (or who had defended their positions as mothers from Sula's scorn for the role) now had nothing to rub up against. The tension was gone and so was the reason for the effort they had made. Without her mockery, affection for others sank into flaccid disrepair" (153). As people let go of the bonds that gave them coherence, "[a] falling away, a dislocation was taking place" (153); and this loss of place is realized on National Suicide Day, at the construction site of the proposed tunnel.

As people recognize their absence of relation in that place, they experience firsthand the losses that Sula kept from them. These are primarily, as I mentioned earlier, losses of relation, of any connection between people and the objects they see, any attachment forged by labor or hope or promise. Without such connections, they see things that they hoped for but that never existed: school shoes, repaired teeth; as well as things that existed but that were broken or cut: coal credit, toilets. Like the "leaning porches" and "slurred re-marks" of the employers whose malevolence is "staggering," all these objects are characterized by an indistinction or a slippage of form, so that they are not what they should be.

Without Sula among them, it is as if people must themselves experience the absence of relationship she contained. They lose their place: slipping out of control, breaking all the tools and equip-ment they can, and moving into a sheer absence of relationship:

They didn't mean to go in, to actually go down into the lip of the tunnel, but in their need to kill it all, all of it, . . . they went too deep, too far . . .

A lot of them died there. The earth, now warm, shifted; the first fore-pole slipped; loose rock fell from the face of the tunnel and caused a shield to give way. . . . With the first crack and whoosh of water, the clamber to get out was so fierce that others who were trying to help were pulled to their deaths. (161–162)

Slipping to their deaths, on "ground" that no longer holds together, these people realize Sula's absence. As they move into identity with her, they clarify the need for the spacing that has kept them apart.

MISSING ABSENCES

Finally, I want to stress some of the implications of a spatial reading of *Sula* for conceptions of African American identity and African American history. To do so, I will turn briefly to Morrison's depiction of racist literature in *Playing in the Dark*. From the seventeenth through the twentieth centuries, Morrison argues in *Playing in the Dark*, the African population of the United States was used by European American writers to work through their own fears and insecurities: particularly, early on, those insecurities experienced as members of a new nation in a strange land.

Black slavery enriched the country's creative possibilities. For in that construction of blackness *and* enslavement could be found not only the not-free but also, with the dramatic polarity created by skin color, the projection of the not-me. The result was a playground for the imagination. What rose up out of collective needs to allay internal fears and to rationalize external exploitation was an American Africanism—a fabricated brew of darkness, otherness, alarm, and desire that is uniquely American. (38)

With Africanism as a background, the white American male is able to sort out his own inner conflicts by transferring the unwanted parts of himself onto a "blank darkness" (38) of "rawness and savagery" (44). According to this redistribution, white people can be seen as enlightened, civilized, free, and individual because black people are seen as dark, savage, enslaved, and personally undifferentiated. The white character and the white population are relieved of inner duality and duplicity, and white and black persons both are simplified into "black and white" terms.

Identifying "American Africanism" in American literature written by whites as a background for the distinction of autonomous white men, Morrison sees this background as in fact composed of figures. The distinction of some figures depends on rendering other figures invisible, identifying them as part of an undifferentiated mass; refusing, that is, to see them. Morrison's spatial conception thereby refigures the relation of figure to ground. The ground is itself composed of figures, but with so little space between them as to appear undifferentiated. The figures that appear "against" such a background stand out only because they keep their distance from others.

In *Sula*, people in the Bottom amass an identity of evil called Sula that functions somewhat like the "background" of racism Morrison identifies in white American literature. But the need for such a ground, and its effects, is different. One might say there is a projection of evil within the black community useful to withstanding the projections practiced upon the community by whites. Under pressure from external forces of racism, people in the Bottom distribute their moral variations among themselves in order to contain what they could project into the white population only at the risk of their own lives. What they contain is not only the evil that would more accurately be located outside their community but their own rage, which, because limitless, cannot be stopped once let loose.

To see Sula's experience in these terms allows for the recognition of missing experience of several kinds. Morrison depicts African-American, historical experiences of loss rather than identifying loss, from a poststructuralist perspective, as a necessary and nonindividualized component of experience. In African-American life Morrison identifies both material losses—missing persons, and parts of persons—and nonmaterial losses—lost relations, lost possibilities—whose absence is historically significant. To miss these "things" that never were is to locate historical significance in nonmaterial as well as material experience and to insist, moreover, that the historical experience of loss extends far beyond material suffering.

NOTES

[1]Among the critics who have considered Morrison's depictions of lost or missing experience are Mae G. Henderson, who discusses "the imaginative and reconstructive recovery of the past which characterizes Morrison's fictive process" ("Toni Morrison's *Beloved*" 66). Henderson identifies in *Beloved* a particularly female reconstruction of a past along "motherlines" (76–77). I am pointing to Morrison's recognition of elements of past experience that cannot be reconstructed or recovered because they never were realized in the past.

[2]In the 1976 interview, Morrison goes on to say: "There's a lot of book after she dies, you know. I wanted them to miss her presence in that book as that town missed her presence" (218).

[3]Valerie Smith discusses difficulties posed by poststructuralism for historical understanding and argues that in *Beloved* Morrison "asserts and reasserts the subjectivity of the former slaves and the depth of their suffering" largely by excluding that experience from representation (354). I am trying to pinpoint in *Sula* ways in which Morrison practices a more inclusive representation of missing experience, although I agree with Smith that Morrison repeatedly insists on the missing charac-

ter of missing experience. I would resist, therefore, identifying inclusiveness with fulfillment, and in this I differ from Robert Grant. Grant argues that in *Sula* "memory acts as a cognitive and imaginative synthesizing connector of the lapses, gaps, absences" (100) in the narrative, as the various "lacks become the sources of figurative fulfillment through memory and/or imaginative projection" (96).

[4]Kathryn Bond Stockton discusses the importance of toilet and anal imagery in the novel and argues that "Morrison dares to value 'debasement'" (82).

[5]Historical difficulties with identifying either African American males or females with conventional symbolic and political orders are discussed by Hortense J. Spillers in "Mama's Baby, Papa's Maybe: An American Grammar Book." She argues that "the African-American woman, the mother, the daughter, becomes historically the powerful and shadowy evocation of a cultural synthesis long evaporated—the law of the Mother—only and precisely because legal enslavement removed the African-American male not so much from sight as from *mimetic* view as a partner in the prevailing social fiction of the Father's name, the Father's law" (80).

[6]More specifically, Spillers argues that Sula breaks with two conventions of African-American female heroism, "uninterrupted superiority on the one hand and unrelieved pathology on the other," evident in Margaret Walker's Vyry Ware and Zora Neale Hurston's Janie Starks; but that "Sula, Vyry, and Janie need not be seen as the terms of an either/or proposition. The three characters here may be identified as sub-perspectives, or *angles onto* a larger seeing" ("Hateful Passion" 232).

[7]Recent feminist film critics have debated the role of the female spectator but insisted that women experience looking differently from men. As Mary Ann Doane summarizes differences in gendered spectators,

Male scopophilia has a well-defined and quite specific object—the female body. The male gaze is fixed to the image of the castrated maternal body and obsessed with its implications for the coherence of male identity. . . . The woman, on the other hand, cannot *look* at that body (except in the mirror of her own narcissism) because she *is* it. Female scopophilia is a drive without an object, an undirected and free-floating drive which is conducive to the operation of the phobia. (141)

Doane thereby likens female spectatorship to Julia Kristeva's depiction of abjection.

The degree to which such feminist theory can be applied to the experience of African-American women has been the subject of much discussion. Patricia Hill Collins has suggested that similarities in "values and ideas that Africanist scholars identify as being characteristically 'Black'" and "ideas claimed by feminist scholars as being characteristically 'female'" are due to "the material conditions of oppression." These apparently "can vary dramatically and yet generate some uniformity in the epistemologies of subordinate groups" (756–757).

[8]See Henderson's discussion, in "Speaking in Tongues," of Sula's "deconstructive reading of the black male text" (34–35) and of her ability to transform "unity into diversity, formlessness into form" (36). Henderson's identification in *Sula* of a multivocal and "progressive model for black and female utterance" (35) is in keeping with Deborah E. McDowell's analysis of disruption in the novel. McDowell emphasizes how Sula and her story break connections required of "the 'positive' racial self" (77) as well as those necessary to knowledge. And McDowell argues that because the novel "opposes a single unified image of the black SELF" it allows "metaphors of self" to "glory in difference" (87–88).

[9]Patricia Klindienst Joplin is one feminist critic to identify weaving as the female antithesis of violent male constructions of meaning. "As an instrument that binds and connects, the loom, or its part, the shuttle, re-members or mends what violence tears apart. . . . War and weaving are antithetical not because when women are weaving we are in our right place, but because all of the truly generative activities of human life are born of order and give rise to order" (51). Jacques Derrida also identifies a "fabric" of differences rather than a fiction of oppositions as the form of meaning. Neither present nor absent, *différance* nevertheless always implies something missing. But the sense that "the diverted presentation continues to be somehow definitively and irreducibly withheld" functions as a binding mechanism. "[D]ifférance holds us in a relation with what exceeds (though we necessarily fail to recognize this) the alternative of presence or absence" (151).

WORKS CITED

Baker, Houston A., Jr. "When Lindbergh Sleeps with Bessie Smith: The Writing of Place in *Sula*." Gates and Appiah 236–260.

Bronfen, Elisabeth. *Over Her Dead Body: Death, Femininity, and the Aesthetic*. New York: Routledge, 1992.

Collins, Patricia Hill. "The Social Construction of Black Feminist Thought." *Signs* 14 (1989): 745–773.

Derrida, Jacques. "Différance." *Speech and Phenomena and Other Essays on Husserl's Theory of Signs*. Trans. David B. Allison. Evanston: Northwestern UP, 1973. 129–160.

Doane, Mary Ann. *The Desire to Desire: The Woman's Film of the 1940s*. Bloomington: Indiana UP, 1987.

Gates, Henry Louis, Jr., and K. A. Appiah, eds. *Toni Morrison: Critical Perspectives Past and Present*. New York: Amistad, 1993.

Grant, Robert. "Absence into Presence: The Thematics of Memory and 'Missing' Subjects in Toni Morrison's *Sula*." *Critical Essays on Toni Morrison*. Ed. Nellie Y. McKay. Boston: Hall, 1988. 90–103.

Henderson, Mae Gwendolyn. "Speaking in Tongues: Dialogics, Dialectics, and the Black Woman Writer's Literary Tradition." *Changing Our Own Words: Essays on Criticism, Theory, and Writing by Black Women*. Ed. Cheryl A. Wall. New Brunswick: Rutgers UP, 1989. 16–37.

——. "Toni Morrison's *Beloved*: Re-Membering the Body as Historical Text." *Comparative American Identities: Race, Sex, and Nationality in the Modern Text*. Ed. Hortense J. Spillers. New York: Routledge, 1991. 62–86.

Joplin, Patricia Klindienst. "The Voice of the Shuttle is Ours." *Stanford Literature Review* 1 (1984): 25–53.

Lemaire, Anike. *Jacques Lacan*. Trans. David Macey. London: Routledge, 1977.

McDowell, Deborah E. "'The Self and the Other': Reading Toni Morrison's *Sula* and the Black Female Text." *Critical Essays on Toni Morrison*. Ed. Nellie Y. McKay. Boston: Hall, 1988. 77–90.

Morrison, Toni. "'Intimate Things in Place': A Conversation with Toni Morrison." With Robert B. Stepto. 1976. *Chant of Saints: A Gathering of Afro-American Literature, Art and Scholarship*. Ed. Michael S. Harper and Robert B. Stepto. Urbana: U of Illinois P, 1979. 213–229.

——. *Playing in the Dark: Whiteness and the Literary Imagination*. Cambridge: Harvard UP, 1992.

——. *Sula*. New York: Knopf, 1973.

Smith, Valerie. "'Circling the Subject': History and Narrative in *Beloved*." Gates and Appiah 342–355.

Spillers, Hortense J. "A Hateful Passion, A Lost Love." Gates and Appiah 210–235.

——. "Mama's Baby, Papa's Maybe: An American Grammar Book." *Diacritics* 17.2 (1987): 65–81.

Stockton, Kathryn Bond. "Heaven's Bottom: Anal Economics and the Critical Debasement of Freud in Toni Morrison's *Sula*." *Cultural Critique* 24 (1993): 81–118.

Wigley, Mark. *The Architecture of Deconstruction: Derrida's Haunt*. Cambridge: MIT P, 1993.

CONTESTED VISIONS/DOUBLE-VISION IN *TAR BABY*[1]

Judylyn S. Ryan

IN HER INCISIVE CRITIQUE OF "THE RACE FOR THEORY," Barbara Christian deplores the "academic hegemony" of "Western philosophers from the old literary elite" (53, 51). Beyond the intense solipsism of this "new" critical discourse, the "takeover" constitutes as well an ideological hegemony since it imposes an interpretive framework that is both Eurocentric and androcentric on literature by "black, women, [and] third world" writers (52). Among the many consequences Christian discusses is the development of an "alien" critical language and its tendency to obscure the political concerns and transformative intentions of the text. Toni Morrison has echoed this critique in *Playing in the Dark* with the observation that "Criticism as a form of knowledge is capable of robbing literature not only of its own implicit and explicit ideology but of its ideas as well" (9). Christian attempts to foil this robbery/displacement and, instead, to resituate the (Black woman) literary artist as conscious and primary theorist, for, she notes, "My folk . . . have always been a race for theory" (52). What distinguishes this tradition, Christian concludes, is that "our theorizing (and I intentionally use the verb rather than the noun) is often in narrative forms, in the stories we create, in riddles and proverbs, in the play with language, since dynamic rather than fixed ideas seem more to our liking" (52). Consequently, this discussion of *Tar Baby* pays particular attention to the "theorizing" within the text in order to explore several interpretive possibilities. First, to illuminate the ways in which the novel rejects the limiting prescription for a unidimensional discussion of gender conflicts, even as it confronts and responds to it as a significant constituent within a multidimensional and complex matrix. Second, to examine the ways in which the novel critiques a European materialist vision without renting the clichéd words, images and plots that are conventionally employed for any analysis of capitalist exploitation and class hierarchies. Third, to evaluate the depiction of individuals who are not permanently quagmired in the seeming immutability of their cultural/class "predicament"—with all its ramifications—but who, along with the readers, are assisted in imagining some form of resolution. And, finally, to suggest some of the ways in which the novel participates in and extends that conscious intertextuality— call-and-response poetics—among Black women literary artists.

Toni Morrison's fiction displays an extensive concern with the erasure of African[2] cultural consciousness and cultural history, and the persisting cultural illness which this erasure precipitates.[3] The cultivated lack of cultural historical consciousness, and the displacement of "peoplehood" which it engenders, is a central theme in several of Morrison's novels. In *Song of Solomon* (1977), for example, Milkman's inadvertent and increasingly captivating quest to literally piece together—to re-*collect*—the story of his ancestors facilitates the reinscription of his own cultural and historical consciousness. Milkman's acknowledgement and reevaluation of his abuse of Hagar and of his disrespect of Pilate, Ruth Foster, and his sisters *following* his recovery of the past is noteworthy. Since the erasure of cultural self-consciousness expresses itself in a range of self-destructive attitudes, Morrison rightly views these factors as central to understanding and, perhaps, resolving the particular tensions that exist between Black women and Black men. Coming after the transformation in Milkman's treatment of women—his relationship with Sweet, for example—which the recovery of his past inspires and facilitates, one might see *Tar Baby* (1981), with its compilation of antagonistic relationships, as the continuing elaboration of a cultural trauma which the earlier novel uncovers. In a 1982 interview with Nellie McKay, Morrison observed that "there is a serious question about black male and black female relationships in the twentieth century. I just think that the argument has always turned on something it should not turn on: gender. I think that the conflict of genders is a cultural illness" ("An Interview" 421). Of her several novels, *Tar Baby* is specifically crafted to explore this "serious question" of relationships between African men and African women in the twentieth century. Significantly, the "contentions" between Black women and Black men—alluded to in the novel's epigraph[4]—fall largely outside the parameters of gender(ed) relationships or heterosexual romance, and within the domain of class antagonisms. Morrison's observation must, therefore, be interpreted in its broader context, as a reference to the connections between the "conflict of genders," "cultural illness" and class conflicts. In light of Morrison's stated analysis of the origin and dimensions of conflicts within the Black community, a useful approach to interpreting the novel would be to examine the means by which it articulates this conviction that "cultural illness" influences and informs gender relationships within the African American community, as well as to evaluate the nature and history of that "cultural illness" so as to discover what possible insights the text offers toward a recovery and/or resolution.

In his turn-of-the-century definition of double-consciousness, W. E. B. DuBois accurately gauges the deleterious impact racism has on cultural self-consciousness and identity in his conclusion that "the Negro is . . . born with a veil, and gifted with second-sight in this American world,—a world which yields him no true self-consciousness, but only lets him see himself through the revelation of the other world" (14). In *The Souls of Black Folk* DuBois notes that "It is a peculiar sensation, this double-consciousness, this sense of always looking at one's self through the eyes of others, of measuring one's soul by the tape of a world that looks on in amused contempt and pity" (14). Although this difference is not articulated—but is implicit—in DuBois's discussion, the term "double-consciousness" refers to two distinct realities. As a process, double-consciousness refers to a state of psychological conflict between opposing cultural world views—what DuBois designates as the internalization of "two thoughts, two unreconciled strivings, two warring ideals." As a final state or outcome, double-consciousness refers to a debilitating resolution in which externally derived and distorted perceptions of the self constitute a *single* but alienated self-consciousness. Some eighty years after DuBois first coined the term, the Kenyan writer/critic Ngũgĩ wa Thiong'o detailed the features and lingering consequences of this outcome, placing it in a global context:

The effect of the cultural bomb is to annihilate a people's belief in their names, in their languages, in their environment, in their heritage of struggle, in their unity, in their capacities and ultimately in themselves. It makes them see their past as one wasteland of non-achievement and it makes them want to distance themselves from that wasteland. It makes them want to identify with that which is furthest removed from themselves; for instance, with other people's languages rather than their own. . . . The intended results are despair, despondency and a collective death-wish. (3)

In referring to these consequences as the *intended* results of a "cultural bomb," wa Thiong'o's analysis identifies the agency behind this double-consciousness which DuBois's discussion only vaguely signals. Wa Thiong'o concludes, "Imperialism is total: it has economic, political, military, cultural and psychological consequences for the people of the world today. . . . But the biggest weapon wielded and actually daily unleashed by imperialism against the collective defiance [of the oppressed] is the cultural bomb" (2-3). This observation illuminates the sociopolitical implications behind Morrison's text which re-presents a social milieu characterized by a prominent economic and political hierarchy, and which is most revealing in its simultaneous contemporaneity and its resemblance to the nineteenth-century southern plantation. Morrison's depiction of relationships in the plantation household of Valerian Street (whose name recalls the sleep-inducing drug extracted from dried roots) contributes to the full exposition of the ways in which the "cultural bomb" inculcates a self-alienating materialist world view, which in turn motivates class and gender conflicts between Black men and Black women.

Diversity among human beings guarantees a potentially beneficial range of different visions. However, when these different visions are manipulated to determine and denote advantages (economic, political and social) and disadvantages, choices available and choices unavailable, then these differences accrue an element of contestation. The contemporary world is characterized by a complex matrix with axes of contestation along dimensions of race/culture, class, gender, territorial/geopolitical nationality, religion, sexual orientation, etc. For obvious historical reasons, contestation has been a central feature of the social, political, and cultural dynamic between Euro-Americans and African Americans. This contestation, because it remains unmediated and unresolved (even now in the post-Civil Rights era), has generated a double-voiced social discourse, characterized by a Euro-American dominant voice/world view and an African-American "minor"/opposing voice/world view, which, in their humanist dimensions and directions, are substantively and categorically different. Interestingly, double-consciousness not only attests to the existence of these contesting visions, but it also reflects a "resolution" of sorts, in the acceptance of the dominant world view on the part of *some* African Americans. (Since the impact of racism and cultural imperialism, and the resistance to these, vary from place to place and over time, it bears mentioning that every African American is *not* equally vulnerable to double-consciousness. Likewise, the opportunities for transformative intervention also vary. Indeed, double-vision originates in some type of transformative intervention.) Double-vision represents an unchauvinistic comprehension of these contesting visions, as a prerequisite for mapping out a wholesome path of emergence—individually and collectively—from this debilitating conflict and irresolution.

Unlike *Song of Solomon*, which depicts Milkman's emergence and recuperation from "cultural illness" through his journey of immersion into the U. S. South,[5] *Tar Baby* is set on an island in the Caribbean owned by a retired Euro-American candy magnate, and focuses on a variety of relationships within Valerian's household: between the butler/maid couple, Sydney and Ondine Childs, dubbed "Kingfish and Beulah," and Valerian and his wife, Margaret, the "Principal Beauty of Maine"; between the Childs and their jet-setting niece, Jadine, "the Copper Venus"; between the indoor/"house" servants and the outdoor/"field" servants, Gideon and Thérèse, whom Sydney, Ondine and Jadine rename "Yardman" and "the Marys." The central focus, however, is on the relationship between the European-educated African American woman, Jadine Childs, and a Florida-born African man, called Son. For the first half of the narrative, there is, however, no "relationship" to speak of between the two. The most striking aspect of the relationship between Jadine and Son is not, however, its delayed beginning, but rather, that each, viewing the other's world as impoverished and/or unsafe, sees it as an occasion to "rescue" the other.

Waiting in New York City for Jadine's arrival from Isle des Chevaliers, the narrator states that Son "saw it all as a rescue: first tearing her mind away from that blinding awe. Then the physical escape from *the plantation*. His first, hers to follow two days later. . . . He thought of it not just as love, but as rescue" (189-190; emphasis added). Son's attempt to "rescue" Jadine from that "blinding awe" of all things European does not begin with the escape to New York. Rather, it begins during the nights he spent undetected in the house, in Jadine's bedroom, "when he crouched there watching her sleep and trying to change her dreams" (112). The narrator recalls that "He had thought hard during those times in order to manipulate her dreams, to insert his own dreams into her . . . the dreams he wanted her to have" (102), dreams that celebrate the day to day rituals of Black people's lives, unfettered by materialist trappings. Nevertheless, "he barely had time to breathe into her the smell of tar and its shiny consistency" (102). And while Son attempts to "insert his own dreams into" Jadine, he also recognizes that "at any moment she might . . . press her dreams of gold and cloisonné and honey-colored silk into him and then who would mind the pie table in the basement of the church?" (103). For Jadine, too, believes that they are *both* at risk, but for her, the danger lies in being claimed/seduced by the vision of a self-loving African woman consciousness embodied in the "diaspora mothers," the "night women." She confronts this possibility when alone in New York, waiting for Son to return from Eloe.[6] And when Son returns, she "fought him . . . but most of the time she knew she was fighting the night women. The mamas who had seduced him and were trying to lay claim to her. It would be the fight of their lives to get away from that coven that had nothing to show but breasts" (226).

While the conflict of genders may originate in cultural illness, the depiction of that illness in *Tar Baby* is both sexualized and gender-inflected. The references to Son's attempt to "insert" a culturally conscious dream into Jadine, and to Jadine's attempt to "press" her class-conscious dreams into Son, reveal the gendered aspects of this conflict. Not only does this sexualized and gendered liaison between Jadine and Son dominate the cast of contentious relationships, but their obsession with rescuing each other recalls several gender- and class-inflected narratives of rescue. On Son's part, these include the narrative of the peasant who rescues the princess from danger or imprisonment, the narrative of the culturally conscious/literate who rescues the culturally unconscious/alienated, the narrative of the supposedly mature elder who rescues the child/ Childs, and the narrative of the formerly enslaved African who returns to rescue another enslaved relative or friend via the Underground Railroad. (The use of Gideon's *pass*port to facilitate Son's departure completes the last motif.) On Jadine's part, the narrative patterns include the sophisticate who rescues/uplifts the "noble" savage from his primitivism; the representative of the "talented tenth" who rescues one of the designated untalented nine-tenths/folk from educational, cultural and sociopolitical stagnation; and the supposedly mature woman who rescues the son/Son.

Son's and Jadine's competing agendas for rescue and conflicting perceptions of the threat facing them underscore the central thematic axis in the novel: the problematic and contested nature of vision as an act and process informed by, and fraught with, historical, social, cultural and political consequences. Indeed, the nature and modes of seeing is a recurring motif in *Tar Baby*. The narrative introduces and develops this motif via the story of the one hundred blind horsemen who roam the hills of Isle des Chevaliers (and for whom the island is named):

Gideon told him a story about a race of blind people descended from some slaves who went blind the minute they saw Dominique. . . . Their ship foundered and sank with Frenchmen, horses and slaves aboard. The blinded slaves could not see how or where to swim so they were at the mercy of the current and the tide. They floated and trod water and ended up on that island along with the horses that had swum ashore. Some of them were only partially blinded and were rescued later by the French, and returned to Queen of France and indenture. The others, totally blind, hid. (130-131)

To determine the significance and source of this "blindness," one has to consider what these enslaved Africans would have seen after emerging from the pit of the slave ship. Two recent texts, both published after *Tar Baby*, and whose attention to a more historically meaningful depiction of Black peoples' lives exemplifies and extends the call-and-response dialectics among African women literary artists, provide an answer to this and other related questions.

In *i is a long memoried woman* (1983), Grace Nichols's titular narrator "had imagined this new world to be— / bereft of fecundity" but "wasn't prepared / for . . . the utter / rawness of life everywhere" (8). The abundance of cruelty, misery and death that was the crossing gave the women, men, and children in the pit of the slave ship the correct understanding that this was not prelude to paradise. For middle passage survivors, therefore, the brilliance and greenery of the "New World" landscape was inconsistent with their preconception of it as "bereft of fecundity." The fact that these Africans "went blind" must be seen as a willed and self-conscious act of survival, inspired by the need to decipher the promise hinted at in that beginning of hell, the slave ship. Hence the subsequent testimony of Nichols's long-memoried woman that "These islands green / with green blades" are "fertile / with brutality" (31). And in Paule Marshall's *Praisesong for the Widow* (1983), this recognition that the landscape which appeared to be blooming with the "rawness of life everywhere" was also "fertile / with brutality" prompted the homeward trek of those long-gone Ibos. As Aunt Cuney tells Avey,

[T]he minute those Ibos was brought on shore they just stopped, my gran' said, and taken a look around. A good long look. Not saying a word. Just studying the place real good. Just taking their time and studying on it.

And they seen things that day you and me don't have the power to see. 'Cause those pure-born Africans was people my gran' said could see in more ways than one. . . . Well, they seen everything that was to happen 'round here that day. . . . Those Ibos didn't miss a thing. Even seen you and me standing here talking about 'em. And when they got through sizing up the place real good and seen what was to come, they turned, my gran' said, and looked at the white folks what brought 'em here. . . . And . . . when they *knew* just from looking at 'em how those folks was gonna do, do you know what the Ibos did? Do you . . . ? [. . .]

   . . . They just turned, my gran' said, all of 'em . . . and walked on back down to the edge of the river here. Every las' man, woman and chile. And they wasn't taking they time no more. They had seen what they had seen and those Ibos was stepping! . . . Those Ibos! Just upped and walked on away not two minutes after getting here! (37-39)

To achieve this vision of the brutality awaiting them, without "missing a thing," these Africans had to blind themselves to the landscape's "cane dancing," "palm waving" come-back-to-Jamaica/Grenada/ Puerto Rico/South Carolina beauty, to close the short-sighted natural eyes in order to see, as Gideon says, "with the eye of the mind." In *Tar Baby*, the ones who "were only partially blinded" went to meet their supposed "rescuers" and were reenslaved. The others, having fully achieved "second sight"/double-vision, understood that "rescue" meant slavery and hid. Son's rejection of Jadine's plans to have Valerian finance his education and/or business venture signals his double-vision of the nexus between "rescue" and slavery/ indebtedness.

   This transformed blindness or second-sight, to return to the language of DuBois's analysis, is the primary feature in the strategies African peoples have devised to survive and overcome the fertile brutality of European/Euro-American imperialism in the "New World." Double-vision or second-sight differs from, but originates in, an *efun*-esque transformation of double-consciousness. (*Efun* is a ritually prepared chalk which is used for cleansing in Yoruba religion. It is said to have the power to transform the negative energy within an entity into a positive potential.) The word "nigger," *as African Americans use it intra-communally* to express, among other things, a benevolent cultural kinship, is a perfect linguistic example of this "cleansing"/transformation. The renaming of Not Doctor Street in *Song of Solomon* is another. It is, therefore, possible to refer to *efun*-esque transformations within African American experience.[7] Both of the examples above arise from an initial contestation: in the first, involving the image and definition of Black peoples, in the second, involving the naming of the territory, a Black neighborhood, to honor someone's ancestor—either Mister Mains (most probably), or Doctor

Foster. Significantly, the transformation does not erase the opposing signification. It simply clears a partial space to allow for an additional meaning, one that, moreover, remembers the history of contestation and the attempted distortion so that both the attempt to impose a distorted meaning and the resistance to that distortion are encoded in the transformed name. While double-consciousness is initially a negative experience characterized by an unreconciled and self-alienating "two-ness of being" in which externally derived distorted perceptions of the African identity are dominant ("measuring one's soul by the tape of a world that looks on in amused contempt and pity"), it can be "cleansed"/transformed into a positive potential—double-vision—which is contiguous with the blues impulse. That is, following this transformation there is a reconciliation and dialectic of the two seemingly antithetical possibilities: the ability to view oneself through one's own culturally informed, historically meaningful and communally affirmative perspective, with simultaneous access to the lenses constructed, and with which one is viewed by the machinators of that "cultural bomb." The person "gifted" with this double-vision achieves an understanding that is greater than the sum of the constituent realities. In its simultaneous presentation and mediation of contested visions of reality, *Tar Baby* extends this double-vision.

Contesting visions are introduced and developed throughout the novel, and in such a manner as to provide the reader with an insight into how they both inform and reflect social relations. The contestation of names that the characters assign to each other is illustrative. While Sydney, Ondine, and Jadine express their own double-consciousness and dehumanize Gideon and Thérèse by naming them "Yardman" and "Mary," respectively, Thérèse reciprocates their contempt for her by renaming them "bow-tie," "machete hair," and the "fast ass." Nevertheless, for the reader with a culturally informed double-vision, the name "Yardman," like the term "swamp women," carries a positive value as a coded reference to the folk, the ordinary and extraordinary Black people of Son's pie-table-in-the-church-basement dream memories. And while Margaret assigns Sydney and Ondine to a subordinate class/cultural status by designating them "Kingfish and Beulah"—a label that conspicuously announces its origin in minstrelsy—they express their contempt for her working-class background and assumed airs by dubbing her the "Principal Beauty of Maine." This depiction provides the reader with a more comprehensive understanding of the reciprocal nature of this contestation of naming. *Both* the superordinate and the subordinate exercise this prerogative of naming.

While the names of the central characters—Son and the Childses—evoke memories of the racist designation of Black men as "boys" and the paternalistic view of all Black people as childlike, Morrison's naming intensifies the contestation and prompts an urgent and introspective interrogation of the characters' maturity. For Jadine and Son, the two would-be mature rescuers, this interrogation escalates into a fierce exchange of accusations on the eve of their breakup, articulated through the narrative consciousness: "Each knew the world as it was meant or ought to be. One had a past, the other a future and each one bore the culture to save the race in his hands. Mama-spoiled black man, will you mature with me? Culture-bearing black woman, whose culture are you bearing?" (232).

Contestation also informs Son's and Jadine's differing perspectives of the world, and creates much of the friction in their relationship. The initial discrepancy in their perceptions sets the stage for the many contentions in their brief romance. Arriving in the United States from Isle des Chevaliers, Son sees that "The black girls in New York City were crying. . . . Crying from a grief so stark you would have thought they'd been condemned to death by starvation in the lobby of Alice Tully Hall" (185-186). Two days later, Jadine brings a different view, that "if ever there was a black woman's town, New York was it" (191). While neither will admit the validity of the other's perspective, for the reader with historically and culturally informed double-vision, both observations are clearly accurate.

Perhaps the most important description of contesting visions comes in the wake of Son's challenge to Valerian over his firing of "two people who had dared to want some of his apples" (175). Valerian is confident in his indignation over Son's impertinence in questioning him because "Somewhere in the back of [his] mind one hundred French chevaliers were roaming the hills on horses. Their swords were in their scabbards and their epaulets glittered in the sun. Backs straight, shoulders high—alert but restful in the security of the Napoleonic Code" (177). Son, on the other hand, is secure in his right to challenge "one of the killers of the world" because

Somewhere in back of [his] mind one hundred black men on one hundred unshod horses rode blind and naked through the hills and had done so for hundreds of years. They knew the rain forest when it was a rain forest, they knew where the river began, where the roots twisted above the ground;

they knew all there was to know about the island and had not even seen it. They had floated in strange waters blind, but they were still there racing each other for sport in the hills behind this white man's house. (177)

Interestingly, while the narrative consciousness registers and confirms the presence of the blind African horsemen, *only* Valerian visualizes the French militia men. Still, this discursive layering indicates a much larger dispute over whose social and cultural praxis is sanctioned by the competing histories contained in the geography.

If contestation characterizes the novel's internal dynamic, supratextually it facilitates a decisive resolution in mediating these differing visions toward the construction of a critically enabling double-vision. Indeed, the narrative structure expresses and participates in this double-vision. The representation and resolution in the botanical world of corresponding relationships and events in the human world demonstrates how double-vision informs the structure of the narrative. Morrison's representation of the botanical world in *Tar Baby* serves several related purposes. First, it allows her to critique a European/Euro-American capitalist apparatus that has unleashed a cycle of destruction on nature which we have only now come to acknowledge, amid the life-threatening realities of acid rain, ozone depletion, toxic waste, the contamination of lakes, rivers and oceans, etc. The description of what happened to the "[p]oor insulted, brokenhearted river" that becomes a swamp, Sein de Vieilles, exemplifies this innovatively articulated critique. Second, it allows her to develop and resolve complex human relationships and situations. The importance of the relationship between Jadine and Son is fully revealed through the double-vision afforded by a botanical representation, which occurs even before the two become lovers. And when, at the end of the novel, Son is "revolted by the possibility of being freed" of his enervating love for Jadine and redirected toward a culturally conscious vision, this dénouement is represented in a fusion of the escape motif from the tar baby story with the complicity of the botanical world with which he is in harmony. Finally, since the "swamp women" and "blind horsemen," who inhabit the natural world exploited and devastated by the capitalist agency of "killers of the world" like Valerian, are identified as Black women and Black men, the novel combines a description of the environmental/ecological consequences of capitalist exploitation with a description of the sociological consequences. The description of Jadine standing "up to [her] kneecaps in rot" in Sein de Vieilles is perhaps an oblique reference to the economic stagnation of Black communities like Eloe and, on a broader scale, to the declining economic condition of the

African American community as a whole. The briar patch "home" that Son remembers as "very dry, green and quiet" (144) has become a swamp.

Sein de Vieilles is the swamp created by the "killers of the world," a by-product of their program for maximizing their own wealth by "civilizing" the planet. While waiting in the stalled jeep for Son to return with the gasoline, Jadine decides to "seek shelter from the sun under the trees to the left of the road, in spite of the unpleasant odor" (155). When Jadine walks toward the swamp, she discovers that

> The trees were not as close together as she'd thought. Tall bushes had made them seem so. She approached the shade and peeped in between the trees. She almost laughed at what she saw. Young trees ringed and soared above the wavy mossy floor. . . . In the center under a roof of green was a lawn of the same dark green the Dutchmen loved to use. . . . It was amazing; the place looked like something by Bruce White or Fazetta—an elegant comic book illustration. She stepped through some bushes that looked like rhododendron and onto the mossy floor. The lawn, the center of the place began only a couple of yards ahead. She walked toward it and sank up to her knees. She dropped the pad and charcoal and grabbed the waist of a tree which shivered in her arms and swayed as though it wished to dance with her. (156)

Son is that "tree that wished to dance with" Jadine, as his magical movement in the narrative indicates.

In a conversation with Robert Stepto, Morrison confessed that "there is an incredible amount of magic and feistiness in black men that nobody has been able to wipe out. But everybody has tried" ("'Intimate Things'" 479). More than the young Cholly Breedlove who falls in love with Pauline's broken foot, more than Ajax—one of the people who could fly—more than Guitar or Milkman, Son, like his prototype, Tea Cake in Hurston's *Their Eyes Were Watching God*, is that Black "magic" man, whom the narrator repeatedly describes as a tree. While waiting for Jadine in New York, Son remembers having "stood in her bedroom, a towel wrapped around his waist. . . . Staring at a heart-red tree desperately in love with a woman he could not risk loving because he could not afford to lose her" (189), suggesting that he *is* the "tree that wished to dance with [Jadine]"! And when his first conversation with Jadine ends with her angry exit, Son

> stood before the mirror looking at his hair. It spread like layer upon layer of wings upon his head, more alive than the sealskin. It made him doubt that hair was in fact dead cells. Black people's hair, in any case, was

definitely alive. Left alone and untended it was like foliage and from a distance it looked like nothing less than the crown of a deciduous tree. (114)

The narrator's reflection on the "left alone and untended" beauty of Black hair contrasts sharply with Jadine's perception of Son's dreadlocked hair as "Wild, aggressive, vicious hair that needed to be put in jail. Uncivilized, reform-school hair. Mau Mau, Attica, chain-gang hair" (97). Typically double-conscious, Jadine acknowledges that "spaces, mountains, savannas—all those were in [Son's] fore-head and eyes" (135), but like her interest in the tamed, trimmed, civilized patch of lawn in the center of the circle of trees, she is only willing to admit her attraction to Son when he is "*clipped* and beautiful" (155; emphasis added). How Jadine responds to the tree whose waist she grabs, illuminates many aspects of the relationship between the two lovers and the influence of that cultural illness on their relationship.

After being disappointed in her advance toward the patch of "lawn of the same dark green the Dutchmen loved to use," Jadine holds on to the tree in desperation. The narrator states that

She struggled to lift her feet and sank an inch or two farther down into the moss-covered jelly. The pad with Son's face badly sketched looked up at her and the women hanging in the trees looked down at her. There is an easy way to get out of this, she thought, and every Girl Scout knows what it is but I don't. . . . Perhaps she was supposed to lie horizontally. She tightened her arms around the tree and it swayed as though it wished to dance with her. Count, she thought. I will count to fifty and then pull, then count again and pull again. She had only to hang on until Son returned and shout— fifteen minutes, not more. And she would spend it edging up the tree that wanted to dance. . . . Count. Just count. Don't sweat or you'll lose your partner, the tree. Cleave together like lovers. Press together like man and wife. Cling to your partner, hang on to him and never let him go. Creep up on him a millimeter at a time, slower than the slime and cover him like the moss. Caress his bark and finger his ridges. Sway when he sways and shiver with him too. Whisper your numbers from one to fifty into the parts that have been lifted away and left tender skin behind. Love him and trust him with your life because you are up to your kneecaps in rot. (156)

The insistent repetition of the tree wanting to dance with Jadine is Morrison's way of inscribing this love affair in a Black cultural context. As the editors of *The Heart of the Race* confirm, "Alongside music, dance has been our most important form of cultural expression. . . . Historically dance has always been integral to Black culture.

There is literally a dance for everything, back in the land of our ancestors—a dance for death, for birth, for weddings, for social occasions, for everything you can imagine" (Bryan et al. 202-203). Given the multifunctionality of dance in African culture, this seems a particularly appropriate coding of the love affair. Indeed the first part of their relationship—before Eloe—is really a dance of cleaving to, caressing, and covering each other. Of their early life in New York, the narrator states,

[H]e let her be still and cry after she told him about her mother and the awful hat she'd worn to the funeral. . . . She poured her heart out to him and he to her. Dumb things, secret things, sin and heroism. They told each other all of it. Or all they could. . . . Gradually she came to feel unorphaned. He cherished and safeguarded her. When she woke in the night from an uneasy dream she had only to turn and there was the stability of his shoulder and his limitless, eternal chest. No part of her was hidden from him. . . . He unorphaned her completely. Gave her a brand-new childhood. (193, 197)

At the beginning of the narrative, Jadine admits to her own "orphanhood," her lack of self-conscious understanding of, and alienation from, an African woman identity in thinking about the woman in yellow she had seen in a grocery store in Paris: "The woman had made her feel lonely in a way. Lonely and inauthentic" (40). Therefore, at the points in their relationship when Jadine seems to be moving toward a recovery of her cultural identity as an African woman, she is, in fact, being "unorphaned" and restored to her role as a *daughter*. When she goes to Eloe, Rosa, in repeatedly referring to her as "daughter," explicitly attempts to unorphan, reclaim, and revise Jadine's identity as a member of the cultural community. As Nanadine belatedly explains, "'A daughter is a woman that cares about where she come from and takes care of them that took care of her'" (242). In terms of the botanical representation, it is, therefore, understandable that the swamp women "were delighted when first they saw her, thinking a runaway child had been restored to them" (157). Back in New York, however, Jadine fiercely rejects this attempt to restore a self-conscious African female identity:

The night women [that is, *all* the Black women named in the narrative: Cheyenne, Rosa, Thérèse, Son's dead mother, Sally Sarah Sadie Brown, Ondine, Soldier's wife Ellen, Francine, her own dead mother, and the woman in yellow] were not merely against her (and her alone—not him), not merely looking superior over their sagging breasts and folded stomachs, they seemed somehow in agreement with each other about her, and were all out to get her, tie her, bind her. Grab the person she had worked hard to become and choke it off with their soft loose tits.

Jadine sipped the grapefruit juice. Its clean, light acid dissolved the morning cloud from her tongue. "No, Rosa. I am not your daughter, and he is not your son." (225)

Perhaps the most revealing sign of Jadine's confusion is her perception of breasts, a symbol of sustenance, as the implement for destroying—"choking off"—what she had become. Jadine is not, I think, unaware of the fact that these women are trying to reveal and nurture another dimension of her identity. Rather, she is afraid that whoever this person might be, she will be faced with the same lack of choice, the same economic and sociopolitical stagnation that these "swamp women" face. In reaching this conclusion, she mistakenly believes that the circumscribed lives these women lead stem from some *intrinsic* quality, some personal weakness on their part, rather than from capitalist exploitation: "The women [including 'Nanadine with the tight-fisted braids looking sorrowful at the kitchen table and accusatory in that room'] had looked awful to her: onion heels, potbellies, hair surrendered to rags and braids. And the breasts they thrust at her like weapons were soft, loose bags closed at the tip with a brunette eye" (225). So she tells Nanadine, "'I don't want to be . . . like you'" (243). Read carefully, however, the metaphor indicates that what Jadine has become is a manifestation of hunger or unconsciousness. Interestingly, this hunger first appears in the narrative in Son's perception that "The black girls in New York City were crying. . . . Crying from a grief so stark you would have thought they'd been condemned to death by starvation in the lobby of Alice Tully Hall. Death by starvation in Mikell's, death by starvation on the campus of C.U.N.Y. And death by starvation at the reception desks of large corporations" (185-186). The text underscores the importance of Jadine's rejection of the opportunity to "feed," and of this name/identity—and, by extension, Son's as well—when Nanadine insists, in her parting conversation with Jadine that

"a girl has got to be a daughter first. . . . And if she never learns how to be a daughter, she can't never learn how to be a woman . . . good enough even for the respect of other women. . . . You don't need your own natural mother to be a daughter. All you need is to feel a certain way, a certain careful way about people older than you are." (242)

Ondine's explanation emphasizes the reciprocal nature of daughter/ mother roles, and the symbiotic relationship between any generation and its elders.

While in Morrison's earlier novel *Song of Solomon*, Milkman lacks a self-conscious *grounding* in an African cultural and historical base,

Jadine is not only rootless but, in receiving a Eurocentric education, has been *grafted* onto a self-alienating cultural base from which to view her own and the experiences of other African peoples.[8] Roberto Fernández Retamar's discussion of cultural imperialism in *Calibán* offers an apt commentary on the character Jadine in his analysis of the figure of Ariel. In order to recover from the self-alienating effects of a Euro-American/European education, Retamar concludes that the "intelligentsia," for whom Ariel's eager subservience is exemplary, "must . . . sever the nexus *of dependence* upon the metropolitan culture from which it has learned, nonetheless, a language as well as a conceptual and technical apparatus. That language will be of profit, to use Shakespearean terminology, in cursing Prospero" (63). In "Friday on the Potomac," the introductory essay for the volume of critical essays on the Thomas/Hill hearings, *Race-ing Justice, En-gendering* Power, Morrison extends this analysis of the diseased relationship between colonizer-cum-"rescuer" and the colonized, noting that "The problem of internalizing the master's tongue is the problem of the rescued. Unlike the problems of survivors who may be lucky, fated, etc., the rescued have the problem of debt" (xxv). A typical representative of "the rescued," Jadine repeatedly expresses a deep (and false) sense of indebtedness to Valerian, telling Son "'a million times'" that "'He put me through school'" (226). Unassisted by helpers who might intervene to facilitate this recovery from the master's tongue and thought, Jadine wants only to *graft* Son into a similar relationship of indebtedness—as part of her "rescue" effort—as the argument over the financing of his college education demonstrates.

Jadine's narcotic dependence on Valerian both impairs her vision and creates an obsessive need to defend him. Son carefully notes the type of "blinding awe" Jadine's dependence on, and indebtedness to, Valerian creates. During the Christmas dinner shoot-out over the firing of Gideon and Thérèse:

Jadine had defended him. Poured his wine, offered him a helping of this, a dab of that and smiled when she did not have to. Soothed down any disturbance that might fluster him; quieted even the mild objections her own aunt raised, and sat next to him more alive and responsive and attentive than even his own wife was, basking in the cold light that came from one of the killers of the world. (175)

And while Valerian's opinion is important to her, her uncle's and aunt's are not: "They were family. . . . Nanadine and Sydney mattered a lot to her but what they thought did not" (41). Jadine completely distorts and denies the truth of the years of sacrifice her aunt and uncle made on her behalf, telling herself that "they had gotten Valerian to pay her tuition while they sent her the rest, *having no one else to spend it on*" (41; emphasis added). As she tells Son, "'[Margaret] and Valerian are my patrons.... They educated me. Paid for my travel, my lodgings, my clothes, my schools'" (101). The truth emerges, however, from Ondine's confession that "'We don't have a place of our own. And the little bit of savings went to Jadine. Not that I regret a penny of it. I don't.... I would have stood on my feet all day all night to put her through that school. And when my feet were gone, I would have cooked on my knees'" (166). Son later summarizes Jadine's responsibility to her uncle and aunt, giving his own corrective evaluation of Valerian's contribution to her education:

> "That was toilet paper, Jadine. He *should* have wiped his ass after he shit over your uncle and aunt.... Why don't you ask me to help you buy a house and put your aunt and uncle in it and take that woman off her feet? Her feet are killing her, killing her, and let them live like people for a change, like the people you never studied, like the people you can't photograph. *They* are the ones who put you through school, woman, they are the ones. Not him. They worked for him all their lives. And you left them down there with him not knowing if they had a job or not. You should cook for *them*. (226, 228)

The fact that Ondine looks much older than Margaret, even though the actual difference in their ages is only four years, perhaps indicates just how much "shit" has covered Ondine and Sydney.

The cultural dimensions and implications of Jadine's impaired vision appear in her actions, comments and conversations throughout the narrative. As an example, her comments on the relative merit of European art versus traditional African art fully reveal someone who, in the language of wa Thiong'o's analysis, viewing her past as "one wasteland of non-achievement," has distanced herself from that putative "wasteland" and clearly identifies with "that which is furthest removed from herself." As she informs Valerian, "'Picasso *is* better than an Itumba mask. The fact that he was intrigued by them is proof of *his* genius, not the mask-makers'" (62). Jadine is here expressing and endorsing an imperialistic view of the artistic production of one culture as mere raw material for the expression of European "genius." As a contemporary parallel, one would also expect her to agree that Paul Simon's music is "better" than the African musicians he *tried* to imitate, his interest being proof of Simon's "genius." These and other similar remarks indicate that

Jadine's formal education has provided her with no knowledge of her own culture and history. For while she claims to understand Picasso's genius, she displays not even passing interest in discovering the genius behind the mask-making tradition, nor even in evaluating the criteria for making these judgments involving different cultural aesthetics. Son's outburst on the paucity of her much-touted education, "'The truth is that whatever you learned in those colleges that didn't include me ain't shit. . . . If they didn't teach you that, then they didn't teach you nothing, because until you know about me, you don't know nothing about yourself. And you don't know anything, anything at all about your children and anything at all about your mama and your papa'" (227-228), is simply a very contemporary demand for a multicultural education. Jadine's response to this demand, "'You want to be a yardman all your life?'" (228), is disturbing in its suggestion that in order to be materially secure, to "ascend" out of the poverty trap, African peoples must dedicate themselves to the knowledge of European/Euro-American culture and that alone; or that knowledge of one's particular cultural history impedes socio-economic progress. Given the previous discussion of the positive reference coded in the name "Yardman," Jadine's question carries, as well, an element of surprise at Son's persistence in clinging to an African cultural identity and self-consciousness.

Jadine's rejection of the choice to heal her own double-consciousness by claiming an African woman consciousness is prefigured in the account of her entry into Sein de Vieilles when the swamp women—who are synonymous with the "night women"—discover, "upon looking closer [that] . . . This girl was fighting to get away from them" (157). Morrison fashions her own coded celebration of the human worth of these swamp women in their silent observation of Jadine's flight:

The women hanging from the trees were quiet now, but arrogant—mindful as they were of their value, their exceptional femaleness; knowing as they did that the first world of the world had been built with their sacred properties; that they alone could hold together the stones of pyramids and the rushes of Moses's crib; knowing their steady consistency, their pace of glaciers, their permanent embrace, they wondered at the girl's desperate struggle down below to be free, to be something other than they were. (157)

This reference to tar as a "sacred property" constitutes yet another example of *efun*esque transformation in the narrative. While most readers are familiar with the folktale—which Son later retells—about the white farmer who made a tar baby as a trap to destroy an allegedly pilfering rabbit,[9] supratextually tar is represented as the symbol for a positive cultural potential—that is, the Black woman's "exceptional femaleness." As Morrison explains in another interview, with Tom LeClair,

"Tar baby" is also a name, like "nigger," that white people call black children, black girls, as I recall. Tar seemed to me to be an odd thing to be in a Western story, and I found that there is a tar lady in African mythology. I started thinking about tar. At one time, a tar pit was a holy place, at least an important place, because tar was used to build things. It came naturally out of the earth; it held together things like Moses' little boat and the pyramids. *For me, the tar baby came to mean the black woman who can hold things together.* ("An Interview" 255; emphasis added)

Or, to use the language of this analysis, the Black woman who can reconcile and attain seemingly antithetical possibilities.

Subverting the standard view of the tar baby as an object created by and for another, Morrison, in yet another *efune*sque transformation, reclaims and represents the autonomous subjectivity of the tar baby. For the Black woman—whose identity as tar baby Morrison revises and validates—some form of initiation is required for the transformation into, and restoration of, her "true and ancient properties." Jadine's entry into Sein de Vieilles symbolizes the beginning of this transformative initiation. Her ability to value Son's human worth and to accept him as a mate, despite her initial estimate of him as a "swamp rat" evidences her beginning initiation. It is, therefore, overwhelmingly significant that the community of swamp women "were delighted when first they saw her, thinking a runaway child had been *restored* to them" (157; emphasis added). The description of Jadine's and Son's life in New York City—before Eloe— provides a parallel depiction of the early phase of Jadine's initiation and of the harmonious interaction of autonomous "tar baby" and "rabbit." In a jazz-like riff on the rabbit's signature, "Lickety-split," Morrison captures their vulnerability, sensitivity, and capacity for empowering each other in this early phase: "She wondered if she should hold back, keep something in store from him, but *he opened the part on her head with his fingers and drove his tongue through the part.* There was nothing to forgive, nothing to win and the future was five minutes away" (197). Once she balks at the initiation, however, Jadine's double-consciousness reasserts itself even more intensely.

Beyond the frequent references to her impaired vision, signalled by her shortcomings as visual artist/photographer, Jadine's distorted view of the world, and the fractured consciousness from which it derives, is fully displayed in her acceptance of reality as consisting of binary oppositions. On the verge of abandoning the initiation (into reconciling antithetical possibilities) which she—a "tar-less" African woman—has not been able to complete, she admits that "This rescue was not going well. She thought she was rescuing him from the night women who wanted him for themselves, wanted him feeling superior in a cradle, deferring to him; wanted her to settle for wifely competence when she could be almighty, to settle for fertility rather than originality, nurturing instead of building" (231). Although there is nothing inherently antithetical in nurturing and building, or in fertility and originality, Jadine has internalized what poet and essayist June Jordan describes in "Toward a Black Balancing of Love and Hatred" as "the white either/or system of dividing the world into unnecessary conflict" (85). Assuming the stance of the Cartesian subject, Jadine therefore posits these as polemical choices: nurturing *versus* building; fertility *versus* originality. Morrison concludes that "When we feel that work and the house are mutually exclusive, then we have serious emotional or psychological problems, and we feel oppressed. But if we regard it as just one more thing you do, it's an enhancement. Black women are both ship and safe harbor" ("An Interview," Lester 49).

Morrison's re-claiming of tar as an ancient property—as evidenced by the novel's dedication[10]—demonstrates that *efun*esque re-visions are both transformative and restorative. Indeed, *Tar Baby* is a novel whose central project involves several restorative dimensions. Apart from those already mentioned, the text restores a critical understanding of the ways in which class conflicts undermine and contaminate relationships between women and men, and of the extent to which the resolution of gender conflicts in the Black community is intimately connected to the struggle against cultural imperialism and the materialist vision it inculcates. As the novel demonstrates and as Morrison has observed,

Many of the problems modern couples have are caused not so much by conflicting gender roles as by the other "differences" the culture offers. . . . Jadine and Son had no problems as far as men and women are concerned. They knew exactly what to do. But they had a problem about what work to do, when and where to do it, and where to live. Those things hinged on what they felt about who they were, and what their responsibilities were in being black. The question for each was whether he or she was really a member of the tribe. ("An Interview," McKay 421-422)

In deciding to return to Paris, in pursuit of her unidimensional "greatness," Jadine offers her own response to the question of her membership in, recognition of, and responsibilities to "the tribe," especially the uncle and aunt who (mis)raised her and who, in their old age, are beginning to need her to hold things together:

She thought [New York City] could be a shelter for her because there the night women could be beaten, reduced to shadows and confined to the briar patch where they belonged. . . . There were no shelters anyway; it was adolescent to think that there were. Every orphan knew that and knew also that mothers however beautiful were not fair. No matter what you did, the diaspora mothers with pumping breasts would impugn your character. And an African woman [Ms. Morrison, perhaps?], with a single glance from eyes that had burned away their own lashes, could discredit your elements. (248)

Indeed, the novel convincingly discredits Jadine's agenda for "rescue," not because financial security is to be disdained, nor because it is maliciously intentioned, but because it is undergirded by a materialist and self-alienating consciousness which recommends selling one's cultural inheritance and "birthright for a mess of pottage" (214), as the narrator of James Weldon Johnson's *The Autobiography of An Ex-Colored Man* phrases it. At the same time, the text validates Son's "rescue" agenda, not because it is coherent or well-planned, but because it perceives and values "the ancient properties" that constitute a communally conscious cultural world view, although this is undermined by his attempt to *impose* rescue. Despite the deliberate omission of a critical commentary on Son's rescue agenda, supratextually he is revealed to be, like Jadine, an "orphan" of sorts and, as such, an incompetent helper. Nowhere is this more clearly depicted than in the violence with which he tries to "convince" Jadine of the correctness of his own view by hanging her out of the window. Indeed, the only successful intervention that the novel depicts is one that is framed by choice. Explaining her decision to bring Son to the far side of Isle des Chevaliers, Thérèse states, "'This is the place. Where you can take a choice. Back there you say you don't. Now you do'" (262). The element of conscious choice makes this not an act of rescue, but an act of survival—without indebtedness.

Toni Morrison develops a multilayered, and deceptively double-voiced discourse within *Tar Baby*. One layer involves the creation of a narrative consciousness that is intimately connected to the character Son but distanced from Jadine. Another involves an extensive exploration of the impact of "cultural illness" on the relationship between Jadine and Son, and an almost cursory, or coded, evaluation of its impact on the relationship between Jadine and her family/parents, Sydney and Ondine. Morrison's creation of a narrative consciousness that seems to acquiesce to, if it does not quite sanction, Son's perspective (shortsightedness and all) leaves the reader taken aback and frustrated, as he is, by Jadine's departure, and the failure of both the love affair and the "rescue" effort. As a result, the reader is emotionally invested in the question of *why* the rescue and initiation failed, and how this might have been prevented. That these questions linger beyond the novel's closure attests to Morrison's dexterity in positioning the reader so that s/he wants/ has to create some meaning out of the text. In "Rootedness: The Ancestor as Foundation," Morrison acknowledges that "to have the reader work *with* the author in the construction of the book—is what's important. What is left out is as important as what is there" (341).

Part of the answer to the reader's lingering questions about the rescue lies in the fact that while the question of *why* prioritize the rescue of Jadine is resoundingly answered, Son, the self-appointed rescuer, never fully considers *how* this might be performed. His handling of the central courtship ritual of taking the beloved to meet the people whom one is trying (or trying not!) to be/become demonstrates his insensitivity to Jadine's quite legitimate concerns and fears. This abandonment is prefigured in the account of Jadine's entry into Sein des Vieilles where she is both bewildered and disoriented, and must—in Son's absence—negotiate her own passage. Similarly then, Eloe is for the uninitiated—of whom Jadine is certainly one, despite her unrecognized cultural kinship to this community— a bewildering and disorienting territory. If double-consciousness is rightly perceived as an unconscious manifestation of involuntary cultural alienation, then some thoughtful intervention and/or initiation, not a sudden baptism or "rescue," is required to facilitate a transformation and recovery.

With regard to the more important question of Jadine's initiation, what needs to be considered is the impact on the two people for whom its incompletion entails the greatest consequence. Perceiving that Jadine has not yet matured into her role and responsibility as a daughter, Sydney and Ondine speculate on the likelihood of her fulfilling one of the most intimate and integral duties owed to one's parents:

> "You think she'll bury us, Ondine?"
> "I think we're going to have to bury ourselves, Sydney." (245)

While the tone here is quite dismal, it is still not definitive. At age twenty-five, with a global community of "night women" waiting, in

Paris, Rome, New York, and elsewhere, if not to rescue, then certainly to challenge and inspire her, Jadine may yet *re-collect* her "true and ancient properties" and move beyond double-consciousness to double-vision.

NOTES

[1]I would like to thank the following friends and colleagues for their comments on earlier drafts of this essay: Jacqui Alexander, Katherine Bassard, Wesley Brown, Abena P. A. Busia, Estella Conwill Májozo, Faith Smith, and especially Cheryl A. Wall.

[2]Throughout this discussion the word "African" is used interchangeably with "Black" to denote cultural identity and praxis, in contradistinction from its usage to denote a collective geopolitical nationality. The term "continental African" is used to indicate the latter.

[3]For New World African peoples the truncation of cultural history deliberately machinated during (and after) slavery has been and continues to be one of the most haunting absences. In *Their Eyes Were Watching God*, Zora Neale Hurston exposes this mutilation/absence when Nanny tells Janie that "'us colored folks is branches without roots'" (31). Hurston further alludes to its debilitating effect in the narrator's observation that "Nanny's head and face looked like the standing roots of some old tree that had been torn away by storm. Foundation of ancient power that no longer mattered" (26). For a discussion of the ways in which images of dismemberment are deployed throughout African American literature to signal psychological and political states, see Májozo.

[4]The epigraph reads in its entirety:

For it hath been declared
unto me of you, my brethen, by them
which are of the house of Chloe, that there are
contentions among you. I Corinthians I:II

[5]Milkman's "journey of immersion" into the South to reconnect with kin and culture exactly follows that of the "articulate kinsman" identified in Robert Stepto's study of African American narrative, *From Behind the Veil*.

[6]Eatonvillle, Hurston's all-Black hometown in South Florida, has been mythologized in her work and in contemporary criticism as a ritual ground that, despite its contradictions and limitations, was the sustaining foundation beneath Hurston's creativity and cultural self-consciousness. In the economically depressed Eloe, Morrison confronts us with the late-twentieth-century version of what that ritual ground, because of economic and political developments of the intervening five or six decades, would have evolved into. Beyond the similar geographies depicted in *Their Eyes Were Watching God* and *Tar Baby*, the drawing of the character Son also recalls Hurston's Tea Cake, who although not from Eatonville (he lives seven miles away in Orlando), is the man with whom Janie finally enjoys a fulfilling relationship, free of materialist obsession, and who assists her in maturing into a full self-confidence and capability. This conscious re-visioning of Hurston again exemplifies double-vision in the novel and contributes another dimension of historicity.

[7]My use of the term *"efun*esque transformation" seeks to advance the goal of inventing culturally informed critical tools for analyzing texts within the African

American literary tradition. Stephen Henderson's coinage of the term "mascon" in his profoundly illuminating interpretive model for *Understanding the New Black Poetry* exemplifies the enabling potential of this project. Henry Louis Gates, Jr., likewise a contributor to this effort with his expert deployment of "signifyin(g)" as a critical term, summarizes the broad objectives of this venture with the observation that "The challenge of black literary criticism is to derive principles of literary criticism from the black tradition itself, as defined in the idiom of critical theory but also in the idiom which constitutes the 'language of blackness,' the signifyin(g) difference which makes the black tradition our very own" (8).

[8]Indeed, Eleanor Traylor's analysis of *Tar Baby* suggests an even more deliberate abandonment: "Ondine and Sydney give Jadine over to Valerian and Margaret, who guide her choices and mold her ways and steer her thinking" (140).

[9]While Son's description confirms the version of the tale that Morrison uses, Trudier Harris offers a useful synopsis of other variants. Whatever the cultural "origin" and initial significance of the tar baby folktale, in the slavery and postslavery context it conveys an important socio-economic analysis. Given the history—begun in feudal Europe—of denying the rights of workers to any of the "carrots" they produced, the rabbit's pilfering, like Gideon's and Thérèse's, actually indicts the exploitative economic and political establishment that systematically overlooks and negates the physical risks experienced by workers, and reserves the harvest for the owners of capital who are identified as the sole risk-takers. Son's challenge to Valerian, "'You didn't row eighteen miles to bring [the apples] here. They did'" (177), explodes the myth, revises the entire episode, and provides us, in the words of Dionne Brand's poetry, with "old pictures of the new world."

[10]The dedication reads:
> For
> Mrs. Caroline Smith
> Mrs. Millie McTyeire
> Mrs. Ardelia Willis
> Mrs. Ramah Wofford
> Mrs. Lois Brooks
> —and each of their sisters,
> all of whom knew
> their true and ancient
> properties.

WORKS CITED

Brand, Dionne. "Old Pictures of the New World." *Chronicles of the Hostile Sun*. Toronto: Wiliams-Wallace Publishers, 1984. 59-61.

Bryan, Beverley, et al. "Self-Consciousness: Understanding Our Culture and Identity." *The Heart of the Race: Black Women's Lives in Britain*. London: Virago Press, 1985. 182-239.

Christian, Barbara. "The Race for Theory." *Cultural Critique* 6 (1987): 51-63.

DuBois, W. E. B. *The Souls of Black Folk*. 1903. *Three Negro Classics*. New York: Avon Books, 1965. 209-389.

Gates, Henry Louis, Jr. "Criticism in the Jungle." *Black Literature and Literary Theory*. New York: Methuen, 1984. 1-24.

Harris, Trudier. *Fiction and Folklore: The Novels of Toni Morrison*. Knoxville: U of Tennessee P, 1991.

Henderson, Stephen. *Understanding the New Black Poetry: Black Speech and Black Music as Poetic References.* New York: Morrow, 1973.

Hurston, Zora Neale. *Their Eyes Were Watching God.* 1937. Urbana: U of Illinois P, 1984.

Johnson, James Weldon. *The Autobiography of An Ex-Colored Man.* 1912. New York: Hill and Wang, 1960.

Jordan, June. "Notes Toward a Black Balancing of Love and Hatred." *Civil Wars.* Boston: Beacon P, 1981. 84-89.

Májozo, Estella Conwill. "From Dismemberment to Regeneration." *Black Books Bulletin* 8 (1991): 143-145.

Marshall, Paule. *Praisesong for the Widow.* New York: Dutton, 1983.

Morrison, Toni. "Friday on the Potomac." *Race-ing Justice, Engendering Power: Essays on Anita Hill, Clarence Thomas, and the Construction of Social Reality.* New York: Pantheon, 1992. vii-xxx.

———. "An Interview with Toni Morrison." With Tom LeClair. *Anything Can Happen: Interviews with Contemporary American Novelists.* Ed. Tom LeClair and Larry McCaffery. Urbana: U of Illinois P, 1983. 252-261.

———. "An Interview with Toni Morrison." With Nellie McKay. *Contemporary Literature* 24 (1983): 413-429.

———. "An Interview with Toni Morrison, Hessian Radio Network, Frankfurt, West Germany." With Rosemarie K. Lester. *Critical Essays on Toni Morrison.* Ed. Nellie McKay. Boston: G. K. Hall, 1988. 47-54.

———. "'Intimate Things in Place': A Conversation with Toni Morrison." With Robert Stepto. *Massachusetts Review* 18 (1977): 473-489.

———. *Playing in the Dark: Whiteness and the Literary Imagination.* Cambridge: Harvard UP, 1992.

———. "Rootedness: The Ancestor as Foundation." *Black Women Writers (1950-1980): A Critical Evaluation.* Ed. Mari Evans. New York: Anchor/ Doubleday, 1984. 339-345.

———. *Song of Solomon.* New York: New American Library, 1977.

———. *Tar Baby.* New York: New American Library, 1981.

Nichols, Grace. *i is a long memoried woman.* London: Karnak House, 1983.

Retamar, Roberto Fernández. "Caliban: Notes Towards a Discussion of Culture in Our America." Trans. Lynn Garafola, et al. *The Massachusetts Review* 15 (1974): 7-72.

Stepto, Robert B. *From Behind the Veil: A Study of Afro-American Narrative.* Rev. ed. Urbana: U of Illinois P, 1991.

Traylor, Eleanor W. "The Fabulous World of Toni Morrison: *Tar Baby.*" *Critical Essays on Toni Morrison.* Ed. Nellie McKay. Boston: G. K. Hall, 1988. 135-150.

wa Thiong'o, Ngũgĩ. *Decolonising the Mind: The Politics of Language in African Literature.* London: Heinemann, 1986.

part two

MORRISON AND THEORIES OF THE POST-

KNITTING AND KNOTTING THE NARRATIVE THREAD—*BELOVED* AS POSTMODERN NOVEL

Rafael Pérez-Torres

BELOVED WEAVES A STORY ON A SINGULAR FRAME: interpretation represents an integral part of black cultural and social identity. In Toni Morrison's book, the fictional characters and communities—as objects of exploitation in both slave and free-market societies—transform an essential absence into a powerful presence. A sense of self emerges from experiences of exploitation, marginalization and denial. Analogously, Morrison's narrative, confronting a facelessness the dominant culture in America threatens to impose on black expression, forges out of cultural and social absence a voice and identity. *Beloved* creates an aesthetic identity by playing against and through the cultural field of postmodernism.

At a very basic level, this engagement with postmodernism manifests itself in the aesthetic play of the novel. Throughout, *Beloved* demonstrates its concern with linguistic expression: the evocation of both oral and written discourses, the shifting from third person narration to omniscient narration to interior monologue, the iteration and reiteration of words and phrases and passages. While this linguistic and narrative variation is' evocative of an oral literature that shapes and retraces various tellings of the same story, it also demonstrates a concern (characteristic of experimental twentieth-century literary discourses) with the production and meaning of language. The text thus spins a story woven of myth that creates a pattern of sophisticated linguistic play. There is a crossing of genres and styles and narrative perspectives in *Beloved* that suggests it filters the absent or marginalized oral discourse of a precapitalist black community through the self-conscious discourse of the contemporary novel. The narrative emerges, then, at the point at which premodern and postmodern forms of literary expression cross.

The action in *Beloved* turns on processes of reinscription and reinterpretation. It intertwines the mythic, folkloric and poetic threads of an oral literature with the rhetorical and discursive trajectories of a postmodern literary landscape. The novel stands amid a cultural context in which play, allusion, quotation serve as privileged aesthetic techniques. *Beloved* and other novels that emerge from multicultural histories diverge from classically postmodern texts—Pynchon's *V,* Barth's *Giles Goat-Boy,* Barthelme's *The Dead Father*—in their relation to socio-historical realities. Henry Louis Gates has, for example, discussed the theoretical basis of black literature. His work has placed in a new light a tired issue: what distinguishes black literary production in the Americas from other literary works? He positions the question thusly: "the problem, for us, can perhaps be usefully stated in the irony implicit in the attempt to posit a 'black self' in the very Western languages in which blackness itself is a figure of absence, a negation. Ethnocentrism and 'logocentrism' are profoundly interrelated in Western discourse as old as the *Phaedrus* of Plato, in which one finds one of the earliest figures of blackness as absence, a figure of negation" (7). The question from this view becomes not how African American literary production distinguishes itself from other forms, but rather how—given socio-historical conditions compelling it towards silence—the literature manages to speak at all. Gates's work looks at the ways linguistic structures at once mask and reveal the social and political structures from which they arise and which they create. How can black writers, Gates questions, use a language in which blackness signifies absence to write about their own "blackness" as a source of identity? Gates will finally come to argue that black writers have had to digest both Western and non-Western forms of literary production. Out of this process they forge a literary discourse that transforms notions of blackness.

The "blackness" of black literary texts, historically read to signify a lack in Western discourse, becomes in Morrison's hands an important thread tying together the sometimes (especially in a North American context) all too disparate realms of politics and aesthetics. The "not" signified by blackness becomes for Morrison a means by which to weave her tale. A process of interpretation and reinterpretation in *Beloved* serves to form an "is" out of the "nots," helps untie the tangled threads by which Morrison knits together her novel. *Beloved* challenges us to rethink the relationship between the postmodern and the marginal, to bind together seemingly separate cultural realms. The novel forces us to retrace the distinct threads of the historically marginal that color the weave of postmodern culture.

Absence informs several levels of the narration and is made tangible from the first page of *Beloved*. The several historical and geographical facts we are given (the action is set near Cincinnati, Ohio; the year is 1873; the address of the house is 124 Bluestone Road) do nothing to obviate the sense of loss that pervades the narrative's opening. We are told that the grandmother, Baby Suggs, is dead and the sons, Howard and Buglar, have run away. Only the escaped slave Sethe, married to Baby Suggs's son Halle, and her daughter Denver remain. Though free, they are scorned by their community and are the victims of a ghostly presence, a "spite" that fills the house at 124 Bluestone Road. The concrete historic and geographic specificity that opens the narrative stands opposed to the equally concrete absences evident in the story: the missing ancestor and the missing descendants. Readers are placed generationally in a space that floats somewhere between an absent past and an absent future. Into this static fictional present a ghostly past perpetually attempts to insert itself.

Absence is also present through to the last page of the novel. The reader is told numerous times that Beloved's story "is not a story to pass on" (275). "Pass on" signifies both rejection and acceptance. Beloved's story cannot be repeated, the narrative warns, cannot be allowed to occur again in the world. The repeated warning also means that this is a story that cannot be forgotten, that cannot be rejected or "passed" on. Thus the close of the novel evokes again the motif of absence and presence by ambiguously suggesting that Beloved's story should neither be forgotten nor repeated.

The interplay between presence and absence, accepting and rejecting, appearing and disappearing, repeats and resurfaces throughout the course of *Beloved*. The demarcation in the text between life and death (the ultimate distinction in the modern world between existence and extinction) blurs and is erased. Obviously this is the case as Beloved, Sethe's murdered child, returns incarnate. It is a motif, however, evident from the very first scene of the book. Though dead, Baby Suggs is from beginning to end a felt and seen presence in the narrative. We are given her image: an old crippled woman, lying in bed, hovering between the memories of an uneasy life and the certainty of a restless death. Too demoralized to care that her grandsons have run off, she is concerned only with the small satisfaction of meditating upon scraps of colored cloth: "suspended between the emptiness of life and the meanness of the dead, she couldn't get interested in leaving life or living it, let alone the fright of two creeping-off boys. Her past had been like her present—intolerable—and since she knew death was anything but forgetfulness, she used the little energy left her for pondering color" (6). We come to learn of Baby Suggs's slave past that had "busted her legs, back, head, eyes, hands, kidneys, womb and tongue" (87). Her son Halle, who had at the old plantation Sweet Home hired himself out every Sunday for five years in order to buy her freedom, has not managed to make it north to be with his mother, wife and daughter. Baby Suggs has had to become accustomed to absences. And in this she is not alone.

The story of slavery invoked by Beloved and endured by Baby Suggs is premised on the absence of power, the absence of self-determination, the absence of a homeland, the absence of a language. The action of the novel incorporates these historical conditions and draws attention to their many results. The absence of Mr. Garner, who had been a temperate force of oppression at Sweet Home, leads to the slaves' flight. The absence of her children who had escaped earlier and gone ahead of their parents drives Sethe to continue her arduous journey north to Ohio. The absence of Halle leads her to wait for his return and is one of the causes for Baby Suggs's withdrawal into her small world of colored cloth. Sethe learns the lessons of absence and refuses to turn her children over to the slave catchers who have come to take her family back to Sweet Home, eluding capture only by murdering her child. The presence of her baby's ghost as well as its eventual reincarnation serve as a constant reminder of the absence and longing that have led Sethe and Denver to take refuge in their isolated world at 124 Bluestone.

Absence thus comprises the past and the present of the characters' lives in Beloved. Before a presence can be forged from all these absences, the logic that equates black with blank needs to be examined. Consistently, the main absences the characters endure lie in the insulting and violating practice of commodification Baby Suggs and all her people have had to learn to survive:

> . . . in all of Baby's life, as well as Sethe's own, men and women were moved around like checkers. Anybody Baby Suggs knew, let alone loved, who hadn't run off or been hanged, got rented out, loaned out, bought up, brought back, stored up, mortgaged, won, stolen or seized. So Baby's eight children had six fathers. What she called the nastiness of life was the shock she received upon learning that nobody stopped playing checkers just because the pieces included her children. (23)

Commodity and exchange serve as the only form of interaction between blacks and whites in *Beloved*. This exchange on its most basic level involves the marketing of human beings, but exchange also occurs in a more subtle though no less invidious manner. The abolitionists who use Sethe's plight to further their cause turn her story into currency. Their concern is not with her as an individual, but with her as a case. Her story disappears in their rush to turn her case into abolitionist propaganda. This causes Sethe to shy away from repeating her narrative and leads her to put her story away so it can neither be misused nor misunderstood. Only later, with Beloved's re-emergence, does the story of a mother driven to desperation and murder too re-emerge. The relation of Sethe's story opens between her, Beloved and Denver channels of exchange (aesthetic, social, personal) similar to the channels of charitable exchange evident among the black community in the novel. The novel thus posits forms of exchange that provide alternatives to modern forms of market exchange.

Morrison's narrative sketches a relation between the black community and material goods that is governed by the use value of those commodities. Her aesthetic creation is spun out of a historical period in which the industrial has not yet infused the lives of the characters. This aspect in some measure explains how many of Morrison's works explicitly or implicitly focus on elements of rural, pre-industrial life. By presenting monetary exchange only through the buying or selling of slaves, the narrative suggests a nostalgia for the premodern that implicitly focuses criticism on contemporary social organization.

The evocation of exchange within the text does not suggest that absences are tied solely to economic exploitation. The reason Baby Suggs's children are used as pieces in the slave traders' game is, of course, because of their color. Thus one begins to grasp a vague pun woven into the text: Baby Suggs's fascination with color comes as the result of her suffering a life of deprivation, a life, like her room, that is absent of color ("except for two orange squares in a quilt that made the absence shout" [38]). Color becomes a metonym for the richness of life. Yet Baby Suggs's suffering is due precisely to the color of her skin. The punning on Baby Suggs's fixation with "color" is an appropriate verbal device for a narrative concerning and arising from a black culture. The word "color" in this context is a sign for the literal concept of hue and visual perception. The concept undergoes a literary transformation whereby color serves as a metonym for luxuriousness, comfort, pleasure. Simultaneously it serves to signal not just a racial group called "black," but also the recent transformation in our language system in which the term "color" and "colored" were replaced by the terms "African American" and "black." The pun helps trace literal as well as historical, political and social patterns within the weave of the narrative. The language of the text, the effect of pun and play, constructs and dissolves structures that are at once linguistic and ideological.

So while Morrison's text shares narrative affinities with classically postmodern texts, it also suggests a connection between its narrative strategies and the socio-historical realities of Africans in the Americas. Gates argues that the signifying of black narratives—the linguistic playing, punning, coding, decoding and recoding found in African American texts—emerges from the pressing necessity for political, social, and economic survival:

Black people have always been masters of the figurative: saying one thing to mean something quite other has been basic to black survival in oppressive Western cultures. Misreading signs could be, and indeed often was, fatal. "Reading," in this sense, was not play; it was an essential aspect of the "literacy" training of a child. This sort of metaphorical literacy, the learning to decipher codes, is just about the blackest aspect of the black tradition. (6)

The term "play" suggests freedom, innocence, rebellion. The linguistic "play" evident in Beloved results from the crossing of several discourses that have deadly serious political, social, and cultural implications. There is in Beloved no innocence, no aesthetic word play that does not simultaneously trace and erase various structures of political and cultural meaning. In this respect, Beloved and other multicultural novels distinguish themselves from the full-blown fancy found in texts often associated with the postmodern.

The allusions and processes of symbolic exchange evident in Beloved work over and over to re-entrench the narrative in a painful social and historical reality. Late in the novel, for example, Denver goes among the community in search of food and work in order to support her mother who has been incapacitated by the demanding return of her murdered daughter, Beloved. Seeking to enter the service of the Bodwins, the abolitionist family that helped settle Baby Suggs and Sethe on their arrival in Ohio, Denver notices a small figure of a black boy on the shelf:

> His head was thrown back farther than a head could go, his hands were shoved in his pockets. Bulging like moons, two eyes were all the face he had above the gaping red mouth. His hair was a cluster of raised, widely spaced dots made of nail heads. And he was on his knees. His mouth wide as a cup, held the coins needed to pay for a delivery or some other small service, but could just as well have held buttons, pins, or crab-apple jelly. Painted across the pedestal he knelt on were the words "At Yo Service." (255)

The caricature here is cruel. Its image at once suggests commercial exchange (the coins held for delivery or small service), servitude (the kneeling figure), and the grotesquely twisted neck of a lynching victim. With this brief image the text exhibits a comprehensive critique of the commercial, racist and potentially violent nature of the dominant social order. The passage also evokes a series of puns: the "service" of blacks equated with the "service" of the small cup full of change, the taking of money from out of the black boy's mouth suggestive of the drawing upon the services performed by blacks, the presence of the grotesque boy "At Yo Service" evident just as Denver is going to enter the service of the Bodwins. One meaning slides into the next.

The image of the black figurine suggests an instability of symbolic exchange at work in the novel. The significances of such words as "color" and "exchange" and "service" configured by the image of the subservient change cup move towards a critique of social realities. The "slipperiness" of language is foregrounded in the novel as words glide from one frame of reference to another, just as characters glide from one defining identity to another, and the form of the narrative from one genre to another. This shifting is due to the inadequacy of—the absences left by—previous literary, discursive, and social forms. As multiplicity and transformation come to form the privileged components of *Beloved,* the inadequacies of other avant-garde forms of literary expression are made present. In large part, the reason classically postmodern texts move away from connection with socio-historical reality is their commitment to the hermetic isolation of the aesthetic object. By comparison, multicultural texts place in the foreground the relation between language and power. In order to understand alterity and decentralization as historically grounded phenomena rather than reified fetish, a critical postmodernism needs to take into account the profound relationship between language and power that multicultural texts address.

Morrison's narrative "plays" not just with language but with the traces of ideology that leave their mark in language. At this level, the significance of linguistic play that is not simply play makes itself manifest. Language, never innocent of power, becomes in Morrison's text a central means by which power disperses itself. The language of slavery within *Beloved* is comprised of signs written with whips, fires, and ropes. It is this discourse that is literally inscribed on Sethe's back by the dispassionate and evil figure of schoolteacher.

Schoolteacher appears after the death of Mr. Garner in order to help Mrs. Garner run Sweet Home. Faceless, nameless, he becomes the speaking subject of slavery's discourse. Taking advantage of his position as possessor of language, he notes with scientific detachment the animal-like characteristics of Sweet Home's slaves. He has his nephews, come to the farm to work and study under him, do the same: "'No, no. That's not the way. I told you to put her human characteristics on the left; her animal ones on the right. And don't forget to line them up'" (193). Sethe's identity, circumscribed by these "scientific" practices, is subject to the effects of schoolteacher's discourse. As often happens, the treatment she receives as an object of discourse transforms her into an object of violence. She tells Paul D, the one Sweet Home man to escape slavery alive and whole: "'[T]hose boys came in there and took my milk. That's what they came in there for. Held me down and took it. I told Mrs. Garner on em. . . . Them boys found out I told on em. Schoolteacher made one open up my back, and when it closed it made a tree. It grows there still'" (16-17). Sethe's body is doubly violated: once when its nutriment is stolen, then again when torn open by a whip. Just like the page of schoolteacher's notebook, Sethe is divided and marked, inscribed with the discourse of slavery and violation.

Throughout the narrative, the hard language of its voice is heard: Sethe's mother is hanged; Sixo is burned alive then shot; Paul A, mutilated beyond recognition, swings from the trees of the Sweet Home farm. The bodies of these characters become the texts on which their identity is written. In a lesson brought home again and again, the power of the word is made manifest in the world. Power belongs, as schoolteacher tries to show, to those who define words and not to the defined.

Yet the defined do not entirely lack power. Those who live with the absence of power reserve to themselves the persistent practice of decoding and recoding signs. The result is that the texts on which the masters have inscribed one meaning reinscribe those self-same signs and have them signify something new. The master's text becomes the subject rather than the object of language, a master of rather than a slave to discourse.

Both Sethe as a black slave and Amy Denver as a white indentured servant know the bonds of slavery and sexual violation. The two women meet as they each seek to escape their position as objects of oppressive discursive practices. For Amy—running away to Boston and stumbling on the battered, pregnant Sethe—the woman's bloody back is not a mark of her slavery. Rather she exclaims, "'It's a tree. . . . A chokecherry tree. See, here's the trunk—it's red and split wide open, full of sap, and this here's the parting for the branches. You got a mighty lot of branches. Leaves, too, look like, and dern if there ain't blossoms'" (79). Both women have been marked by their position as owned property. As the marks of slavery inscribed on the one are transformed by the other into signs signifying an image of fruition instead of oppression, Amy gives back to Sethe her identity as a nurturing source.

The power to rename represents a reclamation of agency when many other venues are closed that would help the characters establish a sense of subjectivity. At the center of this need to name stands again the sense of absence found throughout *Beloved*. In this instance, the absence of names returns to haunt African American life. As Toni Morrison explains,

among blacks, we have always suffered being nameless. We didn't have names because ours are those of the masters which were given to us with indifference and don't represent anything for us. It's become a common practice, among the community, to give a name to someone according to their characteristics: it's life that gives you a name, in a way. (Pasquier 12; my translation)

Blacks are "nameless" because given names cannot recover a pre-slave past. The community bestows names upon people, constructing through a communal act of rechristening a self meant to counteract the disempowerment of a slave past. Kimberly Benston explains this practice of renaming as a way of creating a historical self-identity. For the African American, he notes,

self-creation and reformation of a fragmented familial past are endlessly interwoven: naming is inevitably genealogical revisionism. All of African

American literature may be seen as one vast genealogical poem that attempts to restore continuity to the ruptures or discontinuities imposed by
the history of black presence in America. (152)

Naming becomes a means of bridging the violent gaps left by history.

One such gap presents itself to Sethe after her escape to Ohio
and her reunion with her children. Sought out by slave catchers and
schoolteacher, Sethe refuses to allow her children to be taken back
to the inhumanity of slavery. In the face of this threat, Sethe marks
her baby with a most profound form of inscription. She draws a
handsaw across her throat.

Sethe stakes her position in the world of the novel by using the
only form of discourse she has at hand. The power to name is the
power to mark, the power to locate and identify. This is the power
Sethe assumes for herself in deciding the fate of her children. Yet
this power does not emerge from nowhere: the language Sethe uses
to mark her child is a language she had learned early in life and
had nearly forgotten. Only in a moment of desperation does it re-
emerge. Sethe recalls being raised, along with the rest of the slave
children, by the one-armed wet nurse Nan. She was the one who
took care of the children, nursed the babies, did the cooking:

And who used different words. Words Sethe understood then but could
neither recall nor repeat now. . . . The same language her ma'am spoke,
and which would never come back. But the message—that was and had
been there all along. . . . She told Sethe that her mother and Nan were
together from the sea. Both were taken up many times by the crew. "She
threw them all away but you. The one from the crew she threw away on
the island. The others from more whites she also threw away. Without
names, she threw them. You she gave the name of the black man. She
put her arms around him. The others she did not put her arms around.
Never. Never. Telling you. I am telling you, small girl Sethe." (62)

The only baby Sethe's mother accepted bears the name of the
only man she took in her arms. The other babies she rejects. Sethe
learns from Nan not the linguistic code of her African past, but
another code of absence, of silence. This language impresses history
by denying to it another victim of oppression. Sethe's language, like
her mother's language, is one of denial and rejection. Hers is a
discourse—a language of desperation—that says No to that which
is not acceptable. Sethe practices this discourse in a woodshed.
Her instrument is a handsaw; her text is her beloved baby; her sign
is the mark of a great refusal: "If she thought anything, it was No.
No. Nono. Nonono. Simple" (163).

The meaning of Sethe's refusal—and the assertion of her own agency—is, however, lost. Others appropriate her story of desperation in order to serve their own ends. Her actions and the significance of her discourse are misconstrued in the rush to turn her story into other stories that have, ultimately, nothing to do with Sethe and her family. As the telling is altered, the story told is no longer Sethe's. First the events are circumscribed by the newspapers of the day: "A whip of fear broke through the heart chambers as soon as you saw a Negro's face in a paper, since the face was not there because the person had a healthy baby, or outran a street mob" (155-156). After the newspapers, the abolitionists take up Sethe's cause, adding fuel to the fire of anti-slavery passion. Like Owen Bodwin, the man who helped Sethe and her family escape slavery, the abolitionists find in Sethe a cause and not a human being: "The Society managed to turn infanticide and the cry of savagery around, and build a further case of abolishing slavery. Good years, they were, full of spit and conviction" (260). Caught between the sensationalism of the newspapers and the inflammatory rhetoric of the abolitionists, Sethe's story disappears.

To tell her story again, to make clear the meaning of what she's done, Sethe would like every word she heard the preacher say at her baby's funeral engraved on the headstone: "Dearly Beloved. But what she got, settled for, was the one word that mattered. She thought it would be enough, rutting among the headstones with the engraver. . . . That should certainly be enough. Enough to answer one more preacher, one more abolitionist and a town full of disgust" (5). Beloved is thus twice marked: once with a handsaw and once with a chisel. The first sign brings an absence, creates a lack; the second is Sethe's attempt to fill that lack with an explanation of the emotion that prompted the first. Both, we understand, are legitimate expressions of a difficult discourse. Each rushes to fill the absences left by other discourses pressed physically and psychically upon Sethe and her progeny—slavery, patriarchy, exploitation, violation. Together in the novel, these discourses form constellations of meaning that prove insufficient in the face of Sethe's own sense of her family's humanity. The novel follows how the inscription of discourses reveals the necessity for a transformation of meaning and, thus, serves as witness to how the inadequacies of one discourse need be fulfilled by another.

However, the assertion of self through the appropriation of discourse, as Sethe learns, is not a simple matter. She thought the inscription of Beloved's tomb would be enough to quiet the past.

While that single word may have been enough to answer the preacher, the abolitionist, the town full of disgust, it was not enough to answer Beloved. The future for Sethe has been solely a matter of keeping the past at bay, but the past, incarnate in the form of Beloved, finally overwhelms her. Beloved becomes Sethe's personal history— a living and usurping power that controls and subsumes her:

Beloved bending over Sethe looked the mother, Sethe the teething child, for other than those times when Beloved needed her, Sethe confined herself to a corner chair. The bigger Beloved got, the smaller Sethe became; the brighter Beloved's eyes, the more those eyes that used never to look away became slits of sleeplessness. Sethe no longer combed her hair or splashed her face with water. She sat in the chair licking her lips like a chastised child while Beloved ate up her life, took it, swelled up with it, grew taller on it. And the older woman yielded it up without a murmur. (250)

The past mercilessly consumes Sethe. She has not found a language to effectively counteract the intolerance and violation traced by other discourses. Despite her best efforts to respond to a hopeless situation, despite her attempts to assert agency by becoming a speaking subject, Sethe finds herself subject to the tyranny of history.

Over and over, Sethe finds this tyranny associated with signs and language. She becomes a text upon which her white masters inscribe a discourse of slavery. She also becomes a text upon which patriarchy seeks to write. Sethe ponders why Paul D would want her, suddenly, to bear him a child. She suspects that he wants to use her body as a marker for establishing a legacy for himself: he will use her to have a child and thus leave a sign that he had passed that way.

The reason Paul D wants a child is because he hasn't the nerve to tell Sethe he has been having sex with both Beloved and with her. The excuse of a child might be, he reasons, what it takes to cause a rift between Sethe and Beloved and finally drive the strange girl out. Sethe herself comes to suspect the truth as she thinks about some of the things Paul D cannot endure: "'Sharing her with the girls. Hearing the three of them laughing at something he wasn't in on. The code they used among themselves that he could not break. Maybe even the time spent on their needs and not his. They were a family somehow and he was not the head of it" (132). Paul D's sense of self and power is challenged when he confronts a situation unfamiliar to—indeed exclusive of—him. This sense of unfamiliarity and lack of control makes itself manifest in numerous ways. The most striking and disruptive moment occurs when Sethe finally tells him about her murdering her baby.

When Paul D arrives at 124 and runs the spirit of Beloved out of the house, he thinks he has made the house safe for Sethe and Denver. He assumes he can confront and control powers that others cannot. He realizes when Sethe tells him about her baby's death that he has it all wrong:

And because she had not [run the spirit off] before he got there her own self, he thought it was because she could not do it. That she lived with 124 in helpless, apologetic resignation because she had no choice; that minus husband, sons, mother-in-law, she and her slow-witted daughter had to live there all alone making do. The prickly, mean-eyed Sweet Home girl he knew as Halle's girl was obedient (like Halle), shy (like Halle), and work-crazy (like Halle). He was wrong. This here Sethe was new. (164)

Paul D can only judge Sethe by bringing prescribed models of order into play. She needs the direction of a husband/son/mother-in-law in order to do better than "make do." Sethe is measured in Paul D's eyes by how much she is like her husband, Halle, rather than like herself. Under his gaze, her identity is circumscribed. When he learns that her words and her actions can transgress those bounds, Paul D is both surprised and scared that this Sweet Home girl can so effectively tear down the walls of social and familial structures by drawing a handsaw across her child's throat.

The tension between Sethe and Paul D moves towards resolution as he returns to visit Sethe near the close of the narrative. Beloved has been run off. Sethe feels deserted, dissociated from that which was her best part, which she strove so hard to protect, and which has been lost to her once again. The loss of the past, her daughter, and her ability to name and so claim these threatens to destroy Sethe. Beneath Paul D's hands washing her, her body feels as if it will crumble away. She does not know whether she can withstand the touch of contact: "Nothing left to bathe, assuming he even knows how. Will he do it in sections? First her face, then her hands, her thighs, her feet, her back? Ending with her exhausted breasts? And if he bathes her in sections, will the parts hold? She opens her eyes, knowing the danger of looking at him. She looks at him" (272). The narrative marks a moment of commitment on Sethe's part. She realizes the need to connect with and to rely upon another.

For his part, Paul D does not know what to think of Sethe lying on Baby Suggs's bed seemingly—like the old woman before her—waiting only for death: "There are too many things to feel about this woman. His head hurts. Suddenly he remembers Sixo trying to describe what he felt about the Thirty-Mile Woman. 'She is a friend of mine. She gather me man. The pieces I am, she gather them and give them back to me in all the right order. It's good, you know, when you got a woman who is a friend of your mind'" (272). Like the Thirty-Mile Woman of Sixo's affections, Sethe helps form the syntax of Paul D's life. Because of this, "he wants to put his story next to hers" (273). Together they might form a story different from the suffering of Beloved's story, and from the tyranny of history which her story represents.

It is this tyranny to which Paul D refers when he tells Sethe, "'me and you, we got more yesterday than anybody. We need some kind of tomorrow'" (273). Paul D tries to move Sethe away from the destructive past towards a new beginning. Suggesting a movement beyond the structures of patriarchy and the violence of slavery, Paul D realizes the need to rename and re-identify what their past was and, as a result, what their future may be. He wants to put his story next to hers, to rewrite and so reroute the course of their narrative.

After all, Beloved's story "is not a story to pass on" (275). Beloved passes away without a trace so that her memory, like a dream, can be forgotten. Her story needs to be closed off in order for new stories to be created. The world imaged in the narrative is shut off from further scrutiny. The last word of the text merges with the title of the novel. Together they form an inscription that creates a sense of finality even a tombstone could not provide: Beloved.

The drawing together of stories signals the primary strategy of Morrison's text. The novel works to weave together into one narrative stories seemingly as dissimilar as those Sethe and Paul D possess. Throughout, the text highlights the various processes by which stories, both traditional and contemporary, oral and written, are told. The tale of Sethe's escape and Denver's birth, the infanticide and the aftermath, are all told by or remembered through the consciousness of various characters—Denver, Sethe, Stamp Paid, Beloved—as well as through the voice of the modern narrator who frames the entire narrative. From the first page of the novel, this twentieth-century voice creates a tension between the fictional past and the moment of narration. The narrator explains that the site of the novel, 124 Bluestone Road, "didn't have a number then, because Cincinnati didn't stretch that far. In fact, Ohio had been calling itself a state only seventy years . . . " (36). The narrative brings to the fore the temporal disjuncture between the narrative present and the fictional past characteristic of the novelistic form. Beloved also focuses on how stories are told by one person to another as a means of articulating the accumulated wisdom of communal thought and of hearing the dead through the voices of the living. The novel thus evokes numerous forms of narrative as it melds together ancient and contemporary literary forms in a critical postmodern pastiche.

Pastiche has become a loaded term within a contemporary discussion of postmodernism. On one hand the debate, as articulated by such critics as Hal Foster, views artists engaging in pastiche as "foot-loose in time, culture, and metaphor" (16). Fredric Jameson argues that pastiche is a neutral practice of parody "without any of parody's ulterior motives, amputated of the satiric impulse, devoid of laughter. . . . Pastiche is thus blank parody" (65). In another camp, David Antin, discussing postmodern poetry, argues that the "weaker" logical relations between the assembled objects of pastiche allow "a greater degree of uncertainty of interpretation or, more specifically, more degrees of freedom in the reading of the sign-objects and their ensemble relations" (21). Contra Jameson, in *Beloved* the use of pastiche is not a "blank" parody, but rather a liberating technique which frees the signifier from a fixed frame of reference. In *Beloved*, the pastiche suggests that each narrative form evoked by the novel—novelistic, modernistic, oral, preliterate, journalistic— becomes a metanarrative at play in the field of the novel. Each form therefore loses its authoritative status. The leveling this implies— the seeming "blankness" that so concerns Jameson—does not undercut the critique implicit in the novel. By evoking a historically decentered narrative—the communal voice articulating African American experiences, for example—and placing it within the same discursive space as a powerful narrative—an aesthetically decentered but culturally privileged modernism—*Beloved* takes quite literally the decentering impulse that is supposed to inform postmodern culture.

The importance of historically decentered narratives in all of Morrison's works cannot be overestimated. In an interview with Nellie McKay, Morrison talks about the evocation of a community voice in her novels:

The fact is that the stories look as though they come from people who are not even authors. No author tells these stories. They are just told—meanderingly—as though they are going in several directions at the same time. . . . I am not experimental, I am simply trying to recreate something out of an old art form in my books—the something that defines what makes a book "black." And that has nothing to do with whether the people in the books are black or not. The open-ended quality that is sometimes a problematic in the novel form reminds me of the uses to which stories are put in the black community. The stories are constantly being retold, constantly being imagined within a framework. ("An Interview" 427)

Morrison's explanation suggests a reliance upon collective thinking and impersonal memory, the telling and interpretation of stories through multiple voices. Her work does not engage with the infinite progress of aesthetic experimentation. As Andreas Huyssen and other critics have pointed out, one aspect of a culturally resistant postmodernism indicates that the drive for aesthetic avant-gardism betrays a sympathy with the mindset of modernization. The need for endless aesthetic invention can no longer effectively drive contemporary culture: "What has become obsolete . . . are those codifications of modernism in critical discourse which, however subliminally, are based on a teleological view of progress and modernization" (49). Rather than make her art new—a view linked to a belief in the infinite progress of modern civilization—Morrison discusses her works in terms of rewriting and reinterpreting established forms. Her work, in other words, assumes a postmodernist position.

This position resonates with the analysis of storytelling posited by modernist visionary Walter Benjamin. "Experience which is passed on from mouth to mouth," Benjamin writes, "is the source from which all storytellers have drawn. And among those who have written down the tales, it is the great ones whose written version differs least from the speech of the many nameless storytellers" (84). The storyteller draws on the voice of community. Most significantly, the storyteller creates community, uniting, through narrative, the lives of the teller, the listener, and the greater world of experience from which the story is drawn. In this respect, storytelling distinguishes itself from the simple conveyance of information. Storytelling "sinks the thing into the life of the storyteller, in order to bring it out of him again. Thus traces of the storyteller cling to the story the way the handprints of the potter cling to the clay vessel" (Benjamin 91-92). There evolves an organic and authentic interconnectivity between experience, the teller, the auditor.

What separates Morrison's use of storytelling in *Beloved* from Benjamin's romantic vision in "The Storyteller" is pastiche. Rather than confirm storytelling as a singularly "authentic" form of communication, Morrison's text engages with the numerous ways— official and unofficial, central and decentralized, privileged and marginal—narratives function in multicultural spaces. Numerous voices retell the same event, each from different perspectives, none taking precedence over the others. The story of Denver's birth, for example, emerges at different points in the narrative. Each time, a different facet of the story is presented so that together they form the same and yet distinct stories.

The first evocation comes after that moment of vision when Denver looks through the window of 124 Bluestone and sees Beloved hugging Sethe. Denver turns from the window and follows the well-worn path around the house: "Easily she stepped into the told story that lay before her eyes on the path she followed away from the window. . . . And to get back to the part of the story she liked best, she had to start way back: hear the birds in the thick woods, the crunch of leaves underfoot" (29). Though we know that "the magic of her birth, its miracle in fact, testified to . . . friendliness as did her own name," it is not until fifty pages later that we learn the source of Denver's appellation—the white girl in search of velvet, Amy Denver. Sethe too tells a version, though abbreviated, of Denver's birth to Paul D: "'Nothing bad can happen to her. Look at it. Everybody I knew dead or gone or dead and gone. Not her. Not my Denver. Even when I was carrying her, when it got clear that I wasn't going to make it—which meant she wasn't going to make it either—she pulled a whitegirl out of the hill. The last thing you'd expect to help'" (42). Later still, Denver prepares to tell the same story to Beloved: "She swallowed twice to prepare for the telling, to construct out of the strings she had heard all her life a net to hold Beloved" (76). And then the story: "'She had good hands, she said. The whitegirl, she said, had thin little arms but good hands. She saw that right away, she said. Hair enough for five heads and good hands, she said'" (76-77). Presently, the narrative gives way to another voice, the third-person narration told by the omniscient twentieth-century speaker.

Each telling, each version of Denver's birth, shares similar phrases and images: the wild onions into which Sethe falls, the bloody back of the runaway slave, the swollen feet, the river birth. No one telling ultimately takes precedence over the next. Each, rather, adds information through the telling. This repetition and variation creates a sense of the story as always having been present and that one is hearing again a story with which one is already familiar. In this respect, the strategy suggests the quality of orality. The repetition and variation also suggests that there is no authoritative view by which to judge Denver's birth. Despite the potential desire on the part of a sympathetic reader to view the oral elements of *Beloved* as a privileged discourse, its presence within the narrative serves incessantly to disrupt authority.

Authority in *Beloved* becomes subject to a double impulse. One is a move towards an original source, a "true" and powerful form of discourse—the slave narrative, the rural narrative, the folk narrative—as an integral part of Morrison's technique. Simultaneously, there is the implicit and explicit argument made that this is a story that has yet to be told, that cannot be told, cannot be understood. Consequently, numerous forms of narration are called upon to convey the partial information of an inevitably fragmented story. The first move may be characterized as an evocation of the premodern, the second of the postmodern. The decentered and residual tradition of storytelling within *Beloved* is mediated through the complex and decentered form of the postmodern novel. As a result, *Beloved* makes overt the often covert connections between language and power, narrative and politics. It draws upon notions of tradition without yielding to the exigencies of a political, social and cultural conservatism. It resists notions of a centralized authority while not denying that forms of authority—both central and marginal—yet exist in the world. The novel composes a pastiche of discourses intimately tied to forms of power. Simultaneously, it sets those discourses in tension by examining their contested claims to authority. Nowhere is this tension more evident, finally, than in the contested form of the novel itself.

Beloved creates this tension by relying upon the authority of the community in order to speak while employing that most alienated and isolated form of contemporary literary creation—the novel. Walter Benjamin notes that novels are characterized by their peculiar mode of production and consumption. They are formed in solitude for the individual experience of the lone reader:

The novelist has isolated himself. The birthplace of the novel is the solitary individual, who is no longer able to express himself by giving examples of his most important concerns, is himself uncounseled, and cannot counsel others. To write a novel means to carry the incommensurable to extremes in the representation of human life. In the midst of life's fullness, and through the representation of this fullness, the novel gives evidence of the profound perplexity of living. (87)

The novel is born of the tension between the individual psyche and the social world. Yet Morrison's novel stands in a position that evokes an epic structure and an epic purpose: to unite the individual and the world in a meaningful relationship that strengthens individual self-identity and fortifies identity and power for the community. The tension between the modern and the premodern forms the point at which the strategies of Morrison's narrative cross. The work refers to various discourses as it assumes and transforms them. It points towards the alienated world of modern aesthetic production. Simultaneously, it looks towards the narrative authority evident in the marginalized oral literature of the black community. This narrative authority is a critique of the master's authority, a critique of authority altogether. The narrative is born of a dissatisfaction with the present through an invocation of the already present past. *Beloved* can be read, then, as a "rememory" of the discursive powers of community, a metanarrative that critiques the oppressive practices of authority, a postmodern text that profoundly challenges a postmodernism which values reified alterity. *Beloved* knits together various discursive threads in order to counter this reification with a presence premised upon a historical, cultural and political absence. The novel unravels these "nots" of history in order to knit together a new and more inclusive story. The story of absence and exclusion which Beloved's story represents becomes, indeed, not a story to pass on.

WORKS CITED

Antin, David. "Modernism and Postmodernism: Approaching the Present in American Poetry." *Boundary 2* 1.1 (1972): 98-133.

Benjamin, Walter. "The Storyteller: Reflections on the Works of Nikolai Leskov." *Illuminations.* Ed. Hannah Arendt. Trans. Harry Zohn. New York: Schocken, 1969. 83-109.

Benston, Kimberly. "I Yam What I Am: The Topos of (Un)naming in Afro-American Literature." *Black Literature and Literary Theory.* Ed. Henry Louis Gates, Jr. New York: Methuen, 1984. 151-172.

Foster, Hal. "Against Pluralism." *Recodings: Art, Spectacle, Cultural Politics.* Ed. Hal Foster. Port Townsend: Bay Press, 1985. 13-32.

Gates, Henry Louis, Jr. "Criticism in the Jungle." *Black Literature and Literary Theory.* Ed. Henry Louis Gates, Jr. New York: Methuen, 1984. 1-24.

Huyssen, Andreas. "Mapping the Postmodern." *New German Critique* 33 (1984): 5-52.

Jameson, Fredric. "Postmodernism, or the Cultural Logic of Late Capitalism." *New Left Review* 146 (1984): 53-92.

Morrison, Toni. *Beloved.* New York: Knopf, 1987.

____. "An Interview with Toni Morrison." With Nellie McKay. *Contemporary Literature* 14 (1983): 413-429.

Pasquier, Marie-Claire. "Toni Morrison: 'Dans ma famille, on racontait tout le temps des histoires.'" *La Quinzaine Littéraire* 1-15 Mar. 1985: 12-13.

POSTMODERNISM AND POST-UTOPIAN DESIRE IN TONI MORRISON AND E. L. DOCTOROW

Marianne DeKoven

Both utopianism and postmodernism have been seen as quintes-sentially or characteristically American phenomena.[1] This essay will investigate some interrelations between the two. I will begin (appro-priately, I hope, for an essay on "historiographic" fiction)[2] by telling a historical story in order to provide the necessary groundwork for my arguments.

The heyday of American utopianism, in the nineteenth-century antebellum period, saw the blossoming of hundreds of communi-ties, the names of some of them at the heart of our cultural history (Brook Farm, the Shakers, the Icarians, Oneida, Amana, to mention a few of the best known). Socialist and, in the case of the Owenite communities, feminist egalitarian ideals were crucial to these uto-pian communities.[3] This historical utopian cornucopia also coin-cided, of course, with the heyday of slavery. The utopian move-ments overlapped with and sometimes embraced (fostered, were committed to) Abolitionism, with Brook Farm a prime instance. It is clear that utopianism and Abolitionism shared the universalist, En-lightenment ideals of human equality and freedom. I would argue that Radical Reconstruction, including most notably the Freedmen's Bureau (1865–1872), hoped and even attempted to realize the goals of utopianism and Abolition, and that the destruction of Re-construction marked the defeat, at least for that historical moment, of the social goals and visions of both.[4] The period in the 1870s and 1880s following the dissolution of the Freedmen's Bureau, and the ultimate defeat of Reconstruction, was a post-utopian historical mo-ment. It witnessed the breakup and disappearance of most of the antebellum utopian communities, contemporaneous with the institution of slavery by other means in the sharecropping Black Belt South, and of systemic, often murderous racism throughout the country. At the same time, this period encompassed the stunning growth of industrial capitalism in the urban North, with its rampant social miseries as yet unchecked by subsequent radical and reformist movements.

American utopianism had another renaissance in the 1960s, with, again, hundreds of communities (none of them as famous or successful as their nineteenth-century predecessors) springing up all over the country. Like their predecessors, these communities were committed to egalitarianism and crucially linked to a resurgence of socialism, though there were many differences: 1960s communities were generally marked by an anarcho-syndicalist version of socialism, emphasizing personal, individual freedom, pleasure and fulfillment at the expense of group unity or coherence ("the common good").[5] They were therefore much more ephemeral and fragile than the generally more group-oriented, and sometimes rigidly rule-governed, nineteenth-century communities.[6] Despite this difference of emphasis, however, the 60s communes were varyingly, loosely, but consistently committed to ideals of common ownership, equitably shared labor, and an egalitarian power structure based on the New Left ideal of participatory democracy (the hierarchical, guru-governed religious communes were an exception).[7] The antagonisms between the political New Left and the countercultural hippie utopian communes are well documented, but they should not obscure the fact that the New Left and the counterculture were two facets of a broad, general movement that had at its core a commitment to socialist egalitarianism—liberty, equality, community—including racial, class, and, sometimes, gender equality. These issues were highly complex and troubled: most hippies, and therefore most hippie communes, were white and middle-class. Further, because both radicalism and the counterculture were exaggeratedly macho and male dominated until the emergence of second-wave feminism in the final phase of (out of the ashes of) the 60s, they usually reproduced dominant gender inequalities, often in exaggerated versions, despite their egalitarian ideologies.

Like the post-Reconstruction period, the period following the demise and defeat of the 60s—a period, I would argue, continuing into the present—is also a post-utopian moment.[8] This post-utopian moment is the period we now call postmodernism, or postmodernity. Many studies mark the decline or end of egalitarian, socialist-based or -inspired utopianism in postmodernism.[9] In this essay, I want to discuss the status of utopianism in two postmodernist works of fiction, both of them set in the post-utopian early 1870s. I have chosen these two seemingly unrelated novels because they are both set just at the moment of the demise of the Freedmen's Bureau, with, in both cases, that historical moment used at once to account for and also to parallel our current situation: Toni Morrison's *Beloved* and E. L. Doctorow's *The Waterworks*. I will discuss the connections between these novels' visions of utopianism and their deployments of postmodernist narrative strategies.

Both *Beloved* and *The Waterworks* are engaged with utopian visions; in both, history destroys or distorts potential or attempted utopias. Both novels are thoroughly postmodernist in their narrative strategies, interweaving popular with "high literary" modes of fiction writing.[10] In both novels the failure or destruction of utopia is connected to slavery and its racist sequelae: the utopian possibilities of the late 60s—both 1860s and 1960s—are defeated by the intractability of slavery's legacy. For Doctorow, that defeat coincides with the deformations of urban industrial capitalism and its concomitant political corruption (capitalism appears in *Beloved* in the muted or displaced but crucial form of schoolteacher's brutal, dehumanizing, efficiency-oriented rationalism).

Morrison and Doctorow both delineate in the post-utopian 1870s the present of postmodernity. Doctorow saturates his 1870s New York with the crude inequality of vast, ill-gotten elite wealth in dialectic with mass poverty, squalor and wretchedness. Both are linked to the thoroughgoing corruption and degradation of public politics, everywhere suggestive of current post- or neo-Reaganite conditions—what Fredric Jameson, in *Postmodernism, or, the Cultural Logic of Late Capitalism*, calls the global triumph of capitalism in its purest form. *Beloved*, though less explicitly than *The Waterworks*, evokes the aftermath of the 60s by using the end of the Freedmen's Bureau, signaling the nearing defeat of Reconstruction itself, to suggest the failed utopian promise of Civil Rights, Black Power, and early second-wave feminism.

A characteristic postmodernist narrative strategy works in both novels to handle the dilemma of at once representing a powerful utopian desire and at the same time representing a thoroughgoing skepticism concerning the possibility of its fulfillment. This strategy is the refunctioning of sentimental, sensationalist popular genres— melodrama/ghost story for Morrison,[11] detective fiction for Doctorow—along with the traditional heterosexual romance plot, both to resolve and also to refuse to resolve or absolve the tragedy of loss and defeat at the center of each novel.[12] An excess of apocalyptic fictional material that cannot be integrated into the resolutions conventional narrative forms enforce pushes into the ending of each novel, and also erupts through the prose surface of each throughout. This excess connects to the anti-conventional writing in each novel, which I consider the persistence of utopianism as modernist form within the reconfigured formal conventionality of postmodernism.[13] What I am calling modernist writing is most evident in the ellipses Doctorow uses throughout the novel, and also in the explicitly visionary passages in his prose. Morrison's poetic prose in general pushes at the limits of conventional writing; in *Beloved*, the ultimate scene of putative but ultimately murderous utopian fulfillment is written in fully experimental prose.

"Sweet Home" is Morrison's ineluctably clear indictment of the possibility of utopia in a slave country.[14] The acerbic irony of that plantation's name exceeds its allusion to "Home Sweet Home," forcefully undercutting America's claim to Edenic status. As in Eden, the power of naming at Sweet Home belongs to the patriarch; in this case, in this country, he is the white patriarch. The power of naming, both oneself and one's children, is crucial to this novel. Sethe and her mother insist on their right to name their children; Baby Suggs and Stamp Paid insist on the right to name themselves. The fact that all but two of the Sweet Home men are named Paul both highlights the de-individuation of slaves and also provides yet another ironic reference to the master's Christian tradition. The tree planted on Sethe's back by schoolteacher's student's whip is the Edenic tree of knowledge with a vengeance. There is no possibility of antebellum utopia in *Beloved*, because, simply, of slavery.

The novel acknowledges the white utopian aspirations of the antebellum period, in Mr. and Mrs. Garner's enlightened relations to their slaves, in the name "Sweet Home," and in the almost livable life Sethe leads with Halle before the advent of schoolteacher. Utopia, however, is always-already contaminated by slavery: even at their best, the slaves' lives are only almost livable, and nothing like autonomous or free. The unusual (for slavery) autonomy of the "Sweet Home men" proves empty when Mr. Garner dies and Mrs. Garner feels that "she needed her brother-in-law [schoolteacher] and two boys 'cause people said she shouldn't be alone out there with nothing but Negroes" (197). Because their "freedom" was created by Mr. Garner, it died with him.

Toward the end of the novel, Morrison comments, by means of Paul D, on the nonfulfillment of America's Edenic promise:

In five tries he had not had one permanent success. Every one of his escapes . . . had been frustrated. Alone, undisguised, with visible skin, memorable hair and no whiteman to protect him, he never stayed uncaught. . . . And in all those escapes he could not help being astonished by the beauty of this land that was not his. He hid in its breast, fingered its earth for food, clung to its banks to lap water and tried not to love it. (268)

This passage evokes the beautiful (withheld rather than promised) land as the nurturant maternal body. The linkage of the utopian to the maternal, found frequently throughout Western figurations and analyses of utopia, will be an important element of the fictional configurations I analyze here.

Abolition is similarly at once given its due and undercut by Morrison. The Bodwins—the Abolitionists who enable Baby Suggs and her family to find shelter and employment—are clearly "good people." Bodwin remembers with nostalgia, as "heady days," the time "[t]wenty years ago when the Society was at its height in opposing slavery," when " 'bleached nigger' is what his enemies called him, and . . . had caught him and shoe-blackened his face and hair" (260). For Bodwin, the heyday of Abolition was indeed a utopian time, betrayed in the postwar period. His thoughts resemble those of a current veteran of the 1960s: "Those heady days were gone now; what remained was the sludge of ill will; dashed hopes and difficulties beyond repair. . . . Nothing since was as stimulating as the old days of letters, petitions, meetings, debates, recruitment, quarrels, rescue and downright sedition" (260).

The irony of Sethe seeing Bodwin as schoolteacher, when she attacks him with an ice pick at the end of the novel, is nonetheless sharply pointed. While the Bodwins expose themselves to considerable risk in the service of their Abolitionist beliefs, and they manage Sethe's release from prison, they do not see or treat African Americans as equal to whites. Baby Suggs and, later, her granddaughter Denver both enter the Bodwin house through the back door. Denver, having obtained the "Service" (see below) employment in the Bodwin house that will allow her and Sethe to survive, affirms that the Bodwins are "good whitefolks." As she is about to leave through that back door, she sees,

sitting on a shelf . . . a blackboy's mouth full of money. His head was thrown back farther than a head could go, his hands were shoved in his pockets. Bulging like moons, two eyes were all the face he had above the gaping red mouth. His hair was a cluster of raised, widely spaced dots made of nail heads. And he was on his knees. His mouth, wide as a cup, held the coins needed to pay for a delivery or some other small service, but could just as well have held buttons, pins or crab-apple jelly. Painted across the pedestal he knelt on were the words "At Yo Service." (255)

Beyond exploitation, dehumanization, degradation, reification, and theft of labor, this remarkable figure suggests the tortures both of slavery and of postwar violence against African Americans that are among Morrison's central concerns in this novel.[15] The "head thrown back farther than a head could go" and the "gaping red mouth . . . wide as a cup" suggest not only lynching (that suggestion reinforced by the bulging eyes)[16] but also the humiliation and torment of the collar and bit suffered by Paul D. The nails driven into the head suggest at once a generalized violence and also the most drastic sort of bodily imprisonment. "At Yo Service" and "on his knees" remind us again of the view of African Americans held by (almost) all whites, even "good whitefolk" Abolitionists like the Bodwins.[17]

Both the New World Eden and white Abolitionism are vitiated by slavery and racism, but there exists in this novel a much more potent, promising, and therefore more tragically destroyed utopian possibility. We see it first in the preaching Baby Suggs, holy, does in the Clearing, during the period between Halle's purchase of her freedom and Sethe's arrival at 124 Bluestone Road with Denver in her arms and the tree of knowledge on her back. Baby Suggs had

decided that, because slave life had "busted her legs, back, head, eyes, hands, kidneys, womb and tongue," she had nothing left to make a living with but her heart—which she put to work at once. Accepting no title of honor before her name, but allowing a small caress after it [holy], she became an unchurched preacher, one who visited pulpits and opened her great heart to those who could use it. . . . Uncalled, unrobed, unanointed, she let her great heart beat in their presence. When warm weather came, Baby Suggs, holy, followed by every black man, woman and child who could make it through, took her great heart to the Clearing—a wide-open place cut deep in the woods nobody knew for what at the end of a path known only to deer and whoever cleared the land in the first place. (87)

The Clearing has strong utopian resonance, with its anonymous provenance, its anti-instrumentality, its spaciousness, and its depth in the woods—the primeval nature of the American Eden. Baby Suggs, self-named, is literally free of tainted institutions, "unchurched." Her congregation is a spontaneous egalitarian bonding, in nature, of the oppressed, for the purpose of mutual salvation.

They achieve this salvation not through any acceptance of dogma or practice of ritual or belief in divine intercession. Morrison explicitly circumvents Christianity: "She did not tell them to clean up their lives or to go and sin no more. She did not tell them they were the blessed of the earth, its inheriting meek or its glorybound pure. She told them that the only grace they could have was the grace they could imagine" (88). They achieve salvation through the inspiration of Baby Suggs's great heart and her moving language, by means of ecstatic laughing, dancing, singing, sobbing. Morrison represents in the Clearing the release through the body into love of the black body despised by white America: " 'Here,' she said, 'in this here place, we flesh; flesh that weeps, laughs; flesh that dances on bare feet in grass. Love it. Love it hard. Yonder they do not love your flesh. They despise it. . . . *You* got to love it, *you!* ' " (88).

We learn of Baby Suggs's ministry in the Clearing only after it is long since lost, when Sethe yearns for it in order to be able to bear the information Paul D has given her about Halle's end—information that has begun to catalyze her "rememory." Baby Suggs renounced her ministry in the wake of the unbearable events at the center of this novel, the "unspeakable unspoken" of slavery itself, whose objective correlative for Morrison is the necessity for a mother to murder her child in order to save her: "no notebook for my babies [to write down their 'animal characteristics'] and no measuring string neither" (198). Baby Suggs says " 'those white things have taken all I had or dreamed . . . and broke my heartstrings too. There is no bad luck in the world but whitefolks.' . . . Her faith, her love, her imagination and her great big old heart began to collapse twenty-eight days after her daughter-in-law arrived" (89).

The event that empties the Clearing and deprives Baby Suggs of faith, love, imagination, and her heart itself, the historical event around which Morrison constructed this novel, takes us back to the linkage of the utopian and the maternal. Beloved is the child Sethe has been driven by the Fugitive Slave Act to kill in order to save her from slavery, the child she then named by paying by the letter with her body for a tombstone inscription. This child returns to claim her mother, into a space opened in Sethe for her by the reappearance of Paul D and the eruption of rememory into Sethe's life. The watery world of death from which Beloved returns is endowed by Morrison with deliberately multiple, ambiguous, undecidable suggestions at once of the womb, the underworld or afterlife, the specific circumstances of Beloved's death, and the general historical circumstances of the Middle Passage. This literally miraculous return restores mother and daughter to one another, and sister to sister (though that relation is largely non-reciprocal, with Denver desiring Beloved and Beloved desiring only Sethe).

Morrison constructs this space of maternal restoration and completion very explicitly as utopian. The three women form a closed whole of perfect mutual gratification. Paul D has decamped, leaving the three women alone at 124 Bluestone. First he had exorcised the ghost Beloved had become, enabling her return in bodily form. When that bodily presence becomes unbearable to him, he repudiates Sethe's action in murdering/saving Beloved by accusing Sethe of precisely the "animal characteristics" ("four feet," as he puts it) attributed to her by schoolteacher. The attribution of "animal characteristics" is what Sethe killed Beloved in order to save her from. In his bitterness at his recognition that Sethe's love for her children outstrips anything she might feel toward him, and in his fear at the danger of a black woman loving her own, therefore herself, with such an absolute claim, he has accused her of a love that is "too thick" (164).

Ultimately, Morrison endorses Paul D's view. At first, the self-contained, absolute, world-excluding mother-daughter bond Sethe forms with Beloved appears to be a redemption not only of the crime against both their lives forced on Sethe by the Law of slavery, but also of the pre-Oedipal connection of the girl child to the mother's body advocated in much feminist theory as the ground for a revolutionary feminist praxis. This bond, however, proves to be monstrous and nearly itself murderous.[18] Beloved's absolute love for and dependence on Sethe gradually, steadily emerges as lethal to Sethe: Beloved is literally sucking away Sethe's life, growing fat on it as Sethe declines (Beloved looks pregnant as Sethe nears death). It is Denver, with her refusal of an absolute bond with Sethe, her link to her father (she looks like and yearns for Halle), her fear of her mother's "too-thick love," and her independence, who pushes outside this self-contained female utopia/dystopia, out into the community, and thereby saves herself and her mother.

Sethe's limitlessly abundant milk is a central figure in the novel of the utopian maternal, suggesting the revolutionary, 60s-inspired feminist utopianism of *écriture féminine*, specifically Hélène Cixous's call to women to write the female body in the "white ink" of mother's milk. In fact, the sequence culminating the bonding of the three women, a bonding so extreme that they become interchangeable with one another, is written in a version of *écriture féminine*, or experimental prose. It is filled with imagery of mother-daughter merging, and is reminiscent of Cixous's own writing:[19]

in the night I hear chewing and swallowing and laughter   it belongs to me
she is the laugh   I am the laugher   I see her face which is mine. . . .   her
face comes through the water   a hot thing. . . .   my face is coming   I have
to have it   I am looking for the join   I am loving my face so much   my dark
face is close to me   I want to join. . . .   she chews and swallows me   I am
gone now I am her face   my own face has left me   I see me swim away   a
hot thing. . . .   I want to be the two of us. . . .   she is my face smiling at me
doing it at last   a hot thing   now we can join   a hot thing (212–213)

This writing is the embodiment, the literalization, of Sethe's "too-
thick" maternal love, the "chewing and swallowing" of mutual en-
gulfment. The theft of self perpetrated by slavery on Africans is represented by the violence of the theft of Sethe's milk—to Sethe this
theft is even more intolerable than the brutal whipping that produces
the "tree" on her back. Despite this theft, her milk is still mirac-
ulously ample and available for both daughters when Sethe arrives
at the home of Baby Suggs, the matriarch of 124's maternal utopia.
When Beloved returns, it appears as if the promise of Sethe's miraculous milk will be fulfilled in the face of, in defiance of, beyond and
outside, the history of slavery and the violent defeat of Radical Reconstruction. But a utopia that excludes Stamp Paid is a utopia that
denies black solidarity, the only hope located within history rather
than, as utopian constructions in post-utopian times inevitably are,
outside it (I refer to the important scene where Stamp Paid, hearing
the three merged voices within the house, feels he cannot enter,
cannot even bring himself to knock on the door when in fact, given
what he has done, he has the right to enter any African-American
house without knocking). Sethe's miraculous milk drains off into the
succubus Beloved has become; its seemingly limitless flow is in fact
limited by the extent of Sethe's own life.

The community of women, catalyzed by Denver, saves Sethe;
Paul D returns to tell her that she, not her children, is her own "best
thing" (273). The radical, absolute mother-daughter bond is broken,
and lighter, thinner, reformist rather than revolutionary bonds take its
place: individualist self-realization ("you your own best thing"), the
romance plot (reconciliation with Paul D), and intermittently acti-
vated, potentially rejecting community (the praying circle of women
who had turned their backs on Sethe's "too-thick love"). Radical
black feminist utopia turned deadly gives way to mildly optimistic
reform (black feminist rather than simply feminist because its maternality is a defiance of and alternative to the deformations of slavery).

Denver's successful move out into the world, her reintegration into the community, bringing Sethe with her, and the return of Paul D, do not end the novel. The reformist, post-utopian ending derived from the conventions of mainstream bourgeois fiction (just as the central narrative structures of the novel are dependent on the ghost story and sentimental, sensationalist melodrama) is succeeded, and to some extent supervened, by the final two-page section. Morrison gives the last word to the uncontainable, apocalyptic excess Beloved represents: "Disremembered and unaccounted for, she cannot be lost because no one is looking for her"; she "erupts into her separate parts"; "They forgot her like a bad dream. . . . Remembering seemed unwise" (274). But "Down by the stream in back of 124 her footprints come and go, come and go" (275), and her name is the last word of the text. The experimental prose cited above and, more pervasively, the dense, magnificent poetic writing Morrison uses throughout, are the footprints of Beloved on the form of this novel. Further, the repeated refrain, "It was not a story to pass on," twice, then "This is not a story to pass on" (274–275), represents, in its contradictory double-entendre of "pass *on*" as transmit and "*pass* on" as walk away from, the persistence of utopian desire in a postmodern fiction that at once passes on it and passes it on.

Where *Beloved*'s evocations of 60s utopianism, and post-60s post-utopianism, are implicit, Doctorow's in *The Waterworks* are explicit, or as nearly so as they can be in a novel set in the 1870s.[20] Morrison deploys refunctioned narrative conventions of sensationalist sentimental melodrama; Doctorow deploys those of sensationalist detective melodrama. I have already alluded to the strong parallel *The Waterworks* establishes between the brutal urban capitalism of the late-nineteenth and the late-twentieth centuries. Augustus Pemberton, one of the novel's villains—the father of one of its heroes, Martin—made his fortune first from the illegal slave trade and then from Civil War profiteering: selling lethally inferior goods to the Union Army. He has built for himself, as the robber barons in fact did, a massive estate on the Hudson, Doctorow's descriptions of which evoke the unnatural monstrosity of the houses on the shore of Fitzgerald's West Egg (*Gatsby* is a profound influence on this novel, as we will see). In his megalomania, his wholehearted belief in his own invulnerability, which corresponds to Boss Tweed's fatal hubris (the breakup of Tammany Hall is one of the novel's subplots), Augustus Pemberton fakes his death and turns all his money over to the amoral genius Dr. Sartorius, who promises him longevity of indefinite term. He thereby impoverishes his young second wife and child, sentimentalized paragons in this stark moral melodrama.

Dr. Sartorius is a figure of scientific/technological modernity, the progress concerning which Doctorow is deeply skeptical. Dr. Sartorius promises Pemberton a version of eternal, or at least indefinitely prolonged life, which he hopes to achieve through his medical "experiments." These fiendish experiments are based on vampirizing the vital essence of poor orphan children and transfusing it into rich old men. Martin begins to unravel the plot when he digs up his father's supposed grave and finds there instead an oddly withered child—"a very shrunken corpse . . . in odd clothing . . . with a tiny leathered face with its eyes closed and lips pursed" (107).[21] Pemberton had consolidated his fortune through Civil War profiteering; Sartorius, in parallel fashion, had established his medical reputation as a brilliant army surgeon: "He had marched and ridden through the worst of our Civil War unscathed . . . either by its cannon and shot or by its issues. The seemingly endless carnage ended upon the table before him in his field surgery . . . as one continuously fascinating . . . wonderfully torn and broken and dying body . . . with endless things to be fixed" (213).

Sartorius's experiments are performed in a secret laboratory constructed within the "Waterworks" of the title, the upstate pumping station for New York City's water supply (the heart for its life-blood). He establishes there what Martin explicitly calls an "obverse Eden" (188). Unlike Yeats's ambiguous utopia, Byzantium, it is a country exclusively for old men—old evil plutocrats who want to live forever by feeding off the lives of the impoverished young. Here is Martin's description of this perverse utopia:

It was in the nature of an indoor park, with gravel paths and plantings and cast-iron benches. It was all set inside a vaulted roof of glass and steel which cast a greenish light over everything. The conservatory was laid out to effect a forbearing harmony and peacefulness. [. . .] Enormous clay urns sprouted profusions of fronds and leaves that I knew on sight were not native. A kind of tepid steam or diffusion of watered air hissed out of ports or valves inset in the floor, so that the atmosphere was cloyingly humid. I could feel through the floor vibrations of the dynamo that was responsible. [. . .] It was as if I had stepped into another universe, a Creation, like . . . an obverse Eden. (187–188)

Late-nineteenth-century capitalism as unchecked greed and exploitation, in unholy alliance with modern science and technology as amoral instrumentalist megalomania, has converted the American Eden into its obverse, an anti-Eden, with the machine dynamo vibrating with a vengeance in the ersatz garden.

Doctorow's post-utopianism is even more explicit elsewhere in the novel. The harbinger of Sartorius's demonic obverse Eden at the Waterworks is his "Home for Little Wanderers," the seemingly benign but in fact lethal orphanage where children are housed in order to die into the unnaturally prolonged lives of plutocrats. The narrator-hero, the journalist McIlvaine, accompanies the policeman-hero, Donne, on a stake-out of the orphanage, which is at 93rd Street and the East River. McIlvaine gives us a long, loving description of the still-pastoral landscape in process of urbanization:

At this time, the city north of Seventy-second Street was no longer country, but not yet city either. The houses were few and far between. Whole blocks had been scraped clear and laid out with surveyor string, but nothing was on them. [. . .] Here was a street set with paving stones that stopped at the edge of a pasture, there was a scaffolded half-risen apartment house through whose unframed windows you saw the sky. [. . .] From Park Avenue and Ninety-third the unpaved road ran downhill in a gentle slope to the river. In the fields on either side pumpkins were scattered and trees were beginning to turn. The sounds of the city were distant, almost imperceptible. Donne and his men were encamped beneath a stand of yellowing weeping willow halfway between First and Second avenues. [. . .] Here and there in the field around us birds were scooting about in their dustbaths or hopping from brush to tree. High up over the river an undulant arrow of geese pointed south. (154–156)

Rearing up out of, and violently negating this bucolic scene, is the Home for Little Wanderers:

a Romanesque structure of red stone trimmed in granite and with the turrets and small windows of an armory. The bottom half was obscured by a brick wall. A cast-iron gate gave on to a courtyard. It looked its part—a very substantial building, lending substance to those who lived there. It was an outpost of our advancing civilization . . . like all our other institutions out at the edges—poorhouses, asylums for fallen women, homes for the deaf and dumb. (156)

McIlvaine so detests this manifestation of "our advancing civilization" that he is moved to the following reflection: "I fervently wished there were no buildings of any kind on this island. I envisioned the first Dutch sailors giving up on the place as a mosquito-infested swamp, and returning in their longboats to the ships . . ." (156).

Doctorow is alluding explicitly here to the famous ending of *The Great Gatsby*, where Nick imagines the Dutch sailors' vision of America, specifically New York, as the "fresh green breast of the new world . . . commensurate to [man's] capacity for wonder." Unlike the modernist Fitzgerald, for whose narrative vision the "inessential houses" of Long Island can "melt away" so that he can see again the "fresh green breast of the new world" that "flowered once for Dutch sailors' eyes," the postmodernist Doctorow sees those Dutch sailors not as surrogate Adams, beholders of utopia, but as emissaries of the "advancing civilization" that destroyed utopia. While Fitzgerald can see utopia again through the Dutch sailors' imagined eyes, Doctorow can only wish that those eyes had perceived not utopia but a "mosquito-infested swamp." Utopia can be reimagined by Doctorow/McIlvaine not through European eyes but only as the pre-Columbian home of Native Americans, those "savage polytheists of [his] mind":

Ever since this day [the day of the vision quoted above at the Home for Little Wanderers] I have dreamt sometimes . . . I, a street rat in my soul, dream even now . . . that if it were possible to lift this littered, paved Manhattan from the earth . . . and all its torn and dripping pipes and conduits and tunnels and tracks and cables—all of it, like a scab from new skin underneath—how seedlings would sprout, and freshets bubble up, and brush and grasses would grow over the rolling hills. [. . .] A season or two of this and the mute, protesting culture buried for so many industrial years under the tenements and factories . . . would rise again . . . of the lean, religious Indians of the bounteous earth, who lived without money or lasting architecture, close to the ground [. . .] always praying in solemn thanksgiving for their clear and short life in this quiet universe. Such love I have for those savage polytheists of my mind . . . those friends of light and leaf . . . those free men and women. . . . (163–164)

The remarkable image of industrial-capitalist Manhattan lifted like a scab to permit the regeneration of a pre-European New World Eden, peopled by what is self-consciously, admittedly a fantasy of pre-rationalist and therefore free "friends of light and leaf," marks Doctorow's post-utopian utopianism: utopia, as for Morrison, can only be imagined outside, and in explicit negation of, history.

As for Morrison, as well, utopian desire persists powerfully in this novel. Like those of *Beloved*, its narrative structures are mainly governed by the popular fictional conventions that make both novels bestsellers, capable of reaching a wide audience. Doctorow uses the conventions of the detective novel (unraveling the crime of the Waterworks, and bringing its perpetrators to justice, controls the plot; the novel's "hero" is a police detective, Donne) and of the closed or neatly resolved heterosexual romantic plot (in this novel's more-or-less happy ending, Donne marries Augustus Pemberton's young widow, and Martin finally marries his long-suffering childhood sweetheart). Also as in *Beloved*, however, the apocalyptic excess of the novel pushes against the closure installed by those conventions. At the most obvious level, McIlvaine himself (like Beloved) cannot be absorbed into the closing structure of heterosexual coupling. Similarly, McIlvaine's language, the prose of the novel itself, is broken throughout, as the lengthy citations here must have made clear, by erratic use of ellipsis. The ellipsis, like Faulkner's use of italics in *The Sound and the Fury*, is inconsistent—sometimes clearly motivated and sometimes not. It is a mark of what Morrison calls "the unspeakable" breaking into, disrupting, the smooth prose surface we would otherwise expect, marking the place of an absented, discredited, historically defeated, but nonetheless persistent utopian desire. The unspeakable, like the Nietzschean abyss of the modernists, deforms and reforms narrative convention. It is precisely this undecidable aggregation of popular convention with anti-conventional, modernist or experimental narrative elements that marks for me the domain of serious or ambitious postmodernist fiction.

In *The Waterworks*, as in *Beloved*, the novel's ending is reserved for such an eruption of fictional excess, in this instance in a passage of powerfully evocative poetic prose reminiscent of the great modernists' and of Morrison's:

I remember how still the city was that afternoon as I walked uptown from the church. It was brilliantly sunny and terribly cold and the streets were empty. The footing was treacherous. Everything was thickly glazed. . . . Horsecars were frozen to their rails, as were the locomotives on their elevated railway of ice. . . . The masts and sheets of the ships in the docks were ensheathed in ice. . . . Ice floes lay in the viscous river. . . . The ironfronts of Broadway seemed in the sun to be burning in ice. . . . The trees on the side streets were of crystal. [. . .] my illusion was that the city had frozen in time. [. . .] all still, unmoving, stricken, as if the entire city of New York would be forever encased and frozen, aglitter and God-stunned. (252–253)

Like the riverside ground behind 124 carrying and erasing Beloved's footprints, this frozen, God-stunned city is marked, by its prose as well as by its figuration of apocalypse outside time and history, as the site of a defeated, absented, inevitably recurring utopian desire.[22]

The maternal is the locus of defeated utopia for Morrison, and maternality itself becomes monstrous in its historical deformation. For Doctorow, it is the paternal that has become the site of the betrayal or defeat of utopian possibility: *The Waterworks* is a father-quest, not for an idealized dead father but for a despised, criminally alive father. *Beloved*'s utopian excess is lodged in the vanishing/returning footprints of a water-lost daughter; *The Waterworks*'s in the curse of frozen water inflicted by God the Father. But in the postmodern destabiliza-tion of the characteristically modern Oedipal configuration and its attendant gender dualism, this difference (the maternal orientation of one novel, the paternal orientation of the other) loses defining signifi-cance. Morrison's maternal feminine African-American world, as vic-tim of history, is no more capable of transcending history's depreda-tions (surviving, defying, but not transcending) than Doctorow's paternal masculine Euro-American world, agent of that victimization, is capable of transcending itself (dissecting, repudiating but not tran-scending).

As postmodern narratives, in which oppositional modernist writ-ing cohabits with popular fictional convention, both novels choose and enact a postmodern form of resistance-from-within. They leave behind the modernist/avant-garde mode of wholesale opposition, in which the new aesthetic stands as representation, harbinger, embod-iment of a world made new. The modernist/avant-garde, utopian model of totalized oppositionality was advocated most forcefully by Marcuse, perhaps the most wholehearted modern believer in the liberatory, transformative power of anti-realist aesthetics. He saw the modernist/avant-garde aesthetic revolution as an avatar of the "new sensibility," the de-repressed human consciousness that would bring into being a "realm of freedom which is not that of the present . . . a liberation which must precede the construction of a free society, one which necessitates an historical break with the past and the present" (*An Essay* viii).

In postmodernity, we are beyond the moment of imagining that revolutionary political/aesthetic intentionality can produce such utter rupture with the past and the present. I would argue, nonethe-less, that we live in the aftermath of a profound historical rupture—postmodernity itself—a rupture that did not break along the lines revolutionary (or any other) intentionality had in mind. Utopia in post-modernity is multiply defeated and discredited, yet it persists in the form not only of desire for elimination of domination, inequality and oppression but also of desire for transcendence itself. Morrison and Doctorow suffuse their post-utopian, genre-inflected bestsellers with high modernist affect and form. Similarly, the political imagina-tion of postmodernity cannot encompass a universal utopia, but it can encompass building "piecemeal . . . a democratic society that will be as imperfect as the people who live in it": an imagination of struggle for local, partial, always-already compromised versions of the freedom, justice and equality that mark the utopian project.

The above quote is from a letter by a victim of Soviet-style utopia, written in Prague two days before the invasion of 1968. He is disgusted by what he considers the romantic unreality of Western radical utopianism of the late 60s, particularly that of Marcuse:

The men I met are all properly repelled by the realities of authoritarian rule, but they keep on preaching the same weary Utopian ideologies that can lead to nothing else. They live in a romantic dream-world in which their dear radical rhetoric is perfectly consistent with their apparently sincere faith in freedom and justice. But do they really think they could apply their radical Utopia in a real world and still respect their libertarian commitments? Do they really think their utopia could be benign if their revolutions were not comic-opera coups on indulgent campuses but real ventures in the exercise of power? . . . It was not until I started visiting the West that I began to understand that a Sartre or a Marcuse can simply afford a great deal of illusion. You all live in a different era—you still believe in Utopia. . . . We've had our fill of Utopia. No more. Now we are building piecemeal, building a democratic society that will be as imperfect as the people who live in it. It will be socialist because it is an industrial and a democratic society—it just doesn't work the other way around. It won't be a Utopia, but it will be a human kind of society, fit for people to live in. ("a student friend in Prague," qtd. in Kohak 389–390).

As for Morrison and Doctorow, the utopian for the "friend in Prague" is not only unrealizable but also utterly discredited, discarded, "of a different era." He not only settles for, but actively prefers, the limited possible. Yet like them, he still desperately desires the freedom and justice, the libertarian, socialist democracy, that have constituted the core vision of modernity's secular utopias. In "a human kind of society, fit for people to live in," the formulation conceived as definitive repudiation of and alternative to utopia, the great emancipatory Enlightenment-humanist project echoes. The intensity of this utopian desire is clear throughout his prose as well, in the very bitterness of his tone, just as the intensity of Morrison's and Doctorow's utopian desire is palpable in the push of their literary writing toward transcendence.

NOTES

[1]For an argument that the United States has been more influenced by utopianism than other societies because of its founding Revolutionary, Enlightenment commitments to liberty and equality, see Goodwin and Taylor 183–184. For an argument that postmodernism, as a definitive break with modernism, is quintessentially North American, see Huyssen, "Mapping the Postmodern." My understanding and deployment of the term "utopian" is influenced by a number of utopian discourses, most notably those of Karl Mannheim, Ernst Bloch, and Herbert Marcuse.

[2]I refer to Hutcheon's term, "historiographic metafiction." She uses this term in *The Poetics of Postmodernism* to designate postmodern fiction that "is both metafictionally self-reflexive and yet speaking to us powerfully about real political and historical realities" (5).

[3]For a thorough, highly informative discussion of the importance of feminism in Owenite socialist utopianism in England and the United States, see Taylor.

[4]For a classic and highly influential discussion of the Freedmen's Bureau and its demise, see Du Bois, chapter 2, "Of the Dawn of Freedom," 10–29.

[5]On the continuities of 1960s countercultural communes with nineteenth-century American utopian communities, see, for example, Gilbert.

[6]See Starr. He also discusses the antagonism between hippies and New Left radicals.

[7]For an extended discussion of the centrality of the concept of participatory democracy to the *Port Huron Statement* and to the New Left in general, see Miller.

[8]For an analysis of postmodernism as post-utopian, see Jameson, "Secondary Elaborations (Conclusion)," in *Postmodernism* 297–418, especially 334–340 and 401–406. See also Bammer.

[9]See, perhaps most notably, Lyotard. In his foreword to Lyotard's volume, Jameson claims, "This is the sense in which high modernism can be definitively certified as dead and as a thing of the past: its Utopian ambitions were unrealizable and its formal innovations exhausted" (xvii).

[10]See Hutcheon, *Poetics of Postmodernism*; also, *Politics of Postmodernism*. I take this aggregation of high-literary and popular narrative modes, resulting from the breakdown of the modernist "great divide" between art and popular culture, to be the most important characteristic of postmodernist fictional form (see Huyssen). Unlike modernism, which draws heavily on popular sources but assimilates them to its radically innovative, oppositional, high-art aesthetic practices, postmodernism leaves popular modes more or less intact. While many theorizations of the postmodern valorize popular culture, attacking modernism for its need to transform popular materials into high art, my argument here views the postmodern aggregation of popular and high-literary modes neutrally, descriptively. For an interesting recent discussion of *Beloved* as postmodern fiction, which in part addresses the issue of its composite form, see Pérez-Torres.

[11]Morrison also, of course, deploys the African-American genres of the slave narrative, the folk tale, storytelling and oral tradition in general.

[12]See duCille, especially pages 143–145.

[13]For discussions of modernist form as utopian, see for example Jameson, *The Political Unconscious*; Bloch; Marcuse; DeKoven. Clearly I am disagreeing with characterizations of postmodernism as primarily or typically formally experimentalist. Again, I am neither valorizing popular culture, as many pro-postmodernist arguments do, nor denigrating it, as many pro-modernist arguments do. I agree with Hutcheon that postmodernism is oppositional from a position within convention, in contradistinction to modernism, which defines itself as a negation of and alternative to convention.

[14]See Rhodes.

[15]This girl Beloved, homeless and without people, beat all, though he [Paul D] couldn't say exactly why, considering the coloredpeople he had run into during the

last twenty years. During, before and after the War he had seen Negroes so stunned, or hungry, or tired or bereft it was a wonder they recalled or said anything. Who, like him, had hidden in caves and fought owls for food; who, like him, stole from pigs; who, like him, slept in trees in the day and walked by night; who, like him, had buried themselves in slop and jumped in wells to avoid regulators, raiders, paterollers, veterans, hill men, posses and merrymakers. Once he met a Negro about fourteen years old who lived by himself in the woods and said he couldn't remember living anywhere else. He saw a witless coloredwoman jailed and hanged for stealing ducks she believed were her own babies. (66)

Eighteen seventy-four and whitefolks were still on the loose. Whole towns wiped clean of Negroes; eighty-seven lynchings in one year alone in Kentucky; four colored schools burned to the ground; grown men whipped like children; children whipped like adults; black women raped by the crew; property taken, necks broken. He [Stamp Paid] smelled skin, skin and hot blood. The skin was one thing, but human blood cooked in a lynch fire was a whole other thing. . . . It was the ribbon. Tying his flatbed up on the bank of the Licking River . . . he caught sight of something red on its bottom. . . . [It] was a red ribbon knotted around a curl of wet woolly hair, clinging still to its bit of scalp. . . . "What *are* these people? You tell me, Jesus. What *are* they?" (180)

[16]See Pérez-Torres for another discussion of this passage.

[17]The one exception is Amy Denver, a young destitute girl, escaping indenture, and therefore at the bottom of the white power structure. Like Sethe, she is abused and on the run; also like Sethe, she is almost superhumanly strong and resourceful. She delivers Denver, who is therefore named for her, and saves Sethe's life.

[18]A great deal of feminist psychoanalytic maternalist criticism has been written on this novel. For a useful bibliography of articles on *Beloved*, including many in the above category, see Mix 812–817. My reading emphasizes the deformations of history rather than the problems of the absolute pre-Oedipal maternal bond as analyzed from within a non-historically inflected psychoanalysis. For an argument with an emphasis on writing and constructions of maternity in African-American women's fiction, see Boyce Davies. Henderson's "Toni Morrison's *Beloved*" is another article that has been very important to my understanding of *Beloved*.

[19]Compare, for example, this passage from Cixous:

In woman there is always, more or less, something of "the mother" repairing and feeding, resisting separation. . . . Text, my body: traversed by lilting flows; listen to me. . . . it is the rhyth-me that laughs you; the one intimately addressed who makes all metaphors . . . the part of you that puts space between yourself and pushes you to inscribe your woman's style in language. Voice: milk that could go on forever. Found again. The lost mother/bitter-lost. Eternity: is voice mixed with milk. (93)

[20]For discussions of Doctorow's use of the 1870s to evoke present-day New York, see for example Sante and Solotaroff.

[21]Doctorow incorporates many ellipses into the text of *The Waterworks*. Those ellipses which are mine will be placed in brackets.

[22]Unlike Morrison, Doctorow does not close with this apocalyptic passage. He adds one more sentence, which ominously but ambiguously relocates us in historical time and place: "And let me leave you with that illusion [the illusion of ice-encased New York lifted by God out of time] . . . though in reality we would soon be

driving ourselves up Broadway in the new Year of Our Lord, 1872" (253). This metafictional moment leaves us in the year of the defeat of the Freedmen's Bureau.

WORKS CITED

Bammer, Angelika. *Partial Visions: Feminism and Utopianism in the 1970s*. New York: Routledge, 1991.

Bloch, Ernst. *A Philosophy of the Future*. New York: Herder and Herder, 1970.

Cixous, Hélène. "Sorties." *The Newly Born Woman*. By Cixous and Catherine Clément. Trans. Betsy Wing. Minneapolis: U of Minnesota P, 1986. 61–132.

Davies, Carol Boyce. "Mother Right/Write Revisited: *Beloved* and *Dessa Rose* and the Construction of Motherhood in Black Women's Fiction." *Narrating Mothers: Theorizing Maternal Subjectivities*. Ed. Brenda O. Daly and Maureen T. Reddy. Knoxville: U of Tennessee P, 1991. 44–57.

DeKoven, Marianne. *Rich and Strange: Gender, History, Modernism*. Princeton: Princeton UP, 1991.

Doctorow, E. L. *The Waterworks*. New York: Random House, 1994.

Du Bois, W. E. B. *The Souls of Black Folk*. 1903. New York: Bantam Books, 1989.

duCille, Ann. *The Coupling Convention: Sex, Text and Tradition in Black Women's Fiction*. New York: Oxford UP, 1993.

Fitzgerald, F. Scott. *The Great Gatsby*. 1925. New York: Collier Books, 1991.

Gilbert, James. "New Left: Old America." *The 60s Without Apology*. Ed. Sohnya Sayres, Anders Stephanson, Stanley Aronowitz, and Fredric Jameson. Minneapolis: U of Minnesota P, 1984. 244–247.

Goodwin, Barbara, and Keith Taylor, eds. *The Politics of Utopia*. New York: St. Martin's, 1982.

Henderson, Mae G. "Toni Morrison's *Beloved*: Re-Membering the Body as Historical Text." *Comparative American Identities: Race, Sex, and Nationality in the Modern Text*. Ed. Hortense Spillers. New York: Routledge, 1991. 62–86.

Hutcheon, Linda. *The Poetics of Postmodernism*. New York: Routledge, 1988.

——. *The Politics of Postmodernism*. New York: Routledge, 1989.

Huyssen, Andreas. "Mapping the Postmodern." *After the Great Divide: Modernism, Mass Culture, Postmodernism*. Bloomington: Indiana UP, 1986. 179–221.

Jameson, Fredric. Foreword. Lyotard vii–xxi.

——. *The Political Unconscious: Narrative as a Socially Symbolic Act*. Ithaca: Cornell UP, 1981.

——. *Postmodernism, or, the Cultural Logic of Late Capitalism*. Durham: Duke UP, 1991.

Kohak, Erazim V. "Requiem for Utopia." *Legacy of Dissent: Forty Years of Writing from* DISSENT *Magazine*. Ed. Nicolaus Mills. New York: Simon and Schuster, 1994. 389–401.

Lyotard, Jean-François. *The Postmodern Condition: A Report on Knowledge*. Trans. Geoff Bennington and Brian Massumi. Minneapolis: U of Minnesota P, 1984.

Mannheim, Karl. *Ideology and Utopia*. New York: Harcourt, Brace and World, 1936.

Marcuse, Herbert. *The Aesthetic Dimension: Toward a Critique of Marxist Aesthetics*. Boston: Beacon Press, 1978.

——. *An Essay on Liberation*. Boston: Beacon Press, 1969.

Miller, James. *"Democracy Is in the Streets": Port Huron to the Siege of Chicago*. New York: Simon and Schuster, 1987.

Mix, Debbie. "Toni Morrison: A Selected Bibliography." Peterson 795–817.

Morrison, Toni. *Beloved*. New York: Alfred A. Knopf, 1987.

Pérez-Torres, Rafael. "Knitting and Knotting the Narrative Thread—*Beloved* as Postmodern Novel." Peterson 689–707. Reprinted in this volume.

Peterson, Nancy J., ed. *Toni Morrison*. Special issue of *Modern Fiction Studies* 39.3–4 (Fall/Winter 1993).

Rhodes, Jewell Parker. "Toni Morrison's *Beloved*: Ironies of a 'Sweet Home' Utopia in a Dystopian Slave Society." *Utopian Studies* 1 (1990): 77–92.

Sante, Luc. "The Cabinet of Dr. Sartorius." Rev. of *The Waterworks*, by E. L. Doctorow. *New York Review of Books* 23 June 1994: 10–12.

Solotaroff, Ted. "Of Melville, Poe and Doctorow." Rev. of *The Waterworks*, by E. L. Doctorow. *The Nation* 6 June 1994: 784–790.

Starr, Paul. "The Phantom Community." *Co-ops, Communes and Collectives: Experiments in Social Change in the 1960s and 1970s*. Ed. John Case and Rosemary C. R. Taylor. New York: Pantheon, 1979. 245–273.

Taylor, Barbara. *Eve and the New Jerusalem*. 1983. Cambridge: Harvard UP, 1993.

SPEAKING THE UNSPEAKABLE: ON TONI MORRISON, AFRICAN AMERICAN INTELLECTUALS AND THE USES OF ESSENTIALIST RHETORIC[1]

Dwight A. McBride

Now that Afro-American artistic presence has been "discovered" actually to exist, now that serious scholarship has moved from silencing the witnesses and erasing their meaningful place in and contribution to American culture, it is no longer acceptable merely to imagine us and imagine for us. We have always been imagining ourselves. We are not Isak Dinesen's "aspects of nature," nor Conrad's unspeaking. We are the subjects of our own narrative, witnesses to and participants in our own experience, and, in no way coincidentally, in the experience of those with whom we have come in contact. We are not, in fact, "other." We are choices. And to read imaginative literature by and about us is to choose to examine centers of the self and to have the opportunity to

compare these centers with the "race-less" one with which we are, all of us, most familiar.
—Toni Morrison, "Unspeakable Things Unspoken: The Afro-American Presence in American Literature"

To be a subject means to activate the network of discourse from *where one stands*. Discourse is not a circle with one center, but more like a mycelium with many mushrooms. To be a subject also means to take nourishment from more than one source, to construct a new synthesis, a new discursive ragout.
—Barbara Johnson, "Response"

IN THE WAKE OF DECONSTRUCTION AND poststructuralism's move into the American academy, our fundamental understanding of the role of language in mediating our "reality" has come to the fore. The advent of poststructuralism, then, has also meant a basic shift in the debate around such categories as race and experience. No longer are race and experience assumed to be stable categories of critical discourse, but rather "race" and "experience" themselves become sites of critical contestation. To use Jacques Derrida's language, as "transcendental signifieds" race and experience are "under erasure." The political and rhetorical impact this move has had on African American critical discourse requires some comment. What has this critical shift meant for the authority of African American scholars doing work in African American Studies in often racist institutions? If not on racial experience, on what grounds do they address the study of African American culture? How do they negotiate the relationship between the discourse of multiculturalism, which argues the need for a culturally diversified academy, and poststructuralist discourse, which makes the sign "experience" a site of contestation? Indeed, what, if not some understanding of their cultural experience, do African Americans uniquely bring to critical inquiry?

These opening observations are what I bring to this reading of Toni Morrison's "Unspeakable Things Unspoken: The Afro-American Presence in American Literature." The reason I begin my investigation of these concerns with Morrison is because she is, arguably, the most prominent artist-critic in contemporary American and African American letters, a position that uniquely qualifies her to speak to the variety of impacts that poststructuralist discussions of "race" and "experience" have had for African American artists and intellectuals. It may be precisely this dual role Morrison plays as African American intellectual and artist that allows her to see so clearly the impact of contemporary discussions of race on both imaginative work and critical work. (And this may explain some of the reasons Morrison took the turn into critical work to begin with.) Let me say up front that I believe Morrison's essay implicitly outlines a critique of poststructuralism's treatment of the category of "race." I hope to demonstrate that the essay also enacts a rhetorical strategy African American intellectuals often use to reclaim a racial essentialism based on experience that authorizes or legitimizes their speech in some very politically important ways.

What is simultaneously interesting and difficult about Morrison's "Unspeakable Things Unspoken" is that while the essay is careful to issue an anti-essentialist disclaimer,[2] it does finally argue for, and depend upon, a variety of racial essentialism (grounded in racial experience) that has significant bearing on contemporary debates surrounding the question of essentialism in critical discourse. An example of this, which I will discuss later at greater length, appears in my epigraph where Morrison invokes the first-person-plural pronoun form of address. By "essentialism" I follow here Diana Fuss's admirable treatment of the term in *Essentially Speaking: Feminism, Nature and Difference*. It may be enough for now to refer to what Fuss identifies as the most commonly understood definition of the term—that is, "a belief in the real, true essence of things, the invariable and fixed properties which define the 'whatness' of a given entity" (xi). Morrison's essay is interesting because of the way it reverses the issue of racial essentialism. That is, she demonstrates from the very outset her awareness of contemporary criticism's move to complicate "race" as a category for critical investigation. The essay is also difficult because of the way it boldly enacts a carefully articulated form of racial essentialism even as it understands the critical risks involved in such a move.

For this reason it will be important to consider the rhetorical strategies Morrison uses to deploy racial essentialism as a useful means of analysis, as well as some of the implications this deployment may have for rethinking larger discussions of the status of racial "experience" (as an essentialist grounds for knowledge) in poststructuralist discourse. For the purposes of this project, a consideration of both Morrison's experience (as a high profile African

American, woman, artist/author and critic) and of the worlds she creates in her fiction is crucial. In fact, it is precisely this variety of identity negotiations—self-canonization as author, critical legitimation as artist in the academy, authority to narrate African American experience as African American, etc.—in which Morrison participates that makes her essay more than suitably representative for the kind of rhetorical analysis I wish to undertake.

My project neither takes issue with nor apologizes for Morrison. Let me immediately admit that I believe Morrison's rhetorical strategies not only to be common among African American intellectuals, but politically indispensable as well. Even in the literary and cultural critiques by African Americans which are informed by much poststructuralist thought, these scholars, almost without fail (and out of political necessity), pause to genuflect before the shrine of essentialism. I will not here try to address the ostensibly unspeakable character of these essentialisms to which many African American critics seem to return.[3] Instead, I will limit my remarks to the politics of the difficult negotiations I have been outlining that motivate the intense and recurring return to the essentializing gesture.

1.

"Unspeakable Things Unspoken" is a text that is highly suggestive and large in scope. It may be useful, therefore, to begin with a word on the structure of the opening section (which is my primary focus) to Morrison's three-part essay. First, the essay provides an overview of the stakes involved in the contemporary canon debate with particular regard to the "race" question. The first portion of the essay critically tracks the trajectory of race in intellectual discourse (3), attempts to define a "racially" formed Afro-American "culture" (as distinct from a "race") (3), destabilizes the notion of "taste" (4), and identifies the most disturbing aspect of the resistance to "displacement within or expansion of the canon" in the "virulent passion that accompanies the resistance" and not in the resistance itself (4-5). Also in this section Morrison suggests (using the example of Milan Kundera's The Art of the Novel) the analogous, hierarchical relationship that obtains between European and American literature and American and African American literature. And she compares Martin Bernal's project in Black Athena (to illuminate the process and motives of the fabrication of Ancient Greece) to her own project (or rather the project of "Afro-American critical inquiry") of illuminating the process of silencing the African American presence in American literature. That is, she identifies "canon building" with "empire building" (8). The last gesture in this first portion of the essay is the recognition of the role "serious scholarship" has played in "disentangling received knowledge from the apparatus of control" (8).

The two aspects of Morrison's essay that I want to elaborate on at some length are the way in which she works to deconstruct the dichotomy between critic and scholar, and how this may inform our understanding of how Morrison occupies the language of the racial discourse available to her and locates her liberating possibilities from inside that discourse through her deployment of racial essentialism. Because the former informs the latter, let me begin by discussing how Morrison de-essentializes the categories of artist and critic in ways that ultimately legitimize and empower her position as artist-critic.

Morrison has a keen interest in what she calls the academy's contrived barriers between critic-scholar and artist. In fact, much of her own distinguished career as a writer, teacher, editor, not to mention her more recent forays into criticism, throw such easy divisions into doubt. Even in the essay at hand Morrison is invested in collapsing these barriers in statements like "Certainly a sharp alertness as to *why* a work is or is not worthy is the legitimate occupation of the critic, the pedagogue and the artist" (5). Consider also the essay's closing paragraph:

For an author, regarding canons, it is very simple: in fifty, a hundred or more years his or her work may be relished for its beauty or its insights or its power; or it may be condemned for its vacuousness and pretension— and junked. Or in fifty or a hundred years the critic (as canon builder) may be applauded for his or her intelligent scholarship and powers of critical inquiry. Or laughed at for ignorance and shabbily disguised assertions of power—and junked. It's possible that the reputations of both will thrive, or that both will decay. In any case, as far as the future is concerned, when one writes, as critic or as author, all necks are on the line. (33-34)

Here Morrison makes it clear that, "regarding canons," time will tell not only the story of the reception of the artist, but of the critic as well. By equating the risks of historical permanence involved for writers with the (all too often unspoken) risks involved for critics, Morrison issues an equalizing blow to the power of the critic in his/ her relationship to writers.

The final example of Morrison's deconstruction of the artist-critic dichotomy comes in her discussions of Kundera's *The Art of the Novel* and Terrence Rafferty's review of the same in the *New Yorker*. She writes:

Kundera's views, obliterating American writers (with the exception of William Faulkner) from his own canon, are relegated to a "smugness" that

Terrence Rafferty disassociates from Kundera's imaginative work and ap-
plies to the "sublime confidence" of his critical prose. The confidence of
an exile who has the sentimental education of, and the choice to become,
a European. (5-6)

The amalgamation of this statement with the preceding one accomplishes several things, not the least of which is that it invites us to
take seriously the rhetorical strategies and subtext of Morrison's
discourse. For if Rafferty can distinguish the character of Kundera's
imaginative work from his critical prose, we are certainly invited to
determine how to negotiate the same issue in the case of Morrison.
By challenging the boundary between artist and critic, Morrison
creates a legitimate place in critical literary discourse for her own
voice. She resists the kind of facile distinction Rafferty makes with
Kundera and, in fact, depends upon the play between the artist/
critic dichotomy for her rhetorical positionality in this essay. Nowhere
is this more clearly demonstrated than in the essay's equalizing final
paragraph. I argue later that Morrison is negotiating two kinds of
"otherness"—the otherness of "artist" in the academy and the
otherness of "race" in America. In this way, the rhetorical gesture
of challenging the artist/critic dichotomy becomes a crucial move
for Morrison in order to enshrine herself (as much of this essay
arguably does) as a legitimate critical voice.[4]

But let me return for a moment to Morrison's discussion of
Rafferty's review of Kundera, in order to concentrate on how Morrison's rhetorical strategies function in that instance. It is worth
quoting at length here from Morrison's excerpt from Rafferty:

Kundera's "personal 'idea of the novel,'" he [Rafferty] wrote, "is so profoundly Eurocentric that it's likely to seem exotic, even perverse, to American
readers. . . . *The Art of the Novel* gives off the occasional (but pungent)
whiff of cultural arrogance, and we may feel that Kundera's discourse . . .
reveals an aspect of his character that we'd rather not have known about. . . .
In order to become the artist he now is, the Czech novelist had to discover
himself a second time, as a European. But what if that second, grander
possibility hadn't been there to be discovered? What if Broch, Kafka, Musil—
all that reading—had never been a part of his education, or had entered
it only as exotic, alien presence? Kundera's polemical fervor in *The Art of
the Novel* annoys us, as American readers, because we feel defensive,
excluded from the transcendent 'idea of the novel' that for him seems
simply to have been there for the taking. (If only he had cited, in his
redeeming version of the novel's history, a few more heroes from the New
World's culture.) Our novelists don't discover cultural values within themselves; they invent them." (5)

Now consider Morrison's response to this statement:

> I was refreshed by Rafferty's comments. With the substitution of certain phrases, his observations and the justifiable umbrage he takes can be appropriated entirely by Afro-American writers regarding their own exclusion from the "transcendent 'idea of the novel.'"
>
> For the present turbulence seems not to be about the flexibility of a canon, its range among and between Western countries, but about its miscegenation. (6)

In the course of these two statements Morrison positions herself as a mediator between the competing forces of the defenders of the canonical faith and the more insurgent intellectual voices involved in the present canon polemic. She makes the discussion slightly more palatable (or in her words "not endangering" [4]) for the more conservative interlocutors who may be reluctant to enter this debate. She places all of her readers at ease by creating, via the figure of Rafferty, a sympathy for American literature against European arrogance and European exclusion of American literature from its definition of canonical texts (here represented by Kundera). It is a swift, unifying, and almost patriotic "call to arms." It enlists our sympathies as Americans, and we feel slighted. The crucial move comes, however, at the close of her discussion of Kundera when Morrison draws the parallel between what Kundera (Europe) is doing to American literature and what American literature is doing to African American literature. It is an established rhetorical tactic (initially putting the reader at ease only to make more stark the realization to which you want him/her to come) that proves effective here.[5] The way in which this rhetorical gesture functions at the level of racial and cultural identity politics demands our notice: establishing herself in the eyes of her American reading audience as the critical voice that points out Kundera's Eurocentrism to the detriment of American literature, Morrison also positions herself to be the recipient of the admiration that this critical "call to arms" creates. This then allows her metonymically to enlist those same sympathies for the ways in which African American literature may suffer from the exclusionary impulses of the traditional American literary canon. It is, after all, Morrison (as African American artist-critic) who is able to *read* the connection between European literature and American literature that Rafferty makes for its applicability to the relationship between American literature and African American literature.

This reading of the rhetorical use to which Morrison puts Rafferty is reminiscent of the kind of analysis she performs on white American literature in *Playing in the Dark: Whiteness and the Literary Imag-*

ination. In this text, Morrison outlines a discussion of what she calls "American Africanisms." She considers the Africanist presence in the fiction of white American writers and argues that African Americans are "serviceable" both in these texts and in the lives of the white characters who populate these novels. Morrison demonstrates how the Africanist presence is "serviceable" both in order to address larger identity questions these white writers or characters may have difficulty confronting, and to provide access for these same writers and characters to the realm of permissive lawlessness, seditiousness and danger that is not available when one deals solely in white bodies. Morrison offers minstrelsy as a representative metaphor to demonstrate this point:

In minstrelsy, a layer of blackness applied to a white face released it from law. Just as entertainers, through or by association with blackface, could render permissible topics that otherwise would have been taboo, so American writers were able to employ an imagined Africanist persona to articulate and imaginatively act out the forbidden in American culture. (66)

According to Morrison, the representation of these "serviceable black bodies" (28) accomplishes much for white writers, including what she calls the "economy of stereotype" (67). That is, by invoking a black body in their texts, these writers enact a complex system of signs (that depends upon the reader's preprogrammed complicity in thinking stereotypically about "blackness"), which "allows the writer a quick and easy image without the responsibility of specificity, accuracy, or even narratively useful description" (67). In *Playing in the Dark* Morrison rehearses this assertion with a variety of literary examples from Poe and Melville to Cather and Hemingway, thus proving its power and pervasiveness.

   The kind of analysis Morrison performs on white American literature in *Playing in the Dark* (via the issue of the serviceability of black bodies) suggests a way of reading the similar rhetorical moves she makes in "Unspeakable Things Unspoken" in "writing" the figure of Rafferty. If white American writers—and in some cases their white characters—enlist black bodies to economize stereotype and to "imaginatively act out the forbidden in American culture," then Morrison makes use of Rafferty's rhetorical serviceability in "Unspeakable Things Unspoken" to legitimize her critical voice in an academy where the artist/critic dichotomy has been concretizing for quite some time.

   In moving from this discussion of how Morrison essentializes professional positioning in the academy to her deployment of racial essentialism for the purpose of authorizing her speech about African

Americans, Morrison's tactics will become more evident. As subject, Morrison, in the words of Barbara Johnson, "takes nourishment from more than one source" (43). Johnson's statement becomes even more valuable to our reading of the way Morrison addresses herself to the race question. If Morrison can claim superiority over the critic, as shown in the earlier discussion of her professional essentializing, because of her positionality (that is, where she stands as she activates the network of discourse), then the same is true of her deployment of racial essentialism as a way of authorizing her speech about African American subjects. Before going too far in this direction, however, I will reflect briefly on Morrison's position inside what I term "racialized discourse"—an understanding of which will serve to illuminate the complexity of Morrison's rhetorical moves in regard to racial essentialism.

2.

Obvious examples of racialized discourse are the overly popular catch-all phrases or calls to unity like "Blacks" and "the Black community" often employed by popular media and in a variety of political discussions. Such terms function as totalizing descriptors or appellations. They serve to make us think (if even for the moment and for the very sake of discourse itself) that "the Black community" is knowable, totalizable, locatable and certainly separate from or other than the speaker (Black or non-Black in some cases).[6] The use of such terminology, then, represents not only a false will to power on the part of the speaker who appropriates such language, but carries with it extremely high political stakes as well. Such labels deny heterogeneity among African Americans (class, gender, educational level, sexuality, etc.) and easily seduce us into the language of stereotypes by characterizing in a facile manner the entirety of the experiences of African American people. Further, these labels implicitly assume something called a "white community" which rarely, if ever, gets spoken of in such terms, since it is a priori the norm, the original against which all else must be compared.

I am reminded here of a dialogue I had some time ago with an African American male graduate student and an African American male undergraduate. Our conversation, as is often the case among African Americans, eventually settled on the problems facing "the Black community." We vigorously catalogued the issues in a manner which seemed almost ritualistic and all too facile, when the uninitiated undergraduate chimed in with a query which is understood as forbidden in polite intellectual discourse of this sort: "So, what can we do about any of this?" As the weight of his question settled upon us, we each fell uncharacteristically silent. There we sat on the steps of Perloff Hall at UCLA, three well-educated, young, African American men, feeling powerless to answer this question in a way that would challenge the perfunctory, superficial responses often spoken in such situations. The silence, I am convinced in this case, had much to do with the way we had constructed our positionality in this scenario. The very fact that we had the leisure to engage in such conversation, that we could outline the problems in such eloquent fashion and not include ourselves in the categories we listed (since few of them directly affected the lives of us interlocutors—drugs, access to education, poverty), demonstrates a disjuncture or discontinuity between the speaking Black subject in this case and those in "the Black community" who are being spoken about.[7]

My use of the term "racialized discourse" is consciously employed as opposed to "racial discourse" or simply "race" so that the reader might remain aware of the very constructedness of this discourse. Discourse is not simply "racial," since this term implies an ontology or essence of something that we can know as "race." It does not not simply reproduce "race" because this neglects the critical role of language in the construction of discourse. The only way that the fiction of the category "race" can be called into existence is if, as Walter Benjamin says in another context, it is supported by an elaborate language (187). In other words, no race without a representational discourse, and no discourse without language. My use of the term "racialized discourse" is an attempt to circumvent these problems. The contrived past-participle form "racialized" signifies a political operation on language that makes it *appear* racially determined (which assumes an existence for "race"). One of the goals of this construction, then, is the thematization of the disjuncture between "racialized discourse" (as construct and mediated representation) and "race" (as essence or experience).

I find Paul de Man's "The Rhetoric of Temporality" useful in pointing out the ways in which racialized discourse functions allegorically to define and construct "race," while also demonstrating the inherent politicality of allegory itself. The one caveat I will issue here is that while I am unquestionably invested in understanding the constructedness or inventedness of race (that is, what some poststructuralists have called "race" under "erasure"), I also insist that it is politically irresponsible to speak of race in this way without a consistent awareness of the oppressive material and political implications of such sociolinguistic constructs for the lives of people of color (that is, the real human pain and suffering people endure). It is for these reasons, I am convinced, that we must inevitably speak the terms of "racial identification" in order to articulate our racial struggle even though we are aware of the risk that these terms may also be converted to serve the agenda of our oppressors.

In "The Rhetoric of Temporality" de Man provides an understanding of the development and interrelatedness of symbol, allegory and irony in literary discourse. Instead of the interrelation of these critical tropes, however, it is the distinctions de Man makes between the three by way of the temporality of their structure that concerns me here. Among these, allegory is of particular interest because its structure includes an illusory and fictitious center that, I maintain, is also characteristic of racialized discourse. De Man's paradigm of allegory provides not only a way to explore "the curious dialectic between formal language use and the inscription of metaphorical racial differences" (Gates 6), but also a way of looking analytically at the politicality of the deep structure of racialized discourse itself.[8]

De Man characterizes allegory by saying it "appears . . . dryly rational and dogmatic in its reference to a meaning that it does not itself constitute" (189). In this way allegory, not claiming to know its origins or identification, "designates primarily a distance in relation to its own origin, and, renouncing the nostalgia and desire to coincide, it establishes its language in the void of this temporal difference" (207). The allegorical sign "points to something that differs from its literal meaning and has as its function the thematization of this difference" (209). Allegory has its existence "entirely within an ideal time that is never here and now but always a past or an endless future." Allegory is a "successive mode capable of engendering duration as the illusion of a continuity that it knows is illusionary" (226).

Given de Man's understanding of allegory, how can this function paradigmatically for a deeper understanding of the allegorical structure of racialized discourse? For racialized discourse to function allegorically, we must first ask what abstract quality or phenomenon is being allegorized. In this case "race" would seem the simple response which turns out, of course, not to be so simple as we might at first imagine. When we recognize the very process of allegorization as the thematization or calling into existence of something that, because of its abstract or illusory nature,[9] has never been represented, then the politicality of allegory begins to come into focus. So even in its inception, racial allegory (and with it racialized discourse) is about choices—the choice to focus on skin color, the choice to make it signify immutable difference, and the choice to call it into existence as a critical category in the first place—and is, therefore, thoroughly and inescapably political.

Again, de Man maintains that allegory "appears dryly rational and dogmatic in its reference to a meaning that it does not itself constitute." A similar case could certainly be made for racialized discourse. Recall the earlier example ("Blacks" and "Black community") which presupposes a category called "race" and a locatable, totalizable "community" of some sort. Such phrases are used in a manner that confers an assumed, unproblematic ontology upon a referent that they in themselves do not and cannot constitute. While even the most cursory study of any language would reveal this to be the case, racialized discourse seduces its speakers into an often unwitting compliance with the assumptions inherent in that discourse. This is precisely what the propagation of the racial allegory depends upon—a kind of selective amnesia, a collective forgetting. It is in that forgetting of the assumptions and origins of racialized discourse[10] (that is, that racialized discourse is predicated upon a fallacious, contrived assumption of difference) that the agenda of the dominant culture's hegemony and the normalization and defensibility of "whiteness" can be located.

De Man also asserts that the allegorical sign "points to something that differs from its literal meaning and has as its function the thematization of that difference." This and more can be said of the racial allegory. Racialized discourse functions not only to thematize the difference between the literal meaning of the sign and the racial meaning being pointed to by the same sign; but, since the sign has no real literal meaning (in the sense that the "blackness" of the sign is a convenient contrivance) the discourse is engaging in creating meaning out of what de Man calls "the void of temporal difference." Again, what is at stake has less to do with any kind of real differences between "races" and more to do with buttressing the agenda of the dominant culture and the defensibility of "whiteness." In cases where the racialized discourse is employed in a Black-Black dialectic, this discursive practice alters little. The speaking Black subjects assume superiority and power over those spoken about via language.[11] Although in most cases these speakers possess good intentions, the risk involved is that the same discourse which enables such well-intended articulations will also sustain the articulations of those who may not be so well intended.

The understanding of racialized discourse, as I have outlined it in this essay, also represents an intervention into poststructuralist discourses centered around the critique of the sign of "experience."[12] For I remain convinced that experience can still be called upon as "grounds" for epistemological claims both without critical apology and without suffering dismissal as an essentialist in the prevailing, derogatory sense of the term. I want to preserve a space for "experience" as a way of authorizing certain speech acts over others on issues where systematic human pain and suffering are involved. I contend that even in the realm of mediation, the "experience" of "race" for whites and for people of color is different. The *status of experience* inside racialized discourse need not be viewed as being any more privileged than the *critique of experience* from within that discourse. This allegorical paradigm helps us to perceive better the linguistic and ideological forces at work that mediate experience. It also enables us to see how we are conditioned, prepared, or overdetermined (white or nonwhite) by racialized discourse to read our "experience" in certain racialized ways. That is to say, to reformulate Morrison's words in another context, in the future when we speak of the status of experience either as subjects relying upon the political value of its "authority" and "authenticity" (although fictive and mediated), or as subjects whose desire it may be to destabilize or deauthorize its reliability, all necks are on the line. Neither the "author" of experience nor its "critics" stand on ground that is more or less stable than the other. Indeed, what a rigorous critique of racialized discourse does is to call us back to the recognition that none of our "experiences," white or nonwhite, inside racialized discourse exist outside that discourse. This does not, then, serve to deauthorize experience as a useful category at all. On the contrary, it calls us to recognize how mediated and constructed experience operates, even in a staunchly poststructuralist and social constructionist context, "as a more sophisticated form of essentialism," as Fuss says of constructionism in *Essentially Speaking* (xii).

The final point of interest here that de Man makes about the temporality of allegory is that it has its existence "entirely within an ideal time that is never here and now but always a past or an endless future." It is a "successive mode capable of engendering duration as the illusion of a continuity that it knows is illusionary" (226). The example of Pecola Breedlove in Morrison's *The Bluest Eye* is illustrative here. Pecola is a little Black girl who through racial experience has come to think of herself as ugly, unworthy, and displaced in a society where the image of beauty is the little yellow-haired, blue-eyed, white girl. The novel traces Pecola's journey into insanity as she pursues her desire to have "the bluest eyes"—the symbol of whiteness that she believes will make her beautiful. Morrison writes:

> So it was.
>
> A little black girl yearns for the blue eyes of a little white girl, and the horror at the heart of her yearning is exceeded only by the evil of fulfillment. (158)

The language through which the narrator articulates Pecola's plight is taken from the mouths of the speakers and creators of racialized discourse. As far as Pecola knows, racialized discourse (if, indeed, we can count her as aware of it as such) has always been around and will always be around. The real tragedy, then, is that Pecola, like all of us, has been seduced into believing that "race" is and always has been "real." That is the quality of racialized discourse that is most pernicious and elusive—the way it insures its continued existence through a fabricated past, reaching back to the beginning of time and forecasting an interminable future. It is for these reasons that the here and now is taken care of—because "race" constitutes a "frozen metaphor" in "ideal time" (Nielsen 12).

3.

Let me now return to Morrison and the question of racial essentialism. Consider again the epigraph by Morrison that opens this essay in which she makes initial use of the first-person plural voice. The rhetorical, indeed, the performative use to which Morrison puts the first-person plural is simultaneously problematic, politically useful, and undoubtedly essentialist. Morrison's use of "we" and "our" is not unlike the example of the use of the term "black community" I discussed earlier. Its veiled, or not so veiled, attempt at a unity, which is finally evasive, is one response (and arguably the most politically expedient response) available to African Americans trying to speak/think their experience inside a racialized discourse.

Johnson's remarks on the use of the "shifter," "we," are also instructive here:

> The pronoun "we" has historically proven to be the most empowering and shiftiest shifter of them all. It is through the "we" that discourses of false universality are created. With its cognitive indeterminacy and its performative authority, it is both problematic and unavoidable for the discourses of political opposition. For this structure of the stressed subject with an indeterminant

predicate may well be the structure necessary for empowerment without essentialism. At the same time, it is an empowerment always in danger of presuming too much. But, then, can there be empowerment without presumption? (43)

I am in full agreement with Johnson to a point. Indeed, the indeterminacy of the "shifter" is tantamount to the process of empowerment. Even de Man, citing Schlegel, makes a similar claim defining freedom as "the unwillingness of the mind to accept any stage in its progression as definitive, since this would stop what he [Schlegel] calls its 'infinite agility'" (220). Where I part ways with Johnson is when she states that this use of the shifter is a method of avoiding essentialism. On the contrary, it may be a way of avoiding an *explicit* essentialism, but it hardly escapes lapsing into an *implicit* essentialism. In order for the indeterminate "shifter" to signify empowerment via its indeterminacy on the order of the particular (especially in Morrison's case), it must be read as implicitly signifying, generally speaking of course, some configuration of an essentially African American referent.

One cannot help also noticing, in the epigraph by Morrison, her use of the term "experience." In fact, with little alteration, this epigraph might well serve as a diversity mission statement for any number of universities at the present time. As the academy has moved from the absence to the presence of African Americans, the emphasis in this passage progresses from imagining and theorizing about African Americans to African Americans imagining and theorizing themselves. When we speak in terms of the value of diversity or pluralism, the language of difference, experience and culture is synonymous with these topics. And since we surely do not mean melanin when we speak of the values of diversity, one can imagine little else that we might be referring to if not the value of different experiences and cultural perspectives (shaped by experience). Consider Morrison's statement: "We are the subjects of our own narrative, witnesses to and participants in our own experience, and . . . in the experience of those with whom we have come in contact." What is interesting about this statement is how Morrison complicates racial experience even as she is essentializing it, effectively demonstrating that essentialism cannot always be read as uncritical or facile. For to say that African Americans are "witnesses to and participants in our own experience" is to posit experience as something we are both determined by and determining, both inside and outside of. And it most certainly, according to this statement, is something over which we have ownership. In other words, our experience is shaped by our perspective (the way we read the world). And our perspective is shaped by the overdeterminacy of racialized discourse in which we are all caught up or "interpellated" as subjects. The latter part of Morrison's statement is no less complicated when she states that we are also participants "in the experience of those with whom we have come in contact." Read in all its richness, this statement testifies to the fact that not only do African Americans have racial "experience," but white Americans do as well. They, too, have learned to read race according to their experience, which African Americans play no small part in constructing.

By the time Morrison reaches the section of her essay in which she gives her reading of *Sula*, she has provided us with a context in which to understand her use of the racial descriptor "black":

I always thought of Sula as quintessentially black, metaphysically black, if you will, which is not melanin and certainly not unquestioning fidelity to the tribe. She is new world black and new world woman extracting choice from choicelessness, responding inventively to found things. Improvisational. Daring, disruptive, imaginative, modern, out-of-the-house, outlawed, unpolicing, uncontained and uncontainable. (25)

The "quintessential blackness" to which Morrison refers here is neither, as I say, facile nor uncritical. It is "metaphysical," constructed, overdetermined and informed by experience. The adjectives used to describe Sula's blackness (and, indeed, her black femaleness) are quite similar to the adjectives used earlier in Morrison's essay to describe the language of African American literature: "unpoliced, seditious . . . inventive, disruptive" (11). This similarity is suggestive of the relationship that obtains between racial experience and racialized discourse.

Morrison's use of the shifter, as described above, is only one way that African American intellectuals use essentialism to authorize their critical voices. Another well-established method is through anecdote—the relating of "experience." Testifying and storytelling are methods of self-disclosure that legitimize the critical project as somehow more authentic, bearing a direct relationship to "experience." While contemporary examples of this are numerous—for example, consider Patricia Williams's *The Alchemy of Race and Rights*, any number of essays by bell hooks, Houston Baker's introduction to *Long Black Song*, or my own use of testimonial earlier in this essay—one of the most illustrative examples is presented in the preface of Cornel West's recent book *Race Matters*.

The preface opens with West describing one of his and his wife's biweekly trips to New York from Princeton in September 1993.

His thoughts move from the two lectures he had given that day—one on Plato and the other on DuBois—to speculation about whether he and his wife would have time to eat and relax at their favorite restaurant after their appointments. After dropping his wife off at an appointment on 60th Street between Lexington and Park avenues, West parks his car and stands on the corner in order to catch a cab to Harlem for the cover photo shoot of *Race Matters*. An experience familiar to many African American New Yorkers, and recognized by many others, follows. West, who "waited and waited and waited" on that street corner, is refused by ten cabs (x). He records his feelings in this way:

After the ninth taxi refused me, my blood began to boil. The tenth taxi refused me and stopped for a kind, well-dressed, smiling female fellow citizen of European descent. As she stepped in the cab, she said, "This is really ridiculous, is it not?"

Ugly racial memories of the past flashed through my mind. Years ago, while driving from New York to teach at Williams College, I was stopped on fake charges of trafficking cocaine. When I told the police officer I was a professor of religion, he replied "Yeh, and I'm the Flying Nun. Let's go nigger!" I was stopped three times in my first ten days in Princeton for driving too slowly on a residential street with a speed limit of twenty-five miles per hour. . . . Needless to say these incidents are dwarfed by those like Rodney King's beating. . . . Yet memories cut like a merciless knife at my soul as I waited on that godforsaken corner. Finally I decided to take the subway. I walked three long avenues, arrived late, and had to catch my moral breath as I approached the white male photographer and the white female cover designer. I chose not to dwell on this everyday experience of black New Yorkers. And we had a good time talking, posing, and taking pictures. (x-xi)

What is immediately interesting about West's story for the purposes of this essay is not only what West experiences, but how he recognizes what it is he is experiencing—in this case the taxi drivers reading him as racially black and, therefore, unreliable as a potential customer. West is able to come to this recognition because he has previously experienced this complex of signs. The experience stirs his racial memory and causes him to recall other "ugly racial memories," which in turn enable him to be a better reader of his present experience. Even so, it is, I am convinced, West's awareness of the suspicion under which poststructuralism has placed the reliability of experience that motivates the curious appearance of the white, female witness to his story.

Upon first reading, I was bewildered by the appearance of this "kind, well-dressed, smiling female fellow citizen of European descent.''[13] What rhetorical value did her presence have for the story? How did her comments—"This is really ridiculous, is it not?"—signify? Upon closer inspection, however, the pains to which West goes in his very concise but meaningful description of the woman are suggestive for how we are to read her. She is white, well-dressed and taking a cab. This description suggests that she is not poor and, therefore, unreliable as a witness. She is also "smiling." This is supposed to be a clue that she is sympathetic to what is happening on that street corner, even as she may feel a bit nervous or guilty herself about witnessing West's situation. In any event, she is cast as the credible witness who can legitimize his experience because she reads it apart from West's potentially "biased" or "overly sensitive" racialized reading. While the essentializing gestures West deploys here are effective and politically necessary, they do run the risk of again locating the woman's ability to be a credible, unbiased witness in her whiteness. This is, however, the kind of risk (as I spoke of earlier) that one must take to authorize and legitimize oneself in racialized discourse.

An example from Patricia Williams is relevant to this point. In *The Alchemy of Race and Rights*, Williams relates a story of how a sales clerk at Benetton's discriminated against her by denying her access to the store (whose entrance was secured by a buzzer, a common feature in many New York shops). In addition to publishing her story in a law review journal, she occasionally uses it in speaking engagements. She cites some of the questions she is often asked in the wake of its telling:

Am I not privileging a racial perspective, by considering only the black point of view? Don't I have an obligation to include the "salesman's side" of the story?

Am I not putting the salesman on trial and finding him guilty of racism without giving him a chance to respond to or cross-examine me?

Am I not using the store window as a "metaphorical fence" against the potential of his explanation in order to represent my side as "authentic"?

How can I be sure I'm right?

What makes my experience the real black one anyway?

Isn't it possible that another black person might disagree with my experience? If so, doesn't that render my story too unempirical and subjective to pay any attention to? (50-51)

These are some of the same kinds of questions to which West's story might be subject were it not for the white female who bears witness.

In a footnote to her text, Williams replies to her own questions in the following way:

These questions question my ability to know, to assess, to be objective. And of course, since anything that happens to me is inherently subjective, they take away my power to know what happens to me in the world. Others, by this standard, will always know better than I. And my insistence on recounting stories from my own perspective will be treated as presumption, slander, paranoid hallucination, or just plain lies.

Recently I got an urgent call from Thomas Grey of Stanford Law School. He had used the piece [the Benetton's article] in his jurisprudence class, and a rumor got started that the Benetton's story wasn't true that it was . . . a lie that was probably the product of a diseased mind trying to make all white people feel guilty. At this point, I realized it almost didn't make any difference whether I was telling the truth or not—that the greater issue I had to face was the overwhelming weight of a disbelief that goes beyond mere disinclination to believe and becomes active suppression of anything I might have to say. The greater problem is a powerfully oppressive mechanism for denial of black self-knowledge and expression. And this denial cannot be separated from the simultaneously pathological willingness to believe certain things about blacks—not to believe them, but things about them. (242)

In addition to outlining the institutional risks involved for African Americans trying to speak about and theorize their experiences, Williams also points out that the major risk of vigorous destabilizations of "experience" is that they can ultimately become political tools to silence and deauthorize African American experience. The danger, then, is that since the fundamental way of identifying racism is by narrating its instances, by deauthorizing the witness it could become virtually impossible to ever name "the beast" at all. This is one reason that I think it is important that African American intellectuals continue to learn new ways of strategizing and essentializing in racialized discourse: because what is at stake is nothing less than the ability to narrate our own stories, witness our own experience.

Morrison's characterization of the function of language in African American literature may be a fitting close for now to a project that is very much still in progress. She writes:

And in Afro-American literature itself the question of difference, of essence, is critical. What makes a work "Black"? The most valuable point of entry into the question of cultural (or racial) distinction, the one most fraught, is its language—its unpoliced, seditious, confrontational, manipulative, inventive, disruptive, masked and unmasking language. Such a penetration will entail the most careful study, one in which the impact of Afro-American presence on modernity becomes clear and is no longer a well kept secret. ("Unspeakable" 11)

Notice the adjectives used here to characterize the function of the language of the African American text: "unpoliced," "seditious," "confrontational." They are all words that express craftiness and resistance. This is because language is in many ways the quintessential site of the recurring confrontation with the other. The language of the African American text itself stands as an emblem of the Herculean struggle to represent an experience that the language is not intended to accommodate. Such texts constitute the attempt to write the seemingly unwritable, the unspeakable.

So it is in an attempt to represent one's experience in a language that is not intended to do that work, that a strategic essentialism becomes an almost indispensable tool.[14] Why? Simply put: It allows us to speak categorically in a discourse that seems to demand and respect labels. It enables us to speak to and about a people whose individual lives may be markedly different, but who nonetheless suffer from a common form of racial hegemony. It permits us to hold up the possibility of a unity, albeit fictitious, that makes our burdens more manageable because the load is shared. It empowers us to be able to speak (through the discourse available to us) about the oppressive material and political manifestations of a racialized hegemony on our lives. And, finally, for our purposes in literary studies, it makes possible the development of a critical discourse that centers these concerns in the study of our literature.

NOTES

[1] I must thank Professors Valerie Smith, Vincent Pecora and Sam Weber who read much earlier versions of this essay. I also wish to thank William Handley, Darrell Darrisaw and Professor Arthur Little for their insightful comments.

[2] I use "anti-essentialist" here as opposed to "constructionist" because Morrison never articulates a full-blown argument for constructionism. Rather, she is always guarding against the popular and facile dismissal that is all too often the response to essentialism. See page 3 of "Unspeakable Things Unspoken" for the most notable example of this practice.

[3] By "unspeakable" here I intend the sometimes seeming indefensibility of essentialist categories like race in light of much recent poststructuralist critical work (invested in social constructionism) that has placed "race" under "erasure."

[4] The shrewd enshrining of self here is not unlike the academy's enshrining of traditional canonical texts that Morrison calls into question. That is, if Morrison deconstructs the artist-critic dichotomy to legitimize her critical voice, then academic traditionalists challenge the inclusion of women and "people of color" in the canon to legitimize or to maintain the status of white male domination that obtains in the curriculum and in the membership of the academy as well. While Morrison's rhetorical strategies here seem deconstructive, they still rely on a kind of thinking that essentializes "artist," "critic," and "American literary canon." This may speak to Diana Fuss's larger claim that constructionism really operates as a more sophisticated form

of essentialism. (See Fuss's "Introduction" in *Essentially Speaking*.) Whatever the case, Morrison is not beyond using the "master's" rhetorical process, which has obviously worked so well for him, to perform the same kind of legitimizing function on herself.

[5]I am thinking here particularly of the rhetorical tactics of Phillis Wheatley and of nineteenth-century slave narratives' direct addresses to their readers. Consider also that Morrison's position in this essay by way of audience is complicated in much the same way that the position of the authors of these slave narratives were. She must negotiate the right amount of courting her traditionalist audience without appearing sycophantic and overly accomodationist to her more progressive audience if she is to be heard.

[6]There are at least two ways in which these appellations function for Black speakers: 1) as a totalizing way of associating oneself with a monolithic black community (in which all differences that may obtain between the speaker and the various members of that community are erased or subsumed by the political claim to rhetorical racial unity) and 2) as a way of constructing "the Black community" as always "out there" and, therefore, in its separateness from the speaker functioning as the object of study or critique. The following anecdote functions in the latter fashion.

[7]I contend that this discontinuity represents the kinds of meaningful heterogenous strains within "the Black community" that are subsumed with such naming (for example, class). The question of the utility of such appellations then naturally arises, which the following discussion of "racialized discourse" seeks to address.

[8]Gates's project is to point out that what I have called "racialized discourse" represents "arbitrary constructs, not reports of reality" (6). He historicizes such discourse, locating its nascence in a larger Enlightenment context.

[9]For lack of a better term, I use "illusory" here to signify the status of phenomena present in our human experience that we have yet to recognize as such.

[10]Recall what de Man says about allegory claiming not to know its origins or identification; the noncoincidence and the renunciation of the "desire to coincide" he speaks of can be considered a kind of forgetting.

[11]I intend "speaking" here with all the implications of will to power. While we must recognize that everyone can speak, not everyone is heard. So by speaking Black subjects, I mean those who represent and mediate to the institutions of dominant culture. Speaking Black subjects are those who at least have such positional entrée.

[12]Poststructuralism's critique of experience has a history of its own that is too involved to adequately detail here. Fuss represents the position best, perhaps, when she writes "the poststructuralist objection to experience is not a repudiation of grounds of knowing *per se* but rather a refusal of the hypostatization of experience as *the* ground (and the most stable ground) of knowledge production" (27). For a more detailed discussion of the issues involved in poststructuralism's critique of "experience" see Fuss, chapters 2 and 7; Scott, and de Lauretis, chapter 6.

[13]West's use of the white woman who appears in his narrative is not altogether unlike the use Morrison argues that white writers make of African American characters in their texts. That is not to say that they are the same, however. Indeed, using a white figure to legitimize one's voice and using an African American character for the economy of stereotype it offers in a thoroughly racialized society are two very different things.

[14]I am thinking here of the closing line of a short, comic film called *Hair Piece* by African American, female filmmaker, Ayoka Chenzira which goes something like

this: "If you are having difficulty with your comb, perhaps the comb that you are using was not designed with your hair in mind."

WORKS CITED

Baker, Houston A., Jr. *Long Black Song: Essays in Black American Literature and Culture*. Charlottesville: U of Virginia P, 1972.

Benjamin, Walter. *The Origin of the German Tragic Drama*. New York: Verso, 1977.

Bernal, Martin. *Black Athena: The Afroasiatic Roots of Classical Civilization, Volume 1: The Fabrication of Ancient Greece 1785-1985*. New Brunswick: Rutgers UP, 1987.

de Lauretis, Teresa. *Alice Doesn't: Feminism, Semiotics, Cinema*. Bloomington: Indiana UP, 1984.

de Man, Paul. "The Rhetoric of Temporality." *Blindness and Insight: Essays in the Rhetoric of Contemporary Criticism*. 1971. Minneapolis: U of Minnesota P, 1983. 187-228.

Fuss, Diana. *Essentially Speaking: Feminism, Nature and Difference*. New York: Routledge, 1989.

Gates, Henry Louis, Jr. "Writing 'Race' and the Difference It Makes." *"Race," Writing, and Difference*. Ed. Henry Louis Gates, Jr. Chicago: U of Chicago P, 1985. 1-20.

Johnson, Barbara. "Response" to Henry Louis Gates's "Canon-Formation, Literary History, and the Afro-American Tradition: From the Seen to the Told." *Afro-American Literary Study in the 1990s*. Ed. Houston A. Baker, Jr., and Patricia Redmond. Chicago: U of Chicago P, 1989. 39-44.

Morrison, Toni. *The Bluest Eye*. New York: Washington Square, 1970.

———. *Playing in the Dark: Whiteness and the Literary Imagination*. Cambridge: Harvard UP, 1992.

———. "Unspeakable Things Unspoken: The Afro-American Presence in American Literature." *Michigan Quarterly Review* 28 (1989): 1-34.

Nielsen, Aldon Lynn. *Reading Race: White American Poets and the Racial Discourse in the Twentieth Century*. Athens: U of Georgia P, 1988.

Rafferty, Terrence. "Articles of Faith." *New Yorker* 16 May 1988: 110-118.

Scott, Joan W. "Experience." *Feminists Theorize the Political*. Ed. Judith Butler and Joan W. Scott. New York: Routledge, 1992. 22-40.

West, Cornel. *Race Matters*. Boston: Beacon, 1993.

Williams, Patricia. *The Alchemy of Race and Rights: Diary of a Law Professor*. Cambridge: Harvard UP, 1991.

part three

NARRATIVES AS CULTURAL INTERVENTIONS

"HE WANTS TO PUT HIS STORY NEXT TO HERS": PUTTING TWAIN'S STORY NEXT TO HERS IN MORRISON'S *BELOVED*[1]

Richard C. Moreland

I WANT TO TRY TO UNDERSTAND AN EPISODE in Toni Morrison's *Beloved* that bears a curious resemblance to Mark Twain's *Adventures of Huckleberry Finn*. It is the episode in which a traveling, young, poor white character named Amy Denver helps Sethe in her escape from slavery. The episode is introduced as a familiar and important story for Sethe's daughter Denver, who has been named after this character who helped Sethe deliver Denver during Sethe's escape—deliver her from slavery and from Sethe's womb. Denver remembers and reimagines this story during the course of Morrison's novel in something like the way the novel may suggest her readers reimagine not only Sethe's story but its relation to Twain's, and much of the racialized United States literature and culture that Twain's novel is often taken to represent.

Morrison has described that culture in her nonfiction in terms of the "solitude" and "separate confinement" of canonical American literature, especially as it has tended to be read by a critical tradition that emphasizes its romance, its flight, its individualism, its exceptionalism, and its supposedly ahistorical, apolitical nature ("Unspeakable" 1, 12). But she suggests it is also a literature and culture that in certain ways may not be as separate from history as it has come to appear:

It only seems that the canon of American literature is "naturally" or "inevitably" "white." In fact it is studiously so. In fact these absences of vital presences in Young American literature may be the insistent fruit of the scholarship rather than the text. Perhaps some of these writers, although under current house arrest, have much more to say than has been realized. (14)

As Denver reimagines the story in Morrison's novel that most resembles Twain's, it begins to seem that Morrison's novel is itself taking up again and reimagining this literary tradition of "the American romance." Julia Kristeva has analyzed a similarly naturalized, ahistorical romance of mother and child in psychoanalysis that I will adapt to the more specific contexts addressed in both Twain's and Morrison's novels. These novels address an ongoing cultural crisis as cultural work in progress—the psychic and social power of the discourse of American romance, and the psychic and social polarizations on which that discourse depends. Together, these novels suggest how such romances may also work to enable the reimagining and restructuring of those same psychic and social polarizations.

Morrison's writing in both fiction and nonfiction suggests how such a cultural work in progress might be carried out. In an essay called "Unspeakable Things Unspoken: The Afro-American Presence in American Literature," she recommends "the examination and reinterpretation of the American canon . . . for the ways in which the presence of Afro-Americans has shaped the choices, the language, the structure—the meaning of so much American literature. A search, in other words, for the ghost in the machine" (11). Morrison's essay is an example of recent changes in American studies in general, related to what Henry Louis Gates, Jr., has called "a new black aesthetic movement," consisting especially of close readings of the social text "to reveal cultural contradictions and the social aspects of literature, the larger dynamics of subjection and incorporation through which the subject is produced." Drawing on but escaping "both the social organicism of the black arts movement and the formalist organicism of the 'reconstructionists,'" such readings problematize, Gates says, both the "black" and the "aesthetic": "No longer, for example, are the concepts of black and white thought to be preconstituted; rather, they are mutually constitutive and socially produced" (309). Thus instead of declaring her social or formal

independence from an American cultural context largely characterized by just such declarations of independence, Morrison's essays
and novels have focused on changing, contextualized encounters
and interactions between a racialized culture and the sometimes
unspoken but irrepressible presence she calls here the ghost in the
machine.

Morrison demonstrates in her essay how this ghostly presence
might function in the canonical American romance, particularly Melville's *Moby Dick*. She also mentions Mark Twain, along with Poe,
Hawthorne, Cather, Hemingway, Fitzgerald, and Faulkner, as examples of other canonical American writers whose works are "begging for such attention" (18). As she has written more recently, in
Playing in the Dark, American romance "made possible the sometimes safe and other times risky embrace of quite specific, understandably human, fears" (36). It made such risky embraces possible
by a kind of transference, in the way that it "transferred internal
conflicts to a 'blank darkness,' to conveniently bound and violently
silenced black bodies" (38). Here where it is more common to speak
of disavowal, repression, projection, and denial, Morrison chooses
instead to use the language of transference, suggesting—as I will
propose that her fiction does as well—that this transference may
function as part of an ongoing analysis and elaboration of psychic
and social configurations that may thereby be reimagined and
changed. Morrison's essay goes on to suggest some of the ways
this African and African American presence continues to work in
contemporary American literature, taking as her example the open-
ings of the novels written by herself as a black writer, but a "black
writer, for whom that modifier is more search than fact" ("Unspeakable" 19). What she writes in this essay about the variously haunted
white canon's "begging" for, that is, needing, perhaps somehow
even wanting such searching attention to "the ghost in the machine,"
together with what she writes about her search for a similar influence
in her own work, recalls an intriguing sentence she writes about
one of her haunted black male characters, Paul D, near the end of
Sethe's own haunted story in *Beloved*: "He wants to put his story
next to hers" (273). Unable easily to escape the cultural power of
the discourse of romance—and of the psychic and social divisions
on which its various declarations of independence depend—each
of these stories and identities is "mutually constitutive." Each is
actively and intimately dependent on each other, both for what and
who they are, and for what and who they might become in their
ongoing interactions.

Perhaps, then, the searching attention Morrison gives in the novel *Beloved* to the ghostly influence of slavery, racism, and the dead in the racialized, gendered, class-marked life-stories of her different characters—female, male, black, white—and the attention she gives in this novel to the changing relationships among these characters' different haunted stories, may also suggest useful ways of understanding the changing relationships and possibilities for exchange between stories like Twain's and Morrison's. How do their works read and respond to each other in the ongoing cultural conversation among the different periods and parts of American literature and culture?[2] How does *Beloved* suggest the machine has seen, heard, and responded to its ghost, and the ghost to its machine, both within and between such stories? How does *Beloved* suggest a canonical white male writer of the nineteenth century like Twain might need or perhaps somehow even want to put his story next to Morrison's? Or to put this more practically here, how does *Beloved* suggest Twain's work might be read and taught in the late twentieth century not apart from or against, but next to Morrison's work, and Morrison's work next to Twain's?

Denver's attitude toward the story involving Amy Denver suggests its own version of the solitude and separate confinement described by Morrison in the tradition of American romance: "Denver hated the stories her mother told that did not concern herself, which is why Amy was all she ever asked about. The rest was a gleaming, powerful world made more so by Denver's absence from it" (62). This favorite story of Amy's and Sethe's and her own magical heroism is bordered, lined, punctuated, haunted by a corresponding sense of abject helplessness toward the rest of this "gleaming, powerful world," a world that appears as unchallenged in its omnipotence as the "miracle" of Denver's birth is in hers. Everything depends on whether Denver (or one of her idealized heroes) is or is not at the supposedly all-powerful, magical center of this particular story's world, apparently unconnected to any other. Until she can remember and draw on other stories and other ways to hear them, Denver's own story—like the "gleaming, powerful world" in whose mirror image hers is constructed here as a self-protective fetish—will alternate between the two kinds of American loneliness figured in both Twain's and Morrison's novels, that of control and helplessness, heroism and abjection.

The emotional alternation in Denver's story between heroism and abjection resembles the alternation in Twain's *Huckleberry Finn* between constant revivals of nearly impossible hopes and a repeated depression and sense of powerlessness that is usually unarticulated except as projected onto a cultural other like Jim. In Twain's novel it is a powerlessness toward the more or less respectable, slave-holding society that waits not only on shore and in the direction of the river's current, but even aboard the raft, in the seductive abilities of the King and Duke and even of Huck's socially constituted "conscience" to articulate and effectively to direct the expression of Huck's desire. When Huck seems to triumph against that conscience to make his much applauded, heroic, private moral decision to help Jim escape, he knows at first that the private moral decision, however difficult and important, is not enough to address his and Jim's practical and political situation. So "I set to thinking over how to get at it, and turned over considerable many ways in my mind; and at last fixed up a plan" (271). But like the romance tradition he is often taken to represent, Huck is personally, also culturally, unaccustomed to thinking of natural, social, or certainly psychological limitations on his own freedom and will. He is used to thinking of such limitations in Jim's case or in the case of women, girls, perhaps Pap, but not himself. So he soon forgets the necessity of such strategic mediations between his private decision and the contingencies of history, and without such positive plans, he is soon feeling lonesome, betrayed, and powerless again. He thus drifts all too easily and uncritically into "trusting to Providence" for his course, as if the world must somehow after all arrange itself around his own white, male, American will. Too often, he confuses his own will with the more socially reinforced authority and romance-derived plans of his middle-class friend Tom Sawyer. The last part of Twain's novel demonstrates in intensely tedious and frustrating detail the inadequacy and ineffectiveness of Huck's unmediated private act of will to set Jim free, as it also suggests the inadequacy and ineffectiveness of Miss Watson's will and more broadly of the Emancipation Proclamation and Reconstruction.[3] Such acts of will prove inadequate and ineffective unless they are also followed up with the positive and specific "plans" and narrative plots that would articulate and negotiate Huck and Jim's desires in a relationship and a course of action that would resist and counter Tom Sawyer's cultural powers, rather than allow him to write Huck and Jim into his own private moral adventures—a series of romances into which other stories and plans too often seem to disappear.

Instead of resisting Tom's story and learning more from his own interactions with Jim, positively articulating and negotiating such necessary alternative "plans" in the complexities of language and history, Huck Finn finally gives up on writing, effectively trusting again to Providence (or perhaps in Twain's case, to a purely negative self-critique), and there the novel ends. The sense of an ending, however, is suffused with most readers' lingering sense of the frustration built up throughout the novel's last section. Perhaps this continuing frustration is one reason why modern readers, including Morrison, keep returning to Twain's novel. It is as if we recognize in the frustrating crisis of its ending not only a character flaw in Huck, an artistic error or a despondently satiric realism in Twain, but a continuing cultural work in progress, potentially a positive work in progress of cultural interaction, learning, and exchange across those very cultural and racial boundaries that the novel seems to leave in place. Morrison's and Twain's novels explore this work in progress as it manifests itself in nineteenth-century America and as it continues to manifest itself more than a century later, in the continuing power of Twain's novel and the more recent power of Morrison's. Both novels bring together an escaping white youth who is learning how to love—including the recognition and acceptance of certain plans, commitments, limitations, and ties—and an enslaved adult who knows all about such limitations and ties but is also learning how to escape. Both figures are learning to love in other terms than those of heroism and helplessness based on the nostalgic models often implied by a certain psychoanalytic family romance of a mother-infant dyad without need or interest in any wider social support and opportunity. Both the white youth and the black adult are learning instead to turn this crisis of imagination and love into an ongoing, practical, cultural work in progress.

I want to suggest, in other words, that Morrison's novel engages with Twain's in the way that *Beloved* draws out and expands on conflicts and fears just at the limits of *Huckleberry Finn*'s reach. These are conflicts and fears, for example, about limits, about positive values and commitments to particular people and particular circumstances, even the unwilling but inescapable involvement with particular people and determining circumstances that *Huckleberry Finn* suggests in Jim's situation and character and that *Beloved* explores more thoroughly in Sethe's "too thick" love. In effect inverting and reinscribing Twain's adventure novel, with its focus on the white, free nation's ambiguously innocent moral heroism toward an exceptional, black, enslaved character like Jim, Morrison's novel focuses instead on the runaway slave, her family, and her community, and how some of these figures live on after Sethe's escape from a slavery that Morrison represents not as exceptional but central to their American experience. Morrison's novel thus attempts to work through what Twain's novel both reaches toward and keeps at arm's length, on the darkened underside of American romance. At its limit, Morrison's novel describes this abject, depressed loneliness as the "loneliness that can be rocked. . . . It's an inside kind—wrapped tight like skin" (274). Her novel deals less directly with the conflicts and fears associated with the other loneliness she describes, the one that "roams," unplanned, unplotted, that "dry and spreading thing that makes the sound of one's own feet going seem to come from a far-off place" (274). But her novel does suggest how these two kinds of loneliness might encounter and interact productively with each other. It is the second, roaming loneliness that characterizes for various reasons Amy Denver, Stamp Paid, Paul D, and others in *Beloved* (and characters more central to her next novel, *Jazz*), and that characterizes Huck and most of the other white characters of *Huckleberry Finn*. This negative freedom also characterizes the emptiness and erotic wandering that Julia Kristeva, among others, has described as a prevailing crisis in late twentieth-century culture, a crisis that much of art, literature, theology, politics, and other signifying practices have attempted to make their own cultural works in progress (*Tales of Love* 380). It is a wandering that has perhaps brought many modern readers to recognize something lost and found again—changed—in *Beloved*.

One place to begin a close reading of this encounter is where Sethe's daughter Denver likes to begin, or where she and most of us have perhaps been variously conditioned and taught to begin, though this is also where Morrison's novel emphatically does not begin. Denver has been taught to begin her own favorite story, again, in "the details of her birth," with "two friendly grown-up women— one . . . helping out the other," so that "the magic of her birth, its miracle in fact, testified to that friendliness as did her own name" (29). Like a romance Hawthorne might have written, this one promises events, names, even miracles, carefully designed by their author or even a higher Author, to signify moral qualities, such as friendliness, or even supernatural intent, such as Denver being, as Sethe says, "a charmed child. From the beginning" (41). Despite this story's silences and shadows, it is a story whose comforting, ritualized magic Denver knows by heart and is careful not to alter or disturb:

Easily she stepped into the told story that lay before her eyes on the path she followed away from the window. There was only one door to the house and to get to it from the back you had to walk all the way around to the front of 124, past the storeroom, past the cold house, the privy, the shed, on around to the porch. And to get to the part of the story she liked best, she had to start way back: hear the birds in the thick woods, and the crunch of leaves underfoot; see her mother making her way up into the hills where no houses were likely to be. (29)

Everything has its ordered place on Denver's path to the front porch and to the part of the story she liked best (liked best "because it was all about herself" [77]). Only gradually will Denver learn more about the fears and desires that this story has helped her to ignore or control, for example, that she will want to leave her own porch and approach other houses, some by doors not at their fronts but in back (253). Other stories are marked by race, gender, class, and loss—elements that her story seems to invoke only to overrule or banish. She will remember and learn more of such stories later, but only insofar as she also learns to read this story and stories like it differently. For now, however, most of the rest of Sethe's past life has been declared "unspeakable; to Denver's inquiries Sethe gave short replies or rambling incomplete reveries" (58). For lack or fear of other stories, then, the young Denver remembers here this incomplete reverie like an unalterable bedtime fairytale.

But Denver's story has been placed not at the beginning of Morrison's novel, nor at the end, but well within the context of other, quite different stories, so that its magic circle of safety is likely to seem to Morrison's readers not natural and inevitable or in the nature of romance or art, but precariously and deliberately incomplete. It is a carefully, desperately guarded refuge that in this way mirrors the very culture whose power it hypnotically flees, what Morrison calls the solitude and separate confinement of canonical American literature. But if some of these canonical writers do "have much more to say than has been realized" ("Unspeakable" 14). Denver's story, too, thus contextualized, has more to offer Denver herself and other readers than only its fragile illusion of safety.

By contrast, what Morrison says she was after in *Beloved*'s "abrupt" beginning, "as the first stroke of the shared experience that might be possible between the reader and the novel's population," is that the reader feel "snatched, yanked, thrown into an environment completely foreign," feel "snatched just as the slaves were from one place to another, from any place to another, without preparation and without defense," "without comfort or succor from the 'author'" ("Unspeakable" 32-33). This sounds like the frightening underside of Denver's more nostalgic version of her own charmed delivery and birth.

Morrison's novel, then, includes two altogether different kinds of stories—the magically or heroically safe and the defenselessly unprepared. Yet her novel will suggest that the differences and encounters between these two different kinds of stories are also played out within each. As she says in her essay, "perhaps some [writers of the canonical romance] were not so much transcending politics, or escaping blackness, as they were transforming it into intelligible, accessible, yet artistic modes of discourse" ("Unspeakable" 14), as she has elsewhere shown that the writers of slave narratives also did for their own, different artistic and political reasons ("The Site of Memory" 299-302). In "creative encounters" with history, she says, "nothing . . . is safe, or should be"; even in Denver's own romance-like story, then, "safety is the foetus of power as well as protection from it" ("Unspeakable" 31). As for the more abrupt and dangerous, almost "unspeakable" story with which *Beloved* begins, it soon becomes clear, she says, "that something is beyond control, but is not beyond understanding since it is not beyond accommodation by both the 'women' and the 'children'" (32). This novel shows how these women and children transform the unspeakable into their own different versions of "intelligible, accessible, yet artistic modes of discourse." Both Denver's safe story and Sethe's more dangerous one are the kinds of story this novel teaches its characters and its readers to listen to "for the holes—the things the fugitives did not say; the questions they did not ask," and to listen "too for the unnamed, unmentioned people left behind" (92). And the novel suggests, I think, that this listening works best by putting quite different stories alongside each other, the heroism alongside the helplessness it denies, and the helplessness alongside the heroism it disavows.

The "told story" Denver remembers her mother telling her casts Denver as an "antelope" ramming and pawing in Sethe's womb, protesting at Sethe's thoughts of resignation and death. Sethe traces this figure of an antelope back to one of her few memories of her own mother, the antelope dance in which the slave men and women "shifted shapes and became something other. Some unchained, demanding other whose feet knew her pulse better than she did. Just like this one in her stomach" (31). But the "demanding other" in Denver's mirror-like story "all about herself" has been relatively tamed; it is for Sethe her own mother, as well as the foetus within Sethe herself as mother, and for Denver it is the foetus that is Denver herself. Thus when Sethe remembers thinking she is "about to be discovered by a whiteboy" and be deprived of even an "easeful death," she can also laugh at how her hunger and imagination turned her into "a snake. All jaws and hungry," as if she could gobble the whiteboy up (31). In the face of disaster, of being trapped on the wrong side of the romance divisions of light and dark, male and female, life and death, heroism and helplessness, Denver's version of Sethe's story almost automatically, desperately transforms this other "demanding other" (Amy) into a form so "intelligible and accessible" as to be easily (omnipotently) devoured. What signals the part of the story "Denver loved the best" is that the whiteboy turns out in fact to be—not edible, maybe, nor black, but at most "a girl" and "[t]he raggediest-looking trash you ever saw," herself hungry like Sethe and looking for huckleberries, then asking Sethe if she likes huckleberries (31-32).

It is a moment of almost comic relief in Morrison's novel to recognize Twain's Huckleberry Finn in girlface. We have seen him as a harmless, transparent girl before, and as a runaway apprentice, and we have seen him put in his place by Jim as "trash." Still, "nothing is safe" in such encounters with history, either in Twain's novel or here, neither Sethe from this whitegirl, Amy Denver, nor Amy from Sethe's appeal for help. Most of what Sethe remembers Amy Denver saying sounds as dangerously insensitive to the plight of this "nigger woman" as Huck is to Jim's. She uses the racist epithet as easily and defensively as Huck does with Jim. She is no more committed by nature or in principle to Sethe's freedom or humanity than Huck is to Jim's. In fact, such natural or moral principles, so confusingly and inadequately articulated by Huck and for Huck by his adopted middle class in Twain's novel, never even seem to arise for Amy. It is as if Morrison's novel re-emphasizes here the incompleteness of such racism *or* such anti-racist moral principles in determining Huck's and Amy's subjectivities, next to the less systematic, more specific repertoire of emotions, gestures, skills, and activities that Foucault would call their "local, discontinuous, disqualified, illegitimate knowledges" ("Two Lectures" 83).

Not by nature or in principle, then, but in the event, and especially in the event of her interaction with Sethe, Amy Denver does find herself drawn, like Huck, unpredictably, almost unaccountably, into helping a slave escape. More than that, she will care for Sethe's swollen feet and beaten back and help deliver her baby. Yet after their first exchange, Amy almost leaves Sethe lying where she found her in the weeds, as if there is nothing in either Sethe's or Amy's stories by themselves that would explain the work they eventually do together. That work depends on the interaction between their stories.

At the prospect of "being left alone without a fang in her head" (32), not omnipotently but powerlessly alone, Sethe asks for more of Amy's story—where she's headed, whether her mother knows: "They slipped effortlessly into yard chat about nothing in particular—except one lay on the ground" (33). The one on the ground, however, is apparently listening that much harder to Amy's talk of velvet from a store in Boston, of her mother's death just after Amy's birth, of her work as an indentured servant to pay for her mother's passage, and again and again of velvet, which, when Sethe asks, Amy describes as being "like the world was just born. Clean and new and so smooth. The velvet I seen was brown, but in Boston they got all colors. Carmine. That means red but when you talk about velvet you got to say 'carmine'" (33). Amy has got it into her head somehow that the utopian answer to her desire is velvet, and she has learned somewhere that "when you talk about velvet you got to say 'carmine'"—perhaps in the ads from the store in Boston, perhaps from a middle-class acquaintance like Tom Sawyer. Amy has learned this convention of her romance of class and velvet as carefully as Tom and Huck have learned certain conventions of their romances, or as carefully as Denver has learned the protective rituals of hers. Similarly, Amy has learned like Tom and Huck from the similarly polarized, naturalized American discourse of race that when she talks about certain people she can say "nigger." But Sethe is listening harder than that, as if for other determinants or other dimensions of Amy's overdetermined language. Because "Sethe didn't know if it was the voice, or Boston or velvet, but while the whitegirl talked, the baby slept. Not one butt or kick, so she guessed her luck had turned" (33). So she warily lets Amy know how weak and injured she is, and with Amy's particular mixture of racist insensitivity, bravery, practical skill, and implied memories of her own and her mother's helplessness (mostly unaddressed except in terms of Sethe's predicament), Amy encourages and walks alongside as Sethe crawls, and "it was the voice full of velvet and Boston and good things to eat that urged [Sethe] along" to the lean-to where Amy "did her magic: lifted Sethe's feet and legs and massaged them until she cried salt tears. 'It's gonna hurt, now,' said Amy. 'Anything dead coming back to life hurts'" (35). Denver's own rendition of her mother's story ends on this ringing note of painful but magical resurrection, which she recites as "a truth for all times" (35). Pain and death are acknowledged here, but they are now so closely attached to resurrection in Denver's guarded imagination that she can safely return her thoughts to the uncanny sight that provoked Denver's retelling herself this "told story": the sight through a window of a dress kneeling next to her mother in prayer, with its sleeve around her mother's waist. If the dress she saw with her mother was in pain, she figures now, it might mean another resurrection of the dead: "it could mean that the baby ghost had plans" (35).

Such "plans" are an unthreatening secret thrill for someone in a state like Denver's, someone who appreciates "the downright pleasure of enchantment, of not suspecting but *knowing* the things behind things," the "safety of ghost company" (37), the sort of assurance romance offers its readers that "plans" (and fictional plots) translate intention and principles directly into events, unimpaired by historical contingencies or the interference of other stories. But for Denver's mother at this point, before Paul D's arrival and the renegotiation with the past and future that his coming sets into motion, plans of any kind are an invitation to disaster, a foolish tampering with a surrounding, external fate so fixed in Sethe's own guarded imagination of time and space that there are places where things that have happened to Sethe will always "'be there for you, waiting for you. So, Denver, you can't never go there. Never'" (36). Denver is aware that her mother "never told me all what happened" (36), but when Denver asks, Sethe says, "'Nothing to tell except schoolteacher'" and his "'book about us,'" and at that, "She stopped. Denver knew that her mother was through with it" (36-37), and Denver depends on this deliberate silence about the world outside their yard and the other stories beyond Denver's own. Denver's story depends on that surrounding silence, but like the romances hers resembles, it is at the same time a way of both warding off and also coming carefully to (different) terms with other, different stories among which hers is set, both schoolteacher's machine-like "book about us" and Morrison's ghostly renditions of "unspeakable things unspoken."

Paul D's arrival at 124 seems to Denver to have destroyed this realm of safety and certainty, and her solitude with her mother. But for Sethe his arrival and the stories he tells have set her thinking again, and differently than Denver has, "about what the word [plans] could mean," the possibility and "temptation to trust and remember . . . to go ahead and feel. . . . Go ahead and *count on something*?"

(38), the possibility, in this case, of making plans that will not discount past experience or be certain of future success, but are either necessary or worth the risk. She and Paul D will come to remember later the elaborate plans they made to escape from Sweet Home: "The plan was a good one, but when it came time. . . . A good plan. . . . But. . . . But. . . . But. . . . But. It is a good plan. . . . But" (197, 222, 223). As Sethe warily begins to take such risks again, both by making plans and by remembering and telling Beloved and herself things "she had forgotten she knew" (58, 61), Denver silently repeats her lesson that all such stories are dangerously off limits: "she clamped her teeth and prayed it would stop. Denver hated the stories her mother told that did not concern herself, which is why Amy was all she ever asked about. The rest was a gleaming, powerful world made more so by Denver's absence from it" (62). But when Denver next resumes her version of Huck Finn's story, she is beginning to learn, partly by imagining how Amy Denver might begin to learn, what Huck Finn never did quite learn—how their various alternations between imagined triumph and powerless abjection might make way for positively different configurations of desire and relationship. Denver has just learned that this "sister-girl," Beloved, the apparent incarnation of the baby ghost's "plans," is a companion dedicated not entirely to Denver herself, but also and primarily to Sethe. For Denver, then, this is no longer the story her mother tells her that is all about Denver herself, no longer a private romance involving at most the two positions of heroism and (denied) helplessness, but a different story involving at least three parties. It begins to resemble what Kristeva describes in psychoanalytic terms as "a third realm supplementing the autoeroticism of the mother-child dyad" (*Tales of Love* 22) which turns this image of a world apart back toward the surrounding worlds of language, society, and history. Kristeva's analysis of a certain nostalgia in the psychoanalytic family romance for a fusion with the mother helps explain how the polarized, protected spaces of other romances may work to ward off but also to prepare for, or open toward, other such "third realms." "The bodily exchange of maternal fondness may take on the imaginary burden of representing love in its most characteristic form," Kristeva writes; "Nevertheless, without the maternal 'diversion' toward a Third Party, the bodily exchange is abjection or devouring" (34), or what I have been calling helplessness or heroism. Apart from the autoerotic romance of such a mother-child dyad, love in other forms requires the mediating presence of some such Third

Party, or another story in which the mother, at least, plays another role, a story in which the mother, at least, is herself other enough to love someone other than the infant itself. Beloved functions as one in a series of such mediating Third Parties for Denver, including her deafness, the baby ghost, her room in the boxwood bushes, and now the stories she tells Beloved. In later replays of this developmental model in psychoanalysis—replays that Kristeva more broadly calls "transference love"—the role of this Third Party may be played by the analyst as an Other who is supposed to know, and know how to love, an Other who speaks society's language, yet listens too for "unspeakable things" unspoken (13). But the role of this Third Party is also played by the imaginative authority and power we tend to transfer and invest in various cultural discourses and, perhaps more self-consciously, in imaginative stories. This authority may function not only as the "gleaming, powerful world['s]" nonnegotiable Law, but also as a power of interaction and love that may continue to differ and change, as in the story of Amy and Sethe that Denver now retells herself and Beloved in Morrison's novel. Denver's retelling of this favorite romance may serve as a model for how we as reader-analysands might also learn from stories that are not stories all about ourselves.[4]

Swallowing "twice to prepare for the telling, to construct out of the strings she had heard all her life a net to hold Beloved" (76), Denver attempts to wean Beloved from her abject attachment to Sethe by interesting her in the story Denver tells. And by concentrating thus on holding the interest of someone not fixated on her but also interested in someone else, Denver is also weaning herself from her own abject attachment to Sethe, just as she is also imagining Sethe's own attempt to distract and hold Amy Denver's interest in something other than her own romance of velvet and Boston. The story feels different now to Denver as she considers her former role in the story as a rescued but powerless victim, able only to identify gratefully with her heroic mother-protectors: "She loved it because it was all about herself; but she hated it too because it made her feel like a bill was owing somewhere and she, Denver, had to pay it. But who she owed or what to pay it with eluded her" (77). She is in a position now, however, to recognize in Beloved's "alert and hungry face" both a mirror of her own desire to hold Beloved and the encouragement she needs to risk a different role than that of either the hero or the powerless victim. She begins "to see what she was saying and not just to hear it," "feeling how it must have felt to her mother," and adding the "fine points" and "details" that give "blood to the scraps her mother and grandmother had told her," so that "the monologue became in fact a duet" (in Kristeva's terms, too, the mother-infant dyad needs a Third Party to avoid becoming a monologue, to become a duet with another, starting perhaps with the mother as a connection with other stories). Denver can begin to appreciate her mother's similar risk and collaboration with Amy Denver, "how recklessly she behaved with this whitegirl— a recklessness born of desperation and encouraged by Amy's fugitive eyes and tenderhearted mouth" (78). Denver imagines Sethe's seeing in Amy's eyes, mouth, and hands signs that Amy's own need and desire may be encouraged to take different forms than only her nonstop, monologic talk of velvet, and signs that Sethe herself may not be as alone and powerless as she fears. Denver's safe story that was "all about herself" becomes a story instead about Sethe's own dangerous interaction with Amy.

Thus Denver, like Sethe, can imagine how that incessant talk of velvet is "struck dumb for a change" when Amy sees Sethe's back (79), and how Amy's talk careens then between two culturally characteristic but increasingly inadequate poles. On the one hand, Amy uses the hypersymbolic language of romance in her "dream-walker's voice" to describe Sethe's back as a chokecherry tree with all the significant detail of Hester Prynne's embroidered letter, and to wonder what God had in mind. On the other hand, Amy draws on the projected, muted "power of blackness" also figured in the American discourse of romance to recall being beaten by her own master, though never like this, for as little as "looking at him straight" (79). But Sethe's groan is enough for Amy to "cut her reverie short," as if she recognizes that neither her dreamy interpretation of Sethe's back nor her own present economic and racial safety from such victimization is adequate either to her own memories or to their present situation. She is then moved to draw on a different, less systematically articulated, more mediated body of knowledge to shift Sethe's feet and gather spiderwebs to clean and drape on Sethe's back, as if to attend to feelings and wounds she knows about in more detail than she admits.

While she works, however, Amy attempts again to use the same racially divided discourse to draw a protective contrast between Sethe and herself: "'You don't know a thing. End up dead, that's what. Not me. I'm a get to Boston and get myself some velvet. Carmine.'" But her contrast does not hold up under the weight of their interaction—though perhaps it works as a temporary reassurance enabling that riskier interaction. She is reminded of "'a old

nigger girl'" who "'don't know nothing'" like Sethe, but who also
"'sews real fine lace,'" perhaps something like the spiderwebs Amy
is herself working with while she talks, or the velvet she talks of
otherwise. She attempts the racial contrast again by thinking of
having twice had what Sethe would probably not have had, the
leisure to "sleep with the sun in [her] face," but she remembers
that this resulted in another beating of her own in Kentucky. So she
turns her thoughts to Boston again, which, it emerges, is where her
now-dead mother was "'before she was give to Mr. Buddy,'" and
here Amy has to ask Sethe for reassurance that Mr. Buddy was not
her own father, as someone has told her he was (80). She asks for
such reassurance, presumably, for her sake but also for her mother's.
Like Huck, Amy cannot love anyone but her lost, dead mother unless
she can imagine a diversion or attraction (at least on her mother's
part, then perhaps on her own part as well) toward some Third Party,
some world beyond herself and her mother that is less abusive and
more trustworthy than their Mr. Buddy, Huck's Pap, or Sethe's
schoolteacher. Amy and Sethe work both practically and imaginatively to provide that Third Party to each other.

In other words, Amy's talk of Boston and velvet, like her singing
her "mama's song" to Sethe, functions here as another dream of
safety haunted by the infant's inevitable loss of that safety, a loss
that has taken the social and legal form in her life, her mother's,
and Sethe's of a powerless surrender to the likes of a Mr. Buddy
or a schoolteacher. But this socially constituted and psychic image
of helplessness is also one among other possible attempts to translate that loss and danger into a different, less fixed, less lonely
language and relationship. By a kind of transference, Sethe's situation gives Amy the opportunity and the courage to address and
rearticulate in her encounter and work with Sethe memories of the
loss of her own mother and of her own past abuse that her dreamy
talk of Boston and velvet usually keep more clumsily and fearfully
at bay. In her encounter and work with Sethe, Amy reimagines and
rearticulates such memories not in the form of a nostalgic return
to an infant's fusion with its mother, but as a moving connection
with her own mother's and with Sethe's stories, which are not "all
about herself" but that move her powerfully nonetheless to translate
and act out those feelings in these different circumstances. And by
a similar transference, Amy's presence gives Sethe the opportunity
and the courage to dare to think for a while at least, strategically,
of velvet, good things to eat, a tenderhearted mouth, and the "de-

manding other" of her own dead mother's antelope dance. It allows her, as well, to think that death for herself and her foetus is not the only possible shape her story can take, placed though it now apparently is on the dark underside of the racialized, gendered, and class-marked, though never quite monolithic, discourse of American romance. Amy's presence apparently helps Sethe to imagine another, different story for a daughter to whom she will give part of Amy Denver's name.

This idea of Sethe's, risky for a former slave, that "there was a world out there and that I could live in it" (182), even love in it, involves risking a language and a community in which to articulate, negate and renegotiate her apparently absolute danger and irretrievable loss. It is an idea that lasts only twenty-eight days, until she decides again there is no place for herself or her children in such a world. Then Paul D arrives eighteen years later and tempts her to think again that "her story was bearable because it was his as well—to tell, to refine, and tell again" (99). She wavers again then on the border between suicidal, murderous, unspeakable depression, and language, transference, and significant interaction with other people, as described in Kristeva's remarks on the relation of depression with language—and the other voices it may connect with one's own:

language starts with a *negation* (*Verneinung*) of loss, along with the depression occasioned by mourning. "I have lost an essential object that happens to be, in the final analysis, my mother," is what the speaking being seems to be saying. "But no, I have found her again in signs, or rather since I consent to lose her I have not lost her (that is the negation), I can recover her in language." Depressed persons, on the contrary, *disavow the negation*: they cancel it out, suspend it, and nostalgically fall back on the real object (the Thing) of their loss, which is just what they do not manage to lose, to which they remain painfully riveted. (*Black Sun* 43-44)

When Sethe tries to tell Paul D what she has done, he is not yet ready to address even in her story, by this process of transference, what he has learned to repress in his, so he falls back himself on the kind of racist distinction between humans and beasts that Amy Denver attempted between herself and Sethe. He will recognize later "how fast he had moved from his shame to hers" (165), but for the moment he is frightened by just how "thick" her love could be, just as he has also been disturbed by how Sethe and Beloved have both managed, since he arrived at 124, to "move him" to do and to say things he "didn't know [were] on his mind" (114), "moved him. Just when doubt, regret and every single unasked question was packed away, long after he believed he had willed himself into being" (221).

Instead of acknowledging and thus negating and translating his own loss of his "red heart" into a language with which he might interact with Sethe, or, less promisingly, "disavowing" any such acknowledgment and negation of loss (thus sinking into depression as Sethe has done), Paul D here draws on the readily available discourse of racialized and gendered romance to deny, repress, project, and transfer his loss onto her. So he and Sethe both return for a while to the two kinds of loneliness to which they are each personally and culturally inclined, as described in the novel's last pages. Like Amy, because she is white, Paul D, because he is male, can better afford than Sethe to trust the dominant drift of their society and at least pretend to the self-sufficient hero's role, much as Huck Finn can speak of drifting naked on the raft for "two or three days and nights" that "swum by, they slid along so quiet and smooth and lovely," even as he and Jim drift farther and farther past Cairo into slaveholding territory (156-158). Paul D can identify with the role of self-sufficient hero on account of his gender (as if he "had willed himself into being") even at the risk (and to deny the risk) of using a racist distinction he also knows can be turned against himself. Thus, too, Amy Denver's talk of velvet invokes class distinctions at the risk (and to deny the risk) of having those same distinctions turned against her as "trash."

For their different reasons, Huck, Amy, and Paul D are thus more prone culturally and personally to what the novel's last pages describe as the "loneliness that roams . . . alive, on its own. A dry and spreading thing that makes the sound of one's own feet going seem to come from a far-off place" (274), the loneliness of the wandering hero or the, supposedly, invulnerable machine. Sethe and Denver, on the other hand, at least in their relations to the world outside their yard, are prone to a more abject, depressed loneliness, what the novel describes as the "loneliness that can be rocked. Arms crossed, knees drawn up; holding, holding on, this motion, unlike a ship's, smooths and contains the rocker. It's an inside kind—wrapped tight like skin" (274)—or, one might add, like the inescapable haunting of a ghost. The discourse of romance holds these two related kinds of loneliness in apparently "separate confinement" from each other, relying heavily on cultural boundaries of gender, race, and class in ways that may both reinforce and otherwise rearticulate those same boundaries.[5]

With apparently no one to help Sethe remember the daughter she named Beloved and to help her to imagine and articulate that memory and loss of hers alongside and in connection to other stories and other plans, Sethe retreats again into this "inside loneliness" with Beloved, this riveting romance of perfect safety isolated and surrounded by unspeakable memories and fears of danger and loss outside. "Without the maternal 'diversion' toward a Third Party," this retreat functions in the way Kristeva describes the mother-infant romance that from two into an indistinguishable one threatens to collapse into abjection and devouring. Denver knows from her own experience that Sethe and Beloved are "locked in a love that wore everybody out." Any parent of an infant understands how much such an intimate relationship also depends on wider social support. Sethe certainly knows from her experience in a context that denied that support: "unless carefree, motherlove was a killer" (132). And now again, like an infant in a relationship that is all about herself, Beloved depends on Sethe for everything, devouring her attention, her time, even her food, demanding complete and absolute protection, accepting no excuses for Sethe's failure to save and protect her before. Both helpless and omnipotent in her demands on her mother, Beloved makes Sethe for her part both responsible for everything and bound helplessly to fail, so that this mother-infant couple become almost indistinguishable. "Whatever was happening," Denver realizes, "it only worked with three—not two" (243), so that Denver "would have to leave the yard; step off the edge of the world, leave the two behind and go ask somebody for help" (243). Although Denver is unaccustomed to this role, and is frightened to remember her grandmother's warnings that there is "no defense" against whitepeople's unpredictable and dangerous behavior, she also hears her grandmother's laugh and her reminder of other stories: "You mean I never told you nothing about Carolina? About your daddy? You don't remember nothing about how come I walk the way I do and about your mother's feet, not to speak of her back? I never told you all that? Is that why you can't walk down the steps?" (244). She implies that just such other, different, but connected stories are what Denver needs to understand not only the powerful truth that there is "no defense" but also what that truth may by itself (like the beginning of *Beloved*) disavow about other, different, but connected stories and plots that may be helpfully placed alongside and discovered within her own. And it is up to Denver now to appeal to a community—including the wider community reading *Beloved*—that has in its own position of relative power denied its connection to Sethe for what she did and for disavowing her connections to them. Sethe and Denver's situation now offers that community, as it did Amy, the opportunity and the courage to begin addressing in the situation at 124 various inarticulate, repressed memories and fears of their own—for example, Stamp Paid's nearly killing and then abandoning his wife Vashti for having been sexually abused by their slavemaster, Ella's being raped and letting the baby die, Paul D's beating "the flirt called life" to death and locking his "red heart" in a box—and modern readers' uneasy memories of American slavery and the history of American race relations. Having denied our loss, by stressing our own helplessness toward and independence from the past, and thus denying our love for the wife, the baby, the life we left for dead, we are here reminded of losses we have ourselves too easily "stamped paid" or denied, reminded by Sethe's "too thick" insistence on her own loss—her disavowal of our negation of loss in what she considers an inadequate language and interaction. To put this differently, she offers us the chance to consider less directly in her case what we have not quite been able to consider in our own language and society, and what she considers all too directly, with almost none of the mediations of language and society that we for our part might offer her. Such characters and readers need and, at some level, want to put our own inadequate stories next to Sethe's story as much as Sethe needs and at some level wants our help in changing the shape of her own story, which otherwise remains isolated and unspeakably depressed.

As the story Denver tells Janey Wagon at the whitefolks' house spreads in the local black community, there are "three groups" of interpreters, "those that believed the worst; those that believed none of it; and those, like Ella, who thought it through" (255). Even Paul D has initially reacted as many white people would and did, with a version of their belief that "under every dark skin was a jungle," or that Sethe, at least, has gotten what she deserved. Morrison's remarks about the American canon, as well as her treatment of Amy Denver in *Beloved*, suggests that this transference is one way of warding off but also, perhaps, beginning to come to terms (as Paul D does) with what Hawthorne and Melville called the "power of darkness" in romance. "Those that believed none of it," like Lady Jones, have more completely than the first group repressed their knowledge of circumstances like those that have driven Sethe to do what she has and to continue suffering for it in silence and isolation. Those who have "thought it through," however, learn how a jungle can grow "inside," not the jungle that whitefolks thought "blacks brought with them to this place from the other (livable) place," but "the jungle whitefolks planted in them" which "grew" and "spread, until it invaded the whites who had made it. Touched them every one" (198-199). As Foucault suggests, domination works not only as oppression *of* individuals or of a group of individuals as subjected objects or victims of power, but also *through* individuals (both perpetrators and victims) as constituted subjects and vehicles of that and other powers, exercising its repressive and constitutive effects both on others and on themselves ("Two Lectures"). Thus Morrison describes racism's effect on both the racist and the victim as different forms of the self's "severe fragmentation . . . a cause (not a symptom) of psychosis" ("Unspeakable" 16).

Paul D remembers Sixo explaining to him that the Thirty-Mile Woman "'is a friend of my mind. She gather me, man. The pieces I am, she gather them and give them back to me in all the right order'" (272-273). And in the passage from which I have taken the title quotation for this essay, Paul D remembers Sethe's "tenderness" about what he still calls "his neck jewelry. . . . How she never mentioned or looked at it, so he did not have to feel the shame of being collared like a beast. Only this woman Sethe could have left him his manhood like that. He wants to put his story next to hers" (273). She and her story help him to understand and feel the careful tenderness and love that his own divided language of manhood and beastliness, like Twain's, almost cannot say but is also maybe learning to say from hers. He has to persuade Sethe, however, that her "best thing" is something not wholly outside or wholly within herself, either in a father's or mother's self-sufficient heroism or in an infant's unspeakable loss, but rather in her ability to remember, articulate, and live out that desire and loss in and alongside other stories as incomplete, as lonely, and as potentially loving again as hers. As I understand it, this is not a fantasy of complementarity and restored wholeness either for individuals or cultures, but a necessary and ongoing project of negotiation, learning, and change.

This last conversation between Sethe and Paul D is the first of what might be called two alternate endings to *Beloved*, and it suggests the possibility that the crisis of this romance may make way for a work in progress of imagination and love, not only in the interaction between Paul D and Sethe but more broadly between others divided or split by their culture's social and discursive structures. In the second of these two endings, the repeated refrain is that this "was not" and still "is not a story to pass on" (275), and indeed the novel has worked to imagine the echoes and circumstances of an historical incident rescued from near oblivion. It is an incident that must remind this novel's readers how many similar incidents have gone untold, because their victims were made into ghosts—either by being denied a full role in the lives and memories of those around them, or by being violently denied a life at all (as in the novel's dedication to "Sixty Million and more"). But even in this more chastened ending there is also the suggestion that these ghosts and stories are less unspeakably lost, less strange, and more uncannily familiar than we tend to think; they survive not as so many facts, identities, or single stories "to pass on" but only and always in the (often feared, denied) interaction or "fit" between different identities, between different but connected stories: "Down by the stream in back of 124 [Beloved's] footprints come and go, come and go. They are so familiar. Should a child, an adult place his feet in them, they will fit. Take them out and they disappear again as though nobody ever walked there" (275). It is in just such connections and interactions between stories like Paul D's and Sethe's, Denver's and Beloved's, Sethe's and Amy Denver's, and Morrison's and Twain's that a multicultural American literature has the most to teach and learn.

In the racialized, gendered, and class-marked discourse of American romance, the elements of this ongoing crisis and work in progress of personal and cultural interaction have been largely split between different social groups and different representative subject positions, so that this work in progress largely depends on interaction between members of groups on all sides of these divisions, or rather between members of different groups who come to recognize how these social and discursive divisions have also isolated, split, and constituted our own subjectivities. No doubt, this American crisis and work in progress has its place in what Kristeva and others have described as a wider state of cultural emptiness and depression in contemporary life. Kristeva points especially to an absence of positive values and beliefs except for "archaic ones derived from religion and incompatible" with other more secular, modern beliefs and identities in a world "filled with hatred, not knowing where it's going. It only knows what it does not want—Stalin, Hitler" (Interview 19). This resembles Michel Serres' description of the crisis left in the wake of an exhausted era of negative critique, and the crisis that many others describe in terms of the negative, apparently depthless, aimless, or "schizophrenic" dimensions of postmodernism, consumerism, or multiculturalism. It is a crisis in contemporary life in general that is arguably more endemic, however, in the violent history and heterogeneous culture of the United States, founded as it has been again and again in terms of its negative difference from European civilization on the one hand and from the "wilderness" on the other, and on its individuals' analogous negative freedom from social or material limitations, ties, or even internal divisions.

Less obviously negative than its cultural commitment to a freedom from European versions of society or the State, its apparently more positive commitment to democracy and equality also evokes concerns more often associated with postmodernism. According to political theorist Claude Lefort, "the important point" about democracy, especially in the face of inequality, is that it

is instituted and sustained by the *dissolution of the markers of certainty*. It inaugurates a history in which people experience a fundamental indeterminacy as to the basis of power, law and knowledge, and as to the basis of relations between *self* and *other*, at every level of social life (at every level where division, and especially the division between those who held power and those who were subject to them, could once be articulated as a result of a belief in the nature of things or in a supernatural principle). (19)

Thus Brian Massumi portrays late capitalist democracies such as that of the United States as a disappointing redistribution of power from such single, disciplinary principles to an array of normalizing "*minidespotisms*: school, office, church, family, police, and a growing number of variations on each" (125). But "the only minidespotism to which every body is required to submit without exception is its Self" (126), which proves under late capitalism to have its own inegalitarian and isolating effects in an ethics and politics of private self-interest and greed (140). Michael Hardt, however, suggests that just such a crisis of certainty about the foundations of power and social relationships might also become "the central project for a democratic political practice": working out "the passage from multiplicity to multitude," seeking to "discern the material mechanisms of social aggregation that can constitute adequate, affirmative, joyful relationships and thus powerful subjective assemblages" (122). Putting Mark Twain's *Adventures of Huckleberry Finn* next to Morrison's *Beloved* shows not only the economic, political, social, and cultural forces (ranging from slavery to patriarchy to capitalism) that make working together in such directions difficult, isolating us from each other and from the others within ourselves; it also shows more particularly how the discourse of American romance both relies on these same disciplinary and normalizing structures and also enables us to reimagine and renegotiate our encounters and interactions.

We will learn to do so only from each other and from the others within ourselves.

NOTES

[1]I want to thank Mary Carruth, Susan Edgerton, Elsie Michie, Dana Nelson, Paul Nielsen, Nancy Peterson, and Reggie Young for suggestions that have helped me to rethink and rewrite this essay, and that have me still rethinking and rewriting this and other work.

[2]See Foucault's "What is an Author?" on the tendency to read the works of literary authors on the model of a biblical and thus of a supernatural author, rather than as participants in a number of changing cultural contexts of constituted, competing, and constituting discursive formations.

[3]Laurence Holland has studied this persistent gap between "the flukish fact of Jim's legal freedom, and the failure of his world to flesh it out with the family, the opportunities, and the community that would give it meaning" (75).

[4]See Meredith Skura: "Freudians tend to put the reader in the place of the psychoanalyst, but for Lacanians the reader is always the patient; the master (analyst)-slave (patient) relation in psychoanalytic transference is thus re-created in reading" (365). I am using Kristeva's work in this latter tradition, with the difference (described by Kelly Oliver) that, unlike Lacan, Kristeva "maintains that the stern oedipal Father [or the master-analyst as this is replayed in transference and reading] with his castration threats is not enough to compel the child [or reader-analysand] to leave the safe haven of the maternal body." Kristeva "develops an account of the narcissistic structure that includes an imaginary agent of love that allows the child to negotiate the passage between the maternal body and the Symbolic order" (Oliver 69), or between a story all about oneself and other people's stories. Against some critics of Kristeva's later work, Oliver argues that Kristeva's notion of the Third Party and the imaginary father "undermines the maternal-paternal dualism" in traditional psychoanalytic theory, and that it is "not a 'race back into the arms of the law'; rather, it is a race back to the outstretched arms before the Law" (69). The latter embrace, again, is not to be read as a fusion with the mother, but as an indispensable relationship with an otherness "always within and originary to the subject, who is always in process" (188). I would agree with Oliver that Kristeva's later work does not reinstate traditional maternity, paternity, compulsory heterosexuality, or religion, but attempts to re-analyze the power of these structures, in terms of a psychology, ethics, and politics not of identity, but of difference, attraction, negotiation, and love.

[5]In terms different from Morrison's, Cora Kaplan suggests another way this "separate confinement" in romance might structure (also disguise, distort, perhaps enable) an interest that exceeds this structure, an interest in interactions across these same boundaries. She argues that a woman reader of romances "identifies with both terms in the seduction scenario, but most of all with the process of seduction" (148). Carol Clover makes a similar argument about the male viewers of "slasher" movies, whose identifications seem to switch more than once between the polarized subject and object positions of slasher and slashed. Kaja Silverman describes similar polarizations of subject positions ("we all function simultaneously as subject and object" [144]) in terms of castration and fetishism.

WORKS CITED

Clover, Carol. *Men, Women, and Chain Saws: Gender in the Modern Horror Film*. Princeton: Princeton UP, 1992.

Foucault, Michel. "Two Lectures." *Power/Knowledge: Selected Interviews and Other Writings 1972-77*. Ed. Colin Gordon. Trans. Colin Gordon, Leo Marshall, John Mepham, Kate Soper. New York: Pantheon, 1980. 78-108.

———. "What Is an Author?" *Language, Counter-Memory, Practice: Selected Essays and Interviews*. Trans. Donald F. Bouchard and Sherry Simon. Ithaca: Cornell UP, 1977. 113-138.

Gates, Henry Louis, Jr. "African American Criticism." *Redrawing the Boundaries: The Transformation of English and American Literary Studies*. Ed. Stephen Greenblatt and Giles Gunn. New York: MLA, 1992. 303-319.

Hardt, Michael. *Gilles Deleuze: An Apprenticeship in Philosophy*. Minneapolis: U of Minnesota P, 1993.

Holland, Laurence B. "A 'Raft of Trouble': Word and Deed in *Huckleberry Finn*." *American Realism: New Essays*. Ed. Eric J. Sundquist. Baltimore: Johns Hopkins UP, 1982. 66-81.

Kaplan, Cora. *Sea Changes: Essays on Culture and Feminism*. London: Verso, 1986.

Kristeva, Julia. *Black Sun: Depression and Melancholia*. Trans. Leon S. Roudiez. New York: Columbia UP, 1989.

———. Interview transcript. *Talking Liberties*. London: Channel Four Television, 1992. 15-20.

———. *Tales of Love*. Trans. Leon S. Roudiez. New York: Columbia UP, 1987.

Lefort, Claude. *Democracy and Political Theory*. Trans. David Macey. Cambridge: Polity, 1988.

Massumi, Brian. *A User's Guide to Capitalism and Schizophrenia: Deviations from Deleuze and Guattari*. Cambridge: MIT P, 1992.

Morrison, Toni. *Beloved*. New York: Knopf, 1987.

———. *Jazz*. New York: Knopf, 1992.

———. *Playing in the Dark: Whiteness and the Literary Imagination*. Cambridge: Harvard UP, 1992.

———. "The Site of Memory." *Out There: Marginalization and Contemporary Cultures*. Ed. Russell Ferguson et al. Cambridge: MIT P, 1990. 299-305.

———. "Unspeakable Things Unspoken: The Afro-American Presence in American Literature." *Michigan Quarterly Review* 28 (1989): 1-34.

Oliver, Kelly. *Reading Kristeva: Unraveling the Double-bind*. Bloomington: Indiana UP, 1993.

Serres, Michel. *Eclaircissements: cinq entretiens avec Bruno Latour*. Paris: François Bourin, 1992.

Silverman, Kaja. *Male Subjectivity at the Margins*. New York: Routledge, 1992.

Skura, Meredith. "Psychoanalytic Criticism." *Redrawing the Boundaries: The Transformation of English and American Literary Studies*. Ed. Stephen Greenblatt and Giles Gunn. New York: MLA, 1992. 349-373.

Twain, Mark. *The Adventures of Huckleberry Finn*. Ed. Walter Blair and Victor Fischer. Berkeley: U of California P, 1985.

TALKING BACK TO SCHOOLTEACHER: MORRISON'S CONFRONTATION WITH HAWTHORNE IN *BELOVED*[1]

Caroline M. Woidat

> It would require a pretty good scholar in arithmetic to tell how many stripes he had inflicted, and how many birch-rods he had worn out, during all that time, in his fatherly tenderness for his pupils. . . . Moreover, he had written a Latin Accidence, which was used in schools more than half a century after his death; so that the good old man, even in his grave, was still the cause of trouble and stripes to idle school-boys.
> —Nathaniel Hawthorne, *The Whole History of Grandfather's Chair*

> Nothing in the world more dangerous than a white schoolteacher.
> —Toni Morrison, *Beloved*

MORE THAN ONE READER OF TONI MORRISON'S *Beloved* (1987) has detected allusions to Nathaniel Hawthorne in the story of Sethe's "crime" and its aftermath. Because of the way Sethe seeks forgiveness yet seems unwilling to relinquish her guilt, a critic remarks that she "appear[s] to be something of a black Hester Prynne" (Otten 91). I will argue that Morrison's Sethe is indeed something of a Hester Prynne, but one that subverts Hawthorne's text by creating marked differences between the characters. Rather than focusing upon the similar themes of innocence and guilt that emerge in *Beloved* and *The Scarlet Letter* (1850), I will examine the relationship between these two novels as part of a sustained debate over American cultural values. In the nineteenth century, Hawthorne spoke *to* and *for* African Americans, asserting his authority as a man of letters and a privileged citizen. Although some African Americans began to exercise their own power as writers within the slave narrative genre, their voices continued to be silenced in both the political arena and America's literary canon. Morrison writes in response to Hawthorne, challenging his politics while claiming her own authority as an African-American writer.

In *Beloved*, we can read an allegory for the process of literary canon formation in the relationship between Sethe and schoolteacher.[2] Schoolteacher stands as the quintessential figure of white male authority, wielding the power of the word as well as the whip. While his students attempt to define Sethe in their notebooks, he tells them to "'put her human characteristics on the left; her animal ones on the right. And don't forget to line them up'" (193). Sethe's assertion of her humanity earns her the scars that form a choke-cherry tree on her back; when she protests the way that schoolteacher has allowed his nephews to milk her—as if she were a cow—he orders them to whip Sethe back into silence. Her body is literally inscribed with this mark of white male dominance, but Sethe ultimately defies schoolteacher's authority by murdering her own child. She kills Beloved so that "no one, nobody on this earth, would list her daughter's characteristics on the animal side of the paper" (251). Reaffirming her own humanity as well as her children's, Sethe denies schoolteacher the right to "possess" her family as slaves.

Sethe's story subtly comments upon that of America's early black women writers, depicting their struggle to claim legitimacy as authors. Schoolteacher, on the other hand, represents only a more extreme version of the formidable opposition that black women authors faced from a literary establishment with both racial and sexual prejudices. While Mae G. Henderson has compared schoolteacher to Hawthorne's Surveyor Pue,[3] it may be more accurate to liken him specifically to Hawthorne himself, whose politics and aesthetic principles reflected such biases. Consider Morrison's description of

the attitude white nineteenth-century American writers such as Hawthorne took toward African Americans: "One could write about them,
but there was never the danger of their 'writing back.' Just as one
could speak to them without fear of their 'talking back.' One could
even observe them, hold them in prolonged gaze, without encoun-
tering the risk of being observed, viewed, or judged in return"
("Unspeakable" 13). Morrison's argument in this and other essays
such as *Playing in the Dark* (1992) is that America's literary history
and its history of slavery cannot be separated. The stance these
white authors assumed toward African Americans is intimately related to that of slave owners such as schoolteacher. In *Beloved*,
when a Sweet Home slave tries to "talk back," schoolteacher "beat
him anyway to show him that definitions belonged to the definers—
not the defined" (190).

As a late twentieth-century author and scholar, Morrison has
much invested in a literary project that addresses Hawthorne's ghost.
Hawthorne and schoolteacher—and, by extension, contemporary
"schoolteachers" who have a role in shaping America's literary
canon—share a similar role as "definers," to whom Sethe and
Morrison respectively must "talk back." *Beloved* draws attention to
the parallels between the antebellum racial politics informing *The
Scarlet Letter* and the contemporary politics of multiculturalism.
Hawthorne, writing in the decade that preceded the Civil War, feared
abolition because he felt that the unity of the nation had to be
preserved at all costs. Morrison's novel appeared in the same year
that two books were published by members of the academic community to voice their own anxiety over the disintegration of America's
cultural unity: Allan Bloom's *The Closing of the American Mind: How
Higher Education Has Failed Democracy and Impoverished the Souls
of Today's Students* (1987) and E. D. Hirsch, Jr.'s *Cultural Literacy:
What Every American Needs to Know* (1987). In stating their opposition to current trends toward diversification in the educational
curriculum, Bloom and Hirsch imply that Americans once enjoyed
a sense of commonality which has since been sacrificed to meet
the special interests of feminists, African Americans, and other
marginalized groups.

Morrison's reinterpretation of *The Scarlet Letter* suggests that
such a golden age of shared American identity existed only as an
illusion that Hawthorne himself worked to create. Her novel is itself
an act of "talking back," part of her project to create literature that
is "irrevocably, indisputably Black" ("Memory" 389). In this response
to white schoolteachers such as Hawthorne, Morrison speaks for

nineteenth-century African Americans whose stories were censored or silenced. Her novel turns to the African-American literary tradition of the slave narrative, which she borrows from but also rewrites. By authoring their own texts, writers of slave narratives performed with the pen what Sethe does with a handsaw: an act of self-definition. Just as Sethe's quest for freedom leaves both her back and her daughter's throat irreparably defaced, however, the authors of slave narratives were often compelled to distort their own features in order to succeed in winning acceptance for their work. *Beloved* enables us to explore the distortions we find in both slave narratives and Hawthorne's fiction by focusing upon those aspects of slavery that nineteenth-century authors tried to conceal. Morrison thus revises both black and white nineteenth-century texts, offering a counternarrative to women's slave narratives and to the works of the "schoolmasters" of young America.

1.

Beloved not only speaks for the slaves whose voices were silenced (alluded to as "Sixty Million and more") but also contributes to Morrison's critique of the aesthetics that have dominated American culture and, likewise, its canon of literature. Expressing her dismay at the Western notion of physical beauty as a virtue, Morrison testifies to the insidious consequences that this idea has had within the black community:

When we are urged to confuse dignity with prettiness, and presence with image, we are being distracted from what *is* worthy about us: for example, our intelligence, our resilience, our skill, our tenacity, irony or spiritual health. And in that absolute fit of reacting to white values, we may very well have removed the patient's heart in order to improve his complexion. ("Rediscovering" 14)

In nineteenth-century women's slave narratives, we encounter this obsession with a white image of virtue by writers who were trying to assert their womanhood to an audience that had long recognized only their "animal characteristics" as "breeders" and "mules." Ironically, in their attempt to prove that they possessed those same virtues that distinguished the "cult of true womanhood," writers such as Harriet Jacobs and Harriet E. Wilson often adopted the literary conventions of white women writers who were themselves disparaged by Nathaniel Hawthorne as "a d—-d mob of scribbling women" (*Letters* 304).

As an African-American woman, Morrison herself writes with an acute awareness of American literary history in creating the figure of schoolteacher. Her approach to reading American literature is "to avert the critical gaze from the racial object to the racial subject; from the described and imagined to the describers and imaginers" (*Playing* 90). The character of schoolteacher is instructive in exploring the relationship between racial and, I would add, gendered objects and subjects, drawing our attention to these dynamics within the literary canon. Assuming the role of a "definer," Hawthorne judged literary merit by "lining up" qualities according to "male" and "female" characteristics. While his condemnation of the "scribbling women" is often quoted, Hawthorne's praise for Fanny Fern (Sara Payson Willis Parton) also helps explain the criteria on which he based such a judgment:

The woman writes as if the Devil was in her; and that is the only condition under which a woman ever writes anything worth reading. Generally women write like emasculated men, and are only to be distinguished from male authors by greater feebleness and folly; but when they throw off the restraints of decency, and come before the public stark naked, as it were,—then their books are sure to possess character and value. (*Letters* 308)

Hawthorne associates social satire with masculinity, whereas most women's fiction is "emasculated" due to a feminine impulse to uphold a code of "decency."[4] If Hawthorne's definition of "good" literature created a double bind for women writers, it put black women writers of the nineteenth century in what Deborah K. King has termed "multiple jeopardy": for their literature to be accepted, they had to overcome prejudice against not only gender, but also race and class.[5]

In order to persuade white, educated readers that slavery was wrong because blacks *were* in fact human, women's slave narratives frequently employed the literary conventions of the sentimental novel scorned by Hawthorne. Many black women writers felt constrained by a code of "decency" that prohibited them from focusing upon the more sordid details of slavery in any real detail. In the preface to *Our Nig* (1859), a narrative written by a free black in the North with the purpose of "Showing That Slavery's Shadows Fall Even There," Harriet E. Wilson acknowledges her self-imposed restraint: "I do not pretend to divulge every transaction in my own life, which the unprejudiced would declare unfavorable in comparison with treatment of legal bondmen; I have purposely omitted what would most provoke shame in our good anti-slavery friends at home" (3). Because she is not legally a slave, Wilson does not wish to create too horrible a tale of oppression at the hands of a cruel northern mistress— even one she claims has "*southern* principles"—for fear that her narrative might harm the abolitionist movement.

The stories of "real" slaves were also edited to suit public decorum: some events remained "too terrible to relate" even as a means of furthering the anti-slavery cause. Lydia Maria Child addresses this issue in her introduction to *Incidents in the Life of a Slave Girl* (1861):

I am well aware that many will accuse me of indecorum for presenting these pages to the public; for the experiences of this intelligent and much-injured woman belong to a class which some call delicate subjects, and others indelicate. This peculiar phase of Slavery has generally been kept veiled; but the public ought to be made acquainted with its monstrous features, and I willingly take the responsibility of presenting them with the veil withdrawn. (8)

In spite of Child's claim, the reader encounters a tale that has been "edited" for a white audience, and whose author's name—Harriet Jacobs—has already been concealed behind the pen name Linda Brent. Wilson's and Jacobs's narratives thus resemble the "mob of scribbling women's" fiction in several ways. They both decline to "throw off the restraints of decency, and come before the public stark naked," acts which Hawthorne believed necessary to producing books of literary value. For their work to be well received by white publishers, critics and readers, these writers had to observe conventional protocols even as they withdrew the veil covering the indecencies of slavery. Like sentimental novels of the day, Jacobs's *Incidents in the Life of a Slave Girl* is imbued with moral purpose and often assumes a didactic tone. Black women writers such as Jacobs and Wilson may thus appear to affirm white society's ideals of womanhood and virtue at the same time they oppose its institution of slavery.

A number of critics have addressed the ways in which *Beloved* attempts to fill these gaps in slave narratives, which is part of Morrison's larger project of reconstructing black history.[6] She acknowledges her responsibility as a writer to "rip that veil drawn over 'proceedings too terrible to relate,'" a process Morrison claims "is also critical for any person who is black, or who belongs to any marginalized category, for, historically, we were seldom invited to participate in the discourse even when we were its topic" ("Site" 110-111).[7] As a slave narrative, *Beloved* is less concerned with the standards of decency that influenced earlier writers. Morrison reveals the horrors of slavery in explicit detail, elaborating upon the physical and psychological abuses suffered by Sethe, Paul D, and the other Sweet Home slaves. *Beloved* also departs from the tradition of the slave narrative by flaunting white society's standards of beauty and womanhood rather than adapting to them. In Sethe, Morrison creates an antidote to the submissive, delicate heroine who once served as an ideal for women, including black writers. Sethe's scars and swollen feet enhance rather than diminish her dignity: her beauty lies in her exceptional ability to endure. Moreover, Sethe's "thick" love for her children is depicted in defiance of traditional conceptions of motherhood. To love a child enough to take its life redefines motherhood from the perspective of a slave. Writing in the twentieth century, Morrison is less defensive than Wilson or Jacobs in portraying her black heroine's unique virtues; she makes no excuses for abominations such as Beloved's death because they result from the white institution of slavery.

The purpose of my comparison between slave narratives and white women's fiction is not to conflate the experiences of black and white women, but rather to show the way that their marginal position in the canon of American literature has been constructed in terms of their ostensible conformity to social norms. To focus upon the ways African American and white women authors reinforced conventional viewpoints—and thus adopt Hawthorne's stance toward such writers—is, however, to overlook their opposition to these same norms. Morrison's strategy in reinterpreting nineteenth-century texts resembles the one that Ella uses when listening to stories told by runaway slaves such as Sethe: she listens "for the holes—the things the fugitives did not say; the questions they did not ask" (92). In *Beloved*, Morrison reconstructs a history of black, female subversiveness using the story of Margaret Garner—the "real" Sethe—as an example of such rebellion.

2.

Morrison's reinterpretation of the slave narrative does more than fill the lacunae in early African-American texts: it offers a reinterpretation of white nineteenth-century texts as well. Like all slave narratives, *Beloved* responds to a white literary tradition. Whereas her predecessors often emulated the white text, however, Morrison works to deconstruct it. In addition to calling attention to the ways in which slave narratives were marked by certain omissions, Morrison's novel forces us to recognize the "holes" in canonical texts such as *The Scarlet Letter*. We can, in fact, read *The Scarlet Letter* in the same way Morrison does Herman Melville's *Moby-Dick* (1851): "for the 'unspeakable things unspoken'; for the ways in which the presence of Afro-Americans has shaped the choices, the language, the structure—the meaning of so much American literature" ("Unspeakable" 11). Hawthorne (and subsequently, many of his critics) would have us preserve a distinction between his work and the more openly didactic writing of his female contemporaries. Yet his monumental novel—which occupies a privileged place in the American literary canon—can be characterized by its own repression of slavery's evils in order to achieve social consensus. By rewriting Hawthorne's narrative as the story of a black slave, Morrison shows us precisely what Hawthorne tried to keep behind a veil.

Although the publication of *The Scarlet Letter* was contemporaneous with the Compromise of 1850 (including the Fugitive Slave Act), as a historical romance the novel seemed to evade the social issues of the day. By contrast, Harriet Beecher Stowe's *Uncle Tom's Cabin* (1852) has been judged more "political" and thus less enduring a work of art than Hawthorne's transcendent, "timeless" classic. Hawthorne's own didacticism becomes apparent, however, when we look at what he does *not* say about slavery in the novel and other writing of the same period. *The Scarlet Letter*'s publication follows that of another text in which Hawthorne seems to shun the topic of slavery in his reconstruction of American history. While working at the Custom House, Hawthorne's financial situation led him to consider writing children's literature for profit. In *The Whole History of Grandfather's Chair* (1841), Hawthorne gives instruction to children using the persona of "Grandfather" to relate his historical tales. These lessons provide us with a context in which we can examine Hawthorne as a schoolteacher at work.

Grandfather mentions slavery only once in tracing American history from 1620 to 1803, but this is not for fear that his young listeners cannot bear stories of severe hardships. When asked whether there were slaves in the eighteenth century, Grandfather replies: "'Yes; black slaves and white. . . . These last were sold, not for life, but for a certain number of years, in order to pay the expenses of their voyage across the Atlantic. . . . As for the little negro babies, they were offered to be given away, like young kittens'" (109). Following Grandfather's comparison of slaves to small pets, one boy suggests that Alice might want one of those babies to play with instead of her doll, in response to which she clutches her doll more tightly, while Grandfather uses the doll as an occasion to change the topic to the women's fashions of this bygone era. Grandfather limits his discussion of slavery to this brief response, though he does offer meticulous details of whippings endured, not by slaves, but by white pupils at the hands of their schoolmaster. Alice begins to cry at Grandfather's graphic accounts of the birch-rod, meant to show how '"in those good old times, a school-master's blows were well laid on'" (84). Likewise, he brings tears to the children's eyes with stories of ocean crossings into the exile of diaspora, speaking not of Africans, but of Acadians torn from their homes in France and British loyalists forced to leave America after the Revolutionary War. Moved by his story of the Acadians, Clara sobs, "'To think of a whole people, homeless in the world! . . . There never was anything so sad!'" (128). Grandfather's sense of decorum does not prevent him from telling stories of injustices against whites, yet he refrains from speaking of white cruelty toward Africans. In his role as a children's teacher, Hawthorne lends dignity to the trials of European settlers in the New World while erasing the plight of African slaves from America's history: when mentioned at all, they are objectified as animals and playthings.

In *The Scarlet Letter*, I will argue, Hawthorne creates another historical tale in which the topic of African slaves is suppressed, this time for mature readers. Although the predominant moral questions of the day centered around the issue of slavery, Hawthorne returns to the time of his Puritan forefathers in order to probe the workings of the human conscience. This is not to say that Hawthorne evades the subject of slavery; rather, it is displaced onto his depiction of the "dark" side of Puritanism—literally configured by Hawthorne with images of blackness.[8] The harshness of Puritanical rule is represented by images and symbols frequently—and, in Hawthorne's day, perhaps more immediately—associated with slavery: imprisonment, whippings, brands, the scaffold, and "darkness" itself, both racial and moral. African Americans may be notably absent from Hawthorne's Puritan community, but allusions to slavery are not. We encounter a (white) slave in the form of Governor Bellingham's bond-servant, although one who will eventually be able to take his place in the community upon fulfilling his work contract. Hester Prynne approximates the black slave's bondage more closely: she is considered "the people's victim and life-long bond-slave" (227). Objectified on the scaffold, marked by a scarlet letter, and separated from the rest of the community, Hester's plight becomes conflated with that of the African-American other seemingly absent from the text.

By leading his reader to reflect that these forms of persecution disappeared after Puritanism had run its course, Hawthorne subtly presents a case for a gradualist approach to slavery. He does not justify the cruelty of the Puritans any more than he would defend slavery; rather, he sees such injustices as an inevitable part of historical process. In their efforts to repoliticize *The Scarlet Letter*, critics have noted that Hawthorne's stand on the issue of slavery is characterized by the same ambiguity surrounding the letter "A."[9] Hawthorne condemned the institution of slavery, yet he also opposed abolition because it threatened to fragment the nation. Rather than remaining trapped in this paradox, however, Hawthorne allowed his concern for the preservation of the Union to take precedence over any repulsion to slavery. In his biography of Franklin Pierce, Hawthorne justified the Compromise of 1850, arguing that Pierce was right "to take his stand as the unshaken advocate of Union, and of the mutual steps of compromise which that great object unquestionably demanded" (*Life* 415). In place of outright abolition, Hawthorne recommended gradualism, promoting the view that slavery is "one of those evils which divine Providence does not leave to be remedied by human contrivances, but which, in its own good time, by some means impossible to be anticipated, but of the simplest and easiest operation, when all its uses shall have been fulfilled, it causes to vanish like a dream" (*Life* 417). As Sacvan Bercovitch has noted, Hawthorne's rhetoric called for "manifest inaction justified by national destiny" (89). Rather than being abolished, slavery would be allowed to play its part in the sweeping course of America's progress.[10]

In *The Scarlet Letter*, Hester Prynne learns to respond to injustice with steady submission rather than outright rebellion, thus offering a preview of Hawthorne's advice to abolitionists. In a desperate moment, Hester wonders whether she and her daughter should ever have been born: "Indeed, the same dark question often rose into her mind, with reference to the whole race of womanhood. Was existence worth accepting, even to the happiest among them?" (165). Her question is one echoed in many slave narratives (including Sethe's) and especially by slave mothers contemplating the birth of a child, although in reference to the African race rather than the "race" of womanhood. In place of such drastic action as suicide or infanticide, Hester comes to endorse gradualism as a solution to female oppression, assuring troubled women of her strong conviction "that, at some brighter period, when the world should have grown ripe for it, in Heaven's own time, a new truth would be revealed, in order to establish the whole relation between man and woman on a surer ground of mutual happiness" (263). The subtext of the novel states that abolitionists and slaves need merely be patient, like Hester, and wait for the "divine operation" that will dissolve the institution of slavery. Hester thus serves as an allegorical figure of patient submission to tyrannical authority—something of a white, female precursor to Stowe's Uncle Tom.[11]

Hester's victimization in fact becomes her salvation: Hawthorne makes it clear that her open suffering is preferable to the guilt that the community's male leaders must endure as perpetrators of oppression. Hawthorne not only blurs the distinction between black and white victims of oppression, he also allows the suffering of these victims to be overshadowed by that of their persecutors. In spite of all that Hester must endure as an object of the community's scorn, Arthur Dimmesdale and Roger Chillingworth meet a worse fate as men who not only share Hester's sin, but are also guilty of hypocrisy and manipulation. While Hester's pregnant, female body signifies her own weakness and transgression of the law, they are able to conceal their guilt from the town. As "unmarked" white men, Dimmesdale and Chillingworth have the power to fashion their own identities by engaging in verbal subterfuge. Hester's husband takes on a new name and history in order to avenge himself, and the minister misleads his congregation with ambiguous confessions that hide his sin and make him into a saint. While these deceptions are at first empowering, however, they eventually lead both men to ruin. In the novel's conclusion, Hawthorne comments upon their decline by warning his readers to be truthful.

Following Morrison's cue, we can explore the ways in which Hawthorne's text reflects his own identity as a racial subject. Dimmesdale's predicament is in many ways reflective of Hawthorne's own ideological struggles as an author. Before the public, Dimmesdale wants to tell the truth that he himself is a sinner, yet still conceal its fuller meaning: specifically, that he is an adulterer and the father of Hester's child. Hawthorne's own narrative is guided by a similar impulse to be both confessional and secretive, to bare his private self and hide it too. What would seem to be a confession appears in his introductory "The Custom-House," where Hawthorne meditates upon the capacity for evil among his own Puritan ancestors, known for their "persecuting spirit." Uncertain whether they ever repented their deeds, Hawthorne seeks forgiveness for them: "I, the present writer, as their representative, hereby take shame upon myself for their sakes, and pray that any curse incurred by them . . . may be now and henceforth removed" (10). Yet *The Scarlet Letter* only indirectly accounts for the actions of Hawthorne's forefathers, the most infamous of which was John Hathorne, one of the three judges presiding in the Salem witch trials of 1692. Hawthorne's decision not to use this subject matter permitted him to obscure his more personal relationship to the Puritans and also the Africanist presence among them. The young girls responsible for crying out "witches" first blamed Tituba, a West Indian slave, for enlisting the power of the devil to bewitch them. Hawthorne's novel suppresses the story of Hathorne and Tituba, thereby removing traces of his own link to America's history of racial conflict.

While claiming responsibility for these inherited sins, Hawthorne can still deflect moral questions specific to his own actions and lifetime. Hawthorne's conditional "confession" allows him to accept blame for a legacy of persecution while still keeping "the inmost Me behind its veil" (4). His creed as an author resembles the moral stated in the novel's conclusion: "Be true! Show freely to the world, if not your worst, yet some trait whereby the worst may be inferred!" (260). Ironically, then, Hawthorne observes the "restraints of decency" that he elsewhere condemns in women writers, refusing to "come before the public stark naked" as Fanny Fern does. Hawthorne's act of self-censoring also calls to mind the strategies used in slave narratives. Whereas the authors of slave narratives spare their readers the worst of their victimization, Hawthorne tries to be honest with his audience while still displacing his own complicity in forms of oppression. Like Dimmesdale, Hawthorne is only comfortable revealing his ideological struggles so long as they can be cloaked in allegorical language.

The veil that Morrison feels must be torn away from the history of slavery thus presents itself in Hawthorne's novel as well. *The Scarlet Letter* enacts Hawthorne's vision of a gradual resolution to the problem of slavery, but it also alludes to the hypocrisy embedded in a pro-Union, anti-slavery position. Dimmesdale can only maintain his balancing act while Hester remains silent, just as Hawthorne's political stance depends upon the effacement of African-Americans. In this novel and in his history for children, Hawthorne denounces slavery only by implication, highlighting the oppression of white rather than black political victims. While white "bond-slaves" such as Hester Prynne can eventually earn acceptance from the community, Hawthorne cannot create a similar movement toward consensus using black characters. Morrison challenges Hawthorne's vision of social unity by showing us how the presence of African Americans tends to thwart his plot and resolution.

3.

Beloved responds to *The Scarlet Letter* by creating alternatives to Hawthorne's politics, whose concern for national unity reverberates in current debates over multiculturalism. In their books published in 1987, Morrison, Bloom and Hirsch still confront questions about the possibility of cultural unity, a recurring issue throughout the course of America's history. While obvious distinctions exist between Hawthorne's views and those of Bloom and Hirsch today, they all share a vision of national unity threatened by the presence of African Americans and various marginalized "others." Morrison's own insistence upon her identity as an African-American woman writer— through her project to create "irrevocably, indisputably Black" literature, to redefine literary criticism, and to reconstruct black history—places her in opposition to any agenda that seeks to suppress racial, cultural, or gender difference for the good of the "majority."

In *Beloved*, she depicts the conflict as one between schoolteacher and his pupils/slaves—the definers and the defined. Sethe chooses to take Beloved's life rather than have it be defined by whites such as schoolteacher: "Whites might dirty *her* all right," but Sethe decides that "she could never let it happen to her own" (251). Schoolteacher asserts his authority by controlling language: unlike Garner, the first master of Sweet Home, he does not allow the slaves to speak their own opinions or to learn to read and write. Instead, he makes them the subjects of his own interpretation— measuring and dissecting them in his notebooks, silencing their voices with an iron bit. Morrison's merging of slavemaster and schoolteacher serves to politicize the process of literary canon formation as an act of "lining up" the qualities of what is and is not American. She alludes not only to the role of Hawthorne and other writers of the American Renaissance, but also to the politics of Bloom, Hirsch, and all those who seek to define a common heritage by erasing difference.

In their arguments for cultural unity, Bloom and Hirsch effectively take on the role of definers who try to contain the multiplicity of American voices. They claim that the late twentieth-century movement toward diversifying the educational curriculum has contributed to the fragmentation of America's "national majority" (Bloom 31) and "national culture" (Hirsch 102). Just as Hawthorne paradoxically defended the Union by minimizing the issue of slavery, Bloom and Hirsch try to establish a core curriculum that unifies American experience in spite of its cultural diversity. Bloom, for example, recalls past definitions of Americanness that depended upon a universal doctrine of natural rights: "by recognizing and accepting man's natural rights, men found a fundamental basis of unity and sameness. Class, race, religion, national origin or culture all disappear or become dim when bathed in the light of natural rights . . ." (27). Speaking of the black power movement and the development of African-American studies, Bloom laments that "just at the moment when everyone else has become a 'person,' blacks have become blacks" (92). He blames the perpetuation of racist attitudes and separatism on African Americans, who have created a "little black empire" in American universities that impedes the establishment of shared goals and values.[12] Hirsch's somewhat different approach attributes the loss of commonality among American students to differences in the background knowledge that they possess. As a first step toward providing all students with a common standard of cultural literacy, Hirsch offers a list of places, events, people, and other information that is meant to illustrate the type of knowledge that "literate" Americans share. In delineating the contours of cultural literacy, Hirsch consulted many colleagues in search of a consensus; he therefore dismisses criticism that the resulting list is "merely academic or male or white, and so on, just because we are" (137). An examination of the list, however, does not yield the name of a single African-American woman.[13]

Once we read *Beloved* in the context of this intellectual debate, schoolteacher's list assumes a new relevance as a symbol of opposition to Morrison's own project of "talking back." Her novel contradicts the notion that race should be subsumed into a more general "Americanness" by rewriting a canonical text (referred to several times on Hirsch's list) that performs such an erasure. Morrison foregrounds the topic of slavery and African-American experience, shifting the narrative perspective so that white men become racial others, men "without skin" (210, 211, 262). While Hawthorne's novel works to make racial differences disappear, Morrison's emphasizes the rift between black and white cultural identities. In *Beloved*, she challenges the myth of consensus that characterizes the white texts of the American Renaissance and provides a foundation for current arguments against multiculturalism.

Morrison's reinterpretation of *The Scarlet Letter* begins with the character of Hester herself. Ostensibly, there are many similarities between Hester and Sethe. Both women commit a "crime" that separates them from society, choose to remain at the scene of their sorrow and guilt, and are at last reconciled with the community. The two characters have a similar type of bond to their daughters, who serve to punish them while also providing their hope for redemption. At each phase of this shared narrative, however, Morrison revises Hawthorne's story, reversing the politics of the text. Unlike Hawthorne's heroine, her black Hester Prynne does not accept compromise: Morrison offers no promise that the scarlet letter will fulfill its purpose. Sethe enacts the revolution that Hester imagines but entrusts to the course of "progress." Whereas Hester patiently submits to her fate, following Hawthorne's prescribed inaction, Sethe uses violence to change her future: her "rough response to the Fugitive Bill" is to kill her children rather than allow them to be slaves (171). If Sethe lives in regret, it is not because she rues her aggression, but that she has been forced to misdirect her attack. Given a second chance, she does not choose to repeat the past as Hester does; this time, she protects her resurrected daughter by trying to kill the white man whom she believes to be schoolteacher. Because she will not resign herself to the fate assigned to her by white society's law, Sethe serves as a foil to Hester and a challenge to Hawthorne's political vision.

Morrison's narrative accentuates the different experiences of European- and African-Americans, whereas Hawthorne's writing often conflates the two. Like Hawthorne, Morrison depicts whippings of white servants and students, acknowledging that such violence is universal. As an indentured servant, Amy Denver is abused by Mr. Buddy, and even schoolteacher's nephews know the touch of his whip. But Morrison is careful to distinguish between the experiences of these victims and those of the Sweet Home slaves. Looking at Sethe's back, Amy comments, "'I had me some whippings, but I don't remember nothing like this'" (79). The difference between the two women is underscored by the separate directions they take: Amy goes to Boston in search of velvet, while Sethe faces the misery of a runaway slave who gets caught. Schoolteacher's nephew cannot understand Sethe's reaction when the slave-catchers arrive, having been beaten "a million times" himself: "But no beating ever made him . . . I mean no way he could have . . . What she go and do that for?" (150). *Beloved* presents a grisly catalog of the physical and psychological abuses against slaves so that African-American experience cannot be subsumed into American history the way it is in *Grandfather's Chair* or even *The Scarlet Letter*.

In Morrison's novel, the legacy of slavery is not one that can be made to "vanish" as Hawthorne suggests. Morrison counters his vision of a gradual movement toward consensus with a testimony to the growth of an encroaching jungle—a threat to social unity arising from the very negation of African American experience that Hawthorne himself performs. As Stamp Paid points out, the savage jungle that whites associated with Africanism was one that they themselves had created and nurtured: "The more coloredpeople spent their strength trying to convince them how gentle they were, how clever and loving, how human, the more they used themselves up to persuade whites of something Negroes believed could not be questioned, the deeper and more tangled the jungle grew inside" (198). The white jungle planted in the black community is responsible for the violent act of infanticide that takes "the Word" away from Baby Suggs and alienates Sethe from her people. In the end, however, the black Word triumphs as the women stand before Sethe's house singing as they used to do at Baby Suggs' meetings in the clearing before schoolteacher's visit changed everything. Likewise, Paul D returns to Sethe and "wants to put his story next to hers" (273). But while Sethe is reunited with the black community, Morrison does not offer a reconciliation with white society or an encompassing, pluralistic "American" society. The black women sing among themselves, for themselves. Their voices are not heard outside the black community, nor are they intended to be.

Beloved depicts a contest for possession of the word at the same time that it engages in one. Reading the novel in the context of a debate over canon formation extending back to Hawthorne's time, we see how America's "schoolteachers" have construed the Africanist (and feminist) presence as a threat to their own authority. One recent critic, for example, writes that "the white male, whether WASP or not, cannot read Toni Morrison's *Beloved* in any other way than 'under siege'" (Todd 43). It would seem that the literary canon is an edifice "under siege" with Morrison at the gates, or, to use Bloom's analogy, that a "black empire" is striking back at America's ivory towers. If the American identity defined by canonical writers such as Hawthorne is not white and male, as Bloom and many others contend, then why this siege mentality? *Beloved* challenges this assumption that Americans share a common culture in which race becomes irrelevant. In rewriting *The Scarlet Letter*, Morrison does more than reveal the Africanist presence in the canon: she reminds us that "the act of enforcing racelessness in literary discourse is itself a racial act" (*Playing* 46).

NOTES

[1]An earlier version of my essay was delivered at the Modern Language Association Convention in December 1992. I am indebted to Ken Cooper for providing me with critical challenges and insights throughout this project. My thanks also to Nancy J. Peterson, Patrick O'Donnell, and Ellen Carol Jones for their comments on later drafts.

[2]The configuration between white instructor and black student is also problematized in Morrison's *The Bluest Eye* (1970), which deconstructs the white "Dick and Jane" text. See Powell 749-753.

[3]Henderson compares the way Hawthorne's Custom-House Surveyor measures each leg of the scarlet letter to the exact quarter-inch with schoolteacher's meticulous data-collecting among the slaves of Sweet Home; see page 70.

[4]Such a view, in fact, characterized the position of later critics who also denigrated nineteenth-century women's fiction because they thought it represented social consensus rather than criticized it. Nina Baym argues this point in "Melodramas of Beset Manhood: How Theories of American Fiction Exclude Women Authors." In *Sensational Designs: The Cultural Work of American Fiction, 1790-1860*, Jane Tompkins asserts that "sentimental" novels were more subversive than critics have been willing to acknowledge.

[5]Although the "triple jeopardy" of racism, sexism, and classism has often been used to conceptualize the status of African-American women, King cautions that "while advancing our understanding beyond the erasure of black women within the confines of the race-sex analogy, it does not yet fully convey the dynamics of multiple forms of discrimination," which she tentatively labels "multiple jeopardy" (46-47).

[6]See Mae G. Henderson, Marilyn Sanders Mobley, and Cynthia Griffin Wolff.

[7]In addition to pursuing this goal in her fiction, Morrison helped edit *The Black Book*, which reconstructs black history using "raw material documents" of black life: newspapers, letters, advertisements, personal recollections, sheet music, etc. See Middleton Harris, et al., eds., *The Black Book*, and Morrison's "Rediscovering Black History."

[8]Hawthorne's text exhibits the ethnocentrism that Henry Louis Gates, Jr., finds broadly characteristic of Western languages, in which "blackness itself is a figure of absence, a negation" (7).

[9]See Jonathan Arac, Sacvan Bercovitch, Jennifer Fleischner, Deborah L. Madsen, and Jean Fagan Yellin.

[10]During the war, Hawthorne's antagonism toward abolitionists surfaced in his essay "Chiefly About War Matters," in which he declares that "nobody was ever more justly hanged" than John Brown and that his death should bring "any common-sensible man . . . a certain intellectual satisfaction" (54). Observing fugitive slaves, Hawthorne describes them as "not altogether human"; he reasons that they could not benefit from the war but would always be forced to "fight a hard battle with the world, on very unequal terms" (50).

[11]Stowe, of course, was writing an abolitionist novel that was not meant to justify Uncle Tom's oppression. His selflessness is linked to the virtue of Christian submission, which Stowe also associates with women. In emphasizing Tom's willing subservience to whites, however, Stowe ironically reinforces a stereotype that was often used to justify slavery.

[12]For a critique of this line of Bloom's argument, see Floyd W. Hayes, III.

[13]I refer here to Hirsch's appendix in *Cultural Literacy*, "What Literate Americans Know: A Preliminary List" (152-215). In 1988, Hirsch published his first *Dictionary of Cultural Literacy*, now in a second, updated and revised edition. Unlike his original list, the new *Dictionary* consciously includes African-American women (and, among them, Toni Morrison); the preface explains that the editors have "taken into account the recent emphasis on the ever more significant area of multiculturalism" by increasing the number of entries covering African-American culture. These new entries were added because they "belong to American (not just African-American) cultural literacy" (vii).

WORKS CITED

Arac, Jonathan. "The Politics of *The Scarlet Letter.*" *Ideology and Classic American Literature*. Ed. Sacvan Bercovitch and Myra Jehlen. Cambridge: Cambridge UP, 1986. 247-266.

Baym, Nina. "Melodramas of Beset Manhood: How Theories of American Fiction Exclude Women Authors." *American Quarterly* 33 (1981): 123-139.

Bercovitch, Sacvan. *The Office of The Scarlet Letter*. Baltimore: Johns Hopkins UP, 1991.

Bloom, Allan. *The Closing of the American Mind: How Higher Education Has Failed Democracy and Impoverished the Souls of Today's Students*. New York: Simon and Schuster, 1987.

Child, Lydia Maria. Introduction. *Incidents in the Life of a Slave Girl, Written by Herself*. Ed. L. Maria Child. 1861. The Schomburg Library of Nineteenth-Century Black Women Writers. Gen. ed. Henry Louis Gates, Jr. New York: Oxford UP, 1988. 7-8.

Fleischner, Jennifer. "Hawthorne and the Politics of Slavery." *Studies in the Novel* 23 (1991): 96-106.

Gates, Henry Louis, Jr. "Criticism in the Jungle." *Black Literature and Literary Theory*. Ed. Henry Louis Gates, Jr. New York: Methuen, 1984. 1-24.

Harris, Middleton, et al., eds. *The Black Book*. New York: Random House, 1974.

Hawthorne, Nathaniel. *The Centenary Edition of the Works of Nathaniel Hawthorne*. 20 vols. Ed. William Chavat, et al. Columbus: Ohio State UP, 1985.

____. "Chiefly About War Matters." *Atlantic Monthly* July 1862: 43-61.

____. *The Letters, 1853-1856*. Vol. 17 of *The Centenary Edition of the Works of Nathaniel Hawthorne*.

____. *Life of Franklin Pierce*. 1852. *Tales, Sketches, and Other Papers*. Vol. 12 of *The Works of Nathaniel Hawthorne*. 347-438.

____. *The Scarlet Letter*. 1850. Vol. 1 of *The Centenary Edition of the Works of Nathaniel Hawthorne*.

____. *The Whole History of Grandfather's Chair*. 1841. *True Stories*. Vol. 6 of *The Centenary Edition of the Works of Nathaniel Hawthorne*. 3-210.

_____. *The Works of Nathaniel Hawthorne*. Riverside Edition. 15 vols. Ed. George Parsons Lathrop. Boston: Houghton Mifflin, 1883.

Hayes, Floyd W., III. "Politics and Education in America's Multicultural Society: An African-American Studies' Response to Allan Bloom." *Journal of Ethnic Studies* 17.2 (1989): 71-88.

Henderson, Mae G. "Toni Morrison's *Beloved*: Re-Membering the Body as Historical Text." *Comparative American Identities: Race, Sex, and Nationality in the Modern Text*. Ed. Hortense J. Spillers. New York: Routledge, 1991. 62-86.

Hirsch, E. D., Jr. *Cultural Literacy: What Every American Needs to Know*. Boston: Houghton Mifflin, 1987.

_____, Joseph F. Kett, and James Trefil, eds. *The Dictionary of Cultural Literacy*. 2nd ed. Boston: Houghton Mifflin, 1993.

Jacobs, Harriet. *Incidents in the Life of a Slave Girl, Written by Herself*. Ed. L. Maria Child. 1861. The Schomburg Library of Nineteenth-Century Black Women Writers. Gen. ed. Henry Louis Gates, Jr. New York: Oxford UP, 1988.

King, Deborah K. "Multiple Jeopardy, Multiple Consciousness: The Context of a Black Feminist Ideology." *Signs* 14 (1988): 42-72.

Madsen, Deborah L. "'A for Abolition': Hawthorne's Bond-Servant and the Shadow of Slavery." *Journal of American Studies* 25 (1991): 255-259.

Mobley, Marilyn Sanders. "A Different Remembering: Memory, History and Meaning in Toni Morrison's *Beloved*." *Toni Morrison*. Ed. Harold Bloom. New York: Chelsea House, 1990. 189-199.

Morrison, Toni. *Beloved*. 1987. New York: Plume, 1988.

_____. *The Bluest Eye*. New York: Washington Square, 1970.

_____. "Memory, Creation, and Writing." *Thought* 59 (1984): 385-390.

_____. *Playing in the Dark: Whiteness and the Literary Imagination*. Cambridge: Harvard UP, 1992.

_____. "Rediscovering Black History." *New York Times* 11 Aug. 1974, sec. 6: 14-24.

_____. "The Site of Memory." *Inventing the Truth: The Art and Craft of Memoir*. Ed. William Zinsser. Boston: Houghton Mifflin, 1987. 101-124.

_____. "Unspeakable Things Unspoken: The Afro-American Presence in American Literature." *Michigan Quarterly Review* 28 (1989): 1-34.

Otten, Terry. *The Crime of Innocence in the Fiction of Toni Morrison*. Columbia: U of Missouri P, 1989.

Powell, Timothy B. "Toni Morrison: The Struggle to Depict the Black Figure on the White Page." *Black American Literature Forum* 24 (1990): 747-760.

Stowe, Harriet Beecher. *Uncle Tom's Cabin*. 1852. New York: New American Library, 1981.

Todd, Richard. "Toni Morrison and Canonicity: Acceptance or Appropriation?" *Rewriting the Dream: Reflections on the Changing American Literary Canon*. Ed. W. M. Verhoeven. Amsterdam: Rodopi, 1992. 43-59.

Tompkins, Jane. *Sensational Designs: The Cultural Work of American Fiction, 1790-1860.* New York: Oxford UP, 1985.

Wilson, Harriet E. *Our Nig; or, Sketches from the Life of a Free Black, In A Two- Story White House, North. Showing that Slavery's Shadows Fall Even There.* 1859. New York: Random House, 1983.

Wolff, Cynthia Griffin. "'Margaret Garner': A Cincinnati Story." *Massachusetts Review* 32 (1991): 417-440.

Yellin, Jean Fagan. "Hawthorne and the American National Sin." *The Green American Tradition: Essays and Poems for Sherman Paul.* Ed. H. Daniel Peck. Baton Rouge: Louisiana State UP, 1989. 75-97.

"SAY MAKE ME, REMAKE ME": TONI MORRISON AND THE RECONSTRUCTION OF AFRICAN-AMERICAN HISTORY

Nancy J. Peterson

> If my work is to be functional to the group (to the village, as it were) then it must bear witness and identify that which is useful from the past and that which ought to be discarded; it must make it possible to prepare for the present and live it out. . . .
> —Toni Morrison, "Memory, Creation, and Writing"

Jazz is a historical novel that "fails" to represent its epoch properly: set for the most part in Harlem, the novel opens in 1926, the heyday of the Harlem Renaissance, but it offers for full view almost none of the artistic, cultural, or political milestones that African Americans achieved in those years. In his review of the novel, Henry Louis Gates, Jr., notes this unexpected treatment, describing *Jazz* as "so near to—yet so far away from—the black literary movement known as the New Negro, or Harlem Renaissance" (52). Gates, perhaps feeling an urgency to fill in the details "missing" in Morrison's novel, spends the next two paragraphs providing references to some of the great black artistic accomplishments of 1926. He cites Langston Hughes, who published both *The Weary Blues* and his influential essay "The Negro Artist and the Racial Mountain" in 1926, as well as Countee Cullen and Zora Neale Hurston, who launched *Fire!!* in that same year; he brings up Duke Ellington and Josephine Baker, who were incredibly popular in the mid-twenties. And if we move beyond Gates's list, we also observe that Morrison's novel does not even mention great black leaders, like W. E. B. Du Bois and Marcus Garvey, who so passionately spoke out about civil rights and equality in those years.

Authors, of course, are not obligated to make overt references to public events and figures from the time in which their novels are set. But Morrison's decision not to include the kind of detail Gates supplies in his review is particularly intriguing because *Jazz* is a historical novel and historical novels typically include these kinds of references. Clearly, as both *Beloved* and *Jazz* indicate, Morrison is not interested in writing a conventional historical novel.[1] As her essential involvement with the design, editing, and production of the unorthodox historical text called *The Black Book* in the early 1970s further suggests, Morrison has spent her career questioning the very premises of history and historical writing, particularly as they pertain to African Americans and the representation of African-American history.[2] The goal of her fiction, as the epigraph to this essay suggests, has been not just to recover details of African-American history, but to choose which details are useful for "the village" or the community in the struggle to create a past that can enable African Americans to have, in the words of *Beloved*, a "livable life" in the present and future (198). While making occasional references to *Beloved*, this essay focuses on *Jazz*, for I argue that the unconventional historicity of *Jazz* is directly linked to Morrison's improvisational exploration of alternative concepts and forms for reconstructing African-American history.

Like *Beloved*, *Jazz* was inspired by an actual document, in this case by a James Van Der Zee photograph of a young black woman, beautifully dressed and coiffed, resting in a satin-lined coffin. The date inscribed on this photograph is 1926, the same year in which Morrison's novel begins. The significance of this photograph first became apparent in Morrison's 1985 interview/conversation with Gloria Naylor. Morrison thought at this time that the stories that form the narrative core of *Beloved* and *Jazz* would be told in the same novel,[3] and so she explained to Naylor that Margaret Garner's decision to kill her children to keep them out of slavery became intertwined for her with the story behind Van Der Zee's funereal photograph. The woman had been shot by her former lover at a party, but did not tell anyone of the shooting, and the people surrounding her noticed only when she collapsed that there was blood on her. She refused medical treatment and refused to summon the police, evidently in order to let her lover escape, and so she died. In both of these stories, Morrison explains to Naylor, "[a] woman loved something other than herself so much. She had placed all of the value of her life in something outside herself" (207).

Morrison was very familiar with Van Der Zee's photographs; in fact, she wrote the foreword to his 1978 collection of death-portraits called *The Harlem Book of the Dead*, in which the photograph and the compelling story behind it that inspired *Jazz* were published. It is striking, however, that when Morrison discusses the subject with Naylor, she dwells on the story and not the image. Van Der Zee's funereal portrait is marked by his characteristic attention to aesthetics: the framing, the lighting, and the composition of the scene engage the viewer in such visual pleasure that the grave subject matter of the photo and its underlying narrative can almost be overlooked. Perhaps it was the dissonance between the beauty of this photo and the singular story of the young black woman featured in it that captured Morrison's attention, for in her foreword to this book, Morrison draws attention to the paradoxical qualities of Van Der Zee's death-portraits: "The narrative quality, the intimacy, the humanity of his photographs are stunning, and the proof, if any is needed, is in this collection of pictures devoted exclusively to the dead about which one can only say, 'How living are his portraits of the dead.'" Morrison focuses neither on the aesthetic or composition aspects of these harmonious photographs, nor on their historical or documentary dimensions in recording a common (but relatively unknown today) practice in Harlem of the twenties and thirties. Rather, she emphasizes their "narrative quality"—their ability to tell a story. Morrison's comments about Van Der Zee are significant in locating the emphasis of her own historical practice, which dwells not on the photograph but on the story that accompanies it, not on mere facts or documents but on the narrative that makes use of them.

The opening of *Jazz* illustrates this distinction. In the first few pages we are given all the facts pertaining to the tragic triangulated relationship at the center of the novel. We learn that Joe and Violet Traces' thirty-some year marriage is troubled: Violet, who has been childless by chance and perhaps by choice, craves a baby now that it is biologically too late for her to have one of her own; and Joe, who has become distanced from her, begins an affair with Dorcas, a young woman of eighteen who seems too self-indulgent through most of the novel to be worthy of Joe's passion and devotion. And most importantly, we are told right away that a desperate Joe has shot and killed Dorcas, after learning that she was stepping out on him, and that Violet, shocked by the knowledge of Joe's betrayal, has become violent, going to Dorcas's funeral with a knife in hand to cut her rival's face. Just when we might think there is nothing left to find out about this story, the narrative takes a peculiar twist: Violet decides to learn everything she can about the dead girl, going so far as to visit Dorcas's aunt, Alice Manfred, and to bring home a picture of Dorcas that she sets prominently on the mantle.

This photograph, however, like the Van Der Zee photograph that inspired *Jazz*, does not by itself provide useful explanations to either Violet or Joe. Although they repeatedly take turns in their restless nights, getting out of bed and going to look at the photograph to try to find clear answers to what has happened to them, they find that they are gazing not on Dorcas, but on their own reconstructions of her:

If the tiptoer is Joe Trace, driven by loneliness from his wife's side, then the face stares at him without hope or regret and it is the absence of accusation that wakes him from his sleep hungry for her company. No finger points. Her lips don't turn down in judgment. Her face is calm, generous and sweet. But if the tiptoer is Violet the photograph is not that at all. The girl's face looks greedy, haughty and very lazy. The cream-at-the-top-of-the-milkpail face of someone who will never work for anything; someone who picks up things lying on other people's dressers and is not embarrassed when found out. It is the face of a sneak who glides over to your sink to rinse the fork you have laid by her plate. An inward face—what it sees is its own self. (12)

Even though this photograph, like any isolated historical fact or document, does not tell them what they need to know, it does provide a sharp desire for some kind of critical understanding, and so Joe and Violet begin to reach back into the more-distant past to re-collect the stories that will enable them to comprehend their present situation.

The problem is that Joe and Violet have spent most of their lives forgetting, or, as Morrison calls it in *Beloved*, "beating back the past" (73). Having left Vesper County, Virginia, in 1906, aboard a train called the Southern Sky heading north, Joe and Violet hoped to leave behind past disappointments and dispossession and begin a new, brighter life. They eventually arrive in Harlem, the promised land for the "wave of black people," like them, "running from want and violence" (33). By 1926, when the novel opens, Harlem seems to be the site of a new historical epoch. The narrator describes the feeling in the air: "Here comes the new. Look out. There goes the sad stuff. The bad stuff. The things-nobody-could-help stuff. The way everybody was then and there. Forget that. History is over, you all, and everything's ahead at last" (7). "History" in this passage is understood as the bad stuff that has happened (in the South) in the past; like slavery, it is something to be gotten over, to be left behind literally in the Great Migration, to be forgotten (like Beloved). Despite the promise of Harlem to be posthistorical, though, Joe and Violet find that the past comes along to haunt them, that they have to reckon with "the sad stuff," "the bad stuff" in order to resuscitate themselves as individuals and as a couple. This narrative movement does, and should, remind us of Beloved.

Morrison's historical novels are structured recursively: that is, the narration of present events is continually interrupted by the telling of "background" stories. The nature of these stories from the past tells us something about Morrison's definition of "historical." Neither Beloved nor Jazz is much interested in narrating fictionalized stories of monumental events. In fact, the tendency in both novels is simply to make passing reference to History with a capital H, as this passage from Beloved shows: "No more discussions, stormy or quiet, about the true meaning of the Fugitive Bill, the Settlement Fee, God's Ways and Negro pews; antislavery, manumission, skin voting, Republicans, Dred Scott, book learning, Sojourner's high-wheeled buggy, the Colored Ladies of Delaware, Ohio, and the other weighty issues that held them in chairs, scraping the floorboards or pacing them in agony or exhilaration" (173). By creating such a list, Morrison is not dismissing the significance of these public and political issues for African Americans, but she is insisting that a useful black history not be solely concerned with such matters. Morrison continually prompts her readers to consider what does not get recorded about the realities of black life in America, as reflected in Stamp Paid's internal historicizing: "Eighteen seventy-four and whitefolks were still on the loose. Whole towns wiped clean of Negroes; eighty-seven lynchings in one year alone in Kentucky; four colored schools burned to the ground; grown men whipped like children; children whipped like adults; black women raped by the crew; property taken, necks broken. He smelled skin, skin and hot blood. The skin was one thing, but human blood cooked in a lynch fire was a whole other thing. The stench stank" (180).[4] Passages in Jazz also summon up images of racist violence against blacks that goes unmentioned in the mainstream newspapers and hence does not become part of the public record or monumental history. These terrible events remain visible only because of a black collective memory that people like Stamp Paid and Ella and Baby Suggs in Beloved or Joe Trace and Felice's father and Alice Manfred in Jazz sustain.

Morrison has described her goal in Jazz as wanting "to tell a very simple story about people who do not know that they are living in the jazz age, and to never use the word" ("Art of Fiction" 117). *Jazz* does refer to various public events of the time, such as the July 1917 East St. Louis riots; the much-celebrated return of the 369th Regiment (an all-black unit) in 1919 from World War I;[5] the vital presence of clubs, leagues, and societies in Harlem during the twenties (the UNIA, the National Negro Business League, the Civic Daughters, and so on); the emergence of print media targeted specifically to a black audience (*The Crisis, Opportunity* magazine, the *Amsterdam News*, the *Messenger*). More often, though, the novel conveys a strong sense of Harlem as a mecca, a promised land for African Americans in the twenties, through generalized descriptions such as this one: "[E]verything you want is right where you are: the church, the store, the party, the women, the men, the postbox (but no high schools), the furniture store, street newspaper vendors, the bootleg houses (but no banks), the beauty parlors, the barbershops, the juke joints, the ice wagons, the rag collectors, the pool halls, the open food markets, the number runner, and every club, organization, group, order, union, society, brotherhood, sisterhood, or association imaginable" (10). This passage acknowledges the inequities that remained in Harlem even during the Renaissance years, but the parentheses bracket them, and so the predominant impression here is of Harlem as a self-sufficient community of black people, the largest community of its kind in America and the world in the twenties.[6] Morrison's novel thus performs an important act of historical recovery by bringing to mind for contemporary readers this exceptional era of (African) American history, when it seemed that, for the first time, blacks would have access to a range of economic, educational, and social opportunities that had previously been denied them.[7]

But in *Jazz*, as in *Beloved*, Morrison's emphasis always moves away from the "big" picture and returns to the everyday lives of black people. Joe declares himself "a new Negro," for instance, which is a reference that might be connected to Alain Locke's important collection of 1925, but Locke himself is never mentioned in Morrison's narrative and so the phrase remains local in its meaning. Most of the novel, in fact, consists of individual stories of the past related to Violet and Joe, and Dorcas and Alice Manfred. Violet reckons with her mother's suicide and what it meant to be raised hearing glorious stories of the light-skinned, fair-haired mulatto child (Golden Gray) that her grandmother helped raise; Joe meditates on his unsuccessful attempts to have Wild acknowledge him as her son; Dorcas sifts through the traumatic memories of her father's and mother's deaths;

Alice faces the intensity of her repressed feelings about her husband's infidelity over thirty years ago. As they recount the stories of their past, Morrison's novel suggests that history is never over, that a conscious historical connection is absolutely necessary for the psychological well-being of the individual and community.[8]

This connection is particularly tenuous because of the historical era in which *Jazz* is set. A time of massive migration from south to north along with a newly conceived image of black selfhood—the New Negro as someone who is self-assertive and militant, who refuses a Booker T. Washington conciliatory stance, who has freed himself from the power of whites to define his life and goals—the Harlem Renaissance might also be seen as a time of rupture, when "newness" became a cultural dominant that marked not only progress, but trauma.[9] Nathan Huggins suggests that the problematic metaphor of "the New Negro" offered a limited and unstable model of assertive black manhood: "[W]hatever promise the new man has for the future, his name and the necessity for his creation imply some inadequacy in the past. Like the New Year's resolution or the 'turning over a new leaf,' the debut of the New Negro announced a dissatisfaction with the Old Negro. And since the New/Old dichotomy is a mere convenience of mind—Afro-Americans were really the same people all along—the so-called Old Negro was merely carried within the bosom of the New as a kind of self-doubt, perhaps self-hate" (65). In Huggins's analysis, this self-doubt eventually contributed to the implosion of the Harlem Renaissance as a movement. Focusing on black women, Houston Baker argues in the opening chapter of *Workings of the Spirit* that this rupture had specific ramifications on the generation of black women writers who came of age in the Harlem Renaissance. Writers such as Nella Larsen and Jessie Fauset, Baker argues, understandably wanted to depart from the constraining images of black women in nineteenth-century literature, but ended up completely sundering all connections to their roots in southern folk wisdom and black vernacular, leaving only the possibility of adopting northern "white-faced minstrelsy" on which to model their literary expressivity. Because of the "daughters' seduction" into "whitemale patriarchy," Baker asserts, "passing" became the predominant trope of their literature.

Although Baker proposes theoretical interventions to suture the gaping wound between northern and southern, urban and rural, male and female black experience, Morrison, it would seem, suggests a different kind of intervention, an intervention involving history and rememory. What is passing if not the repression of one's personal history? Morrison's novel emphasizes historical rememory precisely to move away from passing as the trope that governs contemporary views of the Harlem Renaissance as a historical era.

Both Joe and Violet yearn for some kind of connection with their previous selves in order to deal with the trauma brought on by migration and urban life. Joe cannot tell his best male friends in Harlem, Gistan and Stuck, things he would easily have said to his boyhood friend and near-brother, Victory. He admits, "I changed once too often. Made myself new one time too many. You could say I've been a new Negro all my life" (129)—such continual newness and self-renewal, while made attractive by the rhetoric of the Harlem Renaissance, prove to be problematic and painful. Cut off from Victory and any other connection to his past life in the South, Joe urgently needs someone to listen to all of his unspoken dreams and memories. Violet, who suffers from her own psychological amputations, cannot fulfill this role, and so Joe places his awesome neediness on an eighteen-year-old self-absorbed young woman who reminds him vaguely of Wild, who perhaps is his mother. His desire for Dorcas involves not only sex or beauty or youth, though; perhaps more importantly it involves his desire to articulate, to narrate memories and stories that might connect the past to the present in a meaningful way.

The urgency to make these kinds of connections is also felt by Violet and Alice. Violet suffers "public crazinesses" and "private cracks" in Harlem (22)—fissures in her own self-concept that the novel registers with names signifying her split self: "Violent" and "*that* Violet." She begins to heal these fractures, though, by creating a historical narrative for herself: to Alice, midway through the novel, she says "Everybody I grew up with is down home" (111), and to Felice late in the novel, Violet remarks, " 'Before I came North I made sense and so did the world'" (207), demonstrating her ability to articulate the traumatic effects caused by the profound geographic and emotional dislocations migration entailed.

It is important that Violet's healing, her ability to talk about herself and her life, occurs as a result of the bond she and Alice form after Dorcas's death. Violet initially comes to Alice's apartment to find out what Dorcas was like in an attempt to understand Joe's betrayal, but instead finds herself growing attached to the dead girl and to Alice. Likewise, as Alice stitches up Violet's frayed and torn dress, then her coat, she listens to her closely and repairs her own tattered sense of self. Together they figure out that "sisterhoods" are necessary between black women if they are to avoid becoming wild, armed, and dangerous.

As Morrison observed in a 1977 interview with Ntozake Shange, "What [black] women say to each other and what they say to their daughters is vital information" (50). Without this passing down of wisdom, the daughters cannot have "livable" lives and an entire generation of African Americans will be affected adversely because of the wounds these motherless or sisterless black women carry with them.[10] Morrison's novel dramatizes this predicament by presenting numerous instances of orphaned or abandoned children: Dorcas is raised by her aunt, Alice, after being orphaned; Sweet is raised by his aunt, Malvonne, but despite her best efforts, he joins a gang, robs postal boxes, and disappears from Harlem; Violet's mother, Rose Dear, jumps in a well and drowns herself to escape her pain, and so Violet vows never to have children of her own; Joe's mother is perhaps Wild—he never knows for sure—and his father is totally unknown, so Joe too does not want children of his own. To be sure, young black women like Alice and Violet have learned to exercise a certain kind of strength and willpower to become mature women who have relatively comfortable lives, but their emotional lacks are profound. By giving such close attention to the traumatic lives of Alice and Violet, Morrison's novel both points to the necessary resilience and creativity of black women in trying to make lives for themselves and their families amid tremendous adversities, and suggests the pain that is the underside of such achievement. In this way, Morrison's novel implicitly provides a much different, more complicated explanation of the fractures and fissures in black families than sociological-historical accounts such as Stanley Elkins's 1959 book, which argued that slavery totally dehumanized blacks, or the Moynihan Report of 1965, which produced the cultural image of a controlling and emasculating black matriarch.[11]

Following individual lives closely makes it possible for Morrison to (re)construct a history that remains faithful to the past but is not predetermined. The danger of narrating monumental history lies in creating a master narrative in which there is no space to articulate any local narratives that run counter to it: a historical master narrative has a grand resolution whose outcome has already been decided, and so individual players are unimportant except as they contribute to this final already-determined conclusion. Individual lives, outside of such a grand narrative, however, are much more chaotic, contradictory, and unpredictable—which creates a necessary space for resistance, agency and counternarratives. This issue is taken up specifically in *Jazz*, as the narrator suggests that the City with a capital *C*, an echo of the idea of Harlem during the Renaissance as the capital of the world, predetermines what will happen to Joe: "Take my word for it, he is bound to the track. It pulls him like a needle through the groove of a Bluebird record. Round and round about the town. That's the way the City spins you. Makes you do what it wants, go where the laid-out roads say to. All the while letting you think you're free. . . . You can't get off the track a City lays for you" (120). But does the City with a capital *C* really have the power to define and prescribe individual lives? If it does, Morrison would be close to Richard Wright's naturalism or to totalizing constrictive accounts of black life in America such as Moynihan's or Elkins's. The dominant image of the passage quoted above—the groove of a Bluebird record—suggests a recognition of coercive and oppressive conditions that have adversely restricted African Americans, but it also produces associations that run counter to such predetermination.

The Bluebird label was known for its blues recordings,[12] and blues as a genre is founded on the principle of repetition with subtle variation. So the past (line or lyric) is never repeated exactly in the blues. And if we move on to connect the blues to jazz, as Morrison's novel does, we can see that jazz offers another example of a (narrative) line that resists predetermination: although a jazz composition has a set melody, the room for improvisation and the spontaneity of performance create a fluid and shifting text. Jazz as a genre revisits its own past melody to claim what is useful and make possible further development; it is, in other words, a model of a useful black history. Hence the title of Morrison's novel can be read not only as a reference to its historical setting but more importantly as the model for her historical reconstructive project. Like the narrator's description of the grooved Bluebird record, Morrison's own novel lays down seemingly inescapable tracks—lines of type that logistically must be read on the page from left to right, top of the page to bottom—but contains narrative lines that are patterned after jazz, where each chapter picks up and improvises on a key image or phrase from the end of the previous chapter.

The unfolding of the various strands of the many individual stories in *Jazz* is so intricate and complicated that the novel defies any single totalizing meaning.[13] Part of this intricacy is created by Morrison's curious narrator, who has the detachment and overarching knowledge typically associated with a reliable omniscient narrator, but also has the limited knowledge, biases, and involvement associated with an unreliable first-person narrator. The narrator, for instance, somehow has knowledge of parts of Joe's past and Violet's past that they have never told anyone, let alone each other. At the same time, however, the narrator bluntly admits to many instances of not knowing; remarks like "Anyway, Joe didn't pay Violet or her [boy]friend any notice. Whether she sent the boyfriend away or whether he quit her, I can't say" (4–5), or "I've wondered about it" (71) without any follow-up, or "If I remember right . . ." (71) are not atypical of this narrator. The status of the narrator becomes even more curious, though, when it becomes clear that this narrator will play a greater role than simply relating the stories of the various characters in the novel; she, in fact, unlike any of the narrators found in Morrison's other novels, becomes an individual voice, a quasi character, one who shapes the story as she tells it.[14] At times, she has the voice of a gossip, as in the opening line of the novel: "Sth, I know that woman." Other times, she bluntly interjects her own feelings into the story, exclaiming, for instance, "I'm crazy about this City" (7) early in the novel and beginning a sentence later on with "My own opinion was . . ." (118). Her voice as narrator has a wide range of inflections and levels, moving fluidly from relatively straightforward narrative reportage to lyrical prose to slang to blues lyrics.

One of the most startling attributes of this narrator, though, is her self-reflexivity: she confesses to having serious inadequacies as narrator. Questions about her ability to narrate become particularly pointed in the elaborate story of Golden Gray that unfolds in the novel. The Golden Gray episode is the longest "background" story told in the novel, for various reasons. It reveals parts of Joe's and Violet's past that help to explain the drift and loneliness of their lives in Harlem in 1926.[15] The episode is also a stunning reworking of various Faulknerian motifs, such as long-kept secrets revealed and miscegenation (recall that Morrison's masters thesis at Cornell explored the theme of alienation in Faulkner and Woolf). But perhaps most important, the episode highlights the problems of narrating such an intricate story: the narrator begins the saga of Golden Gray's search for his father, Henry LesTroy (or Le*story*), who is called familiarly Hunters Hunter, on page 143—but the story does not come out right, and so she begins again on page 150.

One of the problems in narrating Golden Gray's story is that he is a racist. Raised by Miss Vera Louise into an ideology of whiteness, Golden Gray is repulsed by black flesh, and so when he witnesses Wild's mad dash into a tree, knocking her unconscious, he can barely bring himself to touch her. And when he arrives at Henry's house, his first concern is to get his trunk inside before he returns to his carriage to see about Wild. These character deficiencies are so glaring that the narrator, who (like Violet) is attracted to the golden young man, begins to loathe him—until she tells the story a second time and adds some slight but influential details: "That is what makes me worry about him. How he thinks first of his clothes, and not the woman. How he checks the fastenings [of his trunk], but not her breath. It's hard to get past that, but then he scrapes the mud from his Baltimore soles before he enters a cabin with a dirt floor and I don't hate him much anymore" (151). These intimate details create a much more complicated picture of Golden Gray, one that makes it impossible to simply dismiss him. The narrator continues to relate the contradictions of Golden Gray's character, how he tries to make up a story for himself or for his father that will exonerate him, that will make him a hero for saving a "wild black girl" (154). The narrator bluntly calls him a "hypocrite" for these efforts (154), but goes on to look at him so closely that she can understand how fear drives his racism and his hypocrisy:

Aw, but he is young, young and he is hurting, so I forgive him his self-deception and his grand, fake gestures, and when I watch him sipping too quickly the cane liquor he has found, worrying about his coat and not tending to the girl, I don't hate him at all. He has a pistol in his trunk and a silver cigar case, but he is a boy after all, and he sits at the table in the single chair contemplating changing into fresh clothes, for the ones he is wearing, still wet at the seams and cuffs, are filthy with sweat, blood and soil. (155)

It is not that the narrator is willing to overlook Golden Gray's faults, so much as that her commitment to looking again brings more details into the picture, which pose new contradictions, and thus her former narrative can no longer offer neat evaluations.

But as the narrator continues to try to tell Golden Gray's story, once again she gets stuck and soon laments, "What was I thinking of? How could I have *imagined* him so poorly? Not noticed the hurt that was not linked to the color of his skin, or the blood that beat beneath it. But to some other thing that longed for authenticity, for a right to be in this place, effortlessly without needing to acquire a false face, a laughless grin, a talking posture. I have been careless and stupid and it infuriates me to discover (again) how *unreliable* I am" (160; emphasis added). The narrator's self-reflexive commentary here might cause readers to wonder if any of the versions of the Golden Gray story is to be trusted: after all, here is a narrator who confesses to imagining Golden Gray and to her own (repeated) unreliability. These questions become even more acute when the narrator reveals how she will arrive at a version of Golden Gray that is fair: "Now I have to think this through, carefully, even though I may be doomed to another misunderstanding. I have to do it and not break down. Not hating him is not enough; liking, loving him is not useful. I have to alter things" (161). How, indeed, will *altering* things lead to a full, complete, or fair story of Golden Gray?

The narrator in the Golden Gray episode is like a historian confronted with pieces of evidence. This evidence can be used to construct many different explanations or stories: the story of Golden Gray as a repulsive racist, the story of Golden Gray as a fearful and confused young man, and so on. But narratives such as these, constructed in a tidy logical way, prove dissatisfying to the narrator as she continues to contemplate these past events. She, paradoxically, is unreliable as a narrator-historian, not because she uses her imagination but because she does not make good enough use of it—she does not "alter" things enough to create a narrative that could be genuinely useful or informative. In fact, the narrator's dilemma and resolution here are strongly reminiscent of the comments Morrison has made about her own goals as an African-American writer. In "Memory, Creation, and Writing," Morrison distinguishes between memory— "the deliberate act of remembering," "a form of willed creation"—and research—"an effort to find out the way it really was" (385). Morrison, of course, does research herself as part of writing her novels, so it is not that she wants to dismiss research altogether. But research material in itself does not provide an intelligent or useful understanding of the past, as Morrison's comments in a later essay, "The Site of Memory," suggest: "[T]he crucial distinction for me is not the difference between fact and fiction, but the distinction between fact and truth. Because facts can exist without human intelligence, but truth cannot" (113). To dwell too much or too soon on the facts, Morrison adds, is to miss the opportunity to explore the "mystery" of the interior lives that she is trying to reconstruct. Fiction offers a kind of truth because, by connecting the world of facts to the world of imagination, it provides a vital understanding of "two worlds—the actual and the possible" (117).

The necessity to create a narrative that is faithful to the actual and yet points toward the possible is what the narrator learns in the Golden Gray episode. She demonstrates that she has learned this lesson when, later in the novel, she corrects the mistaken prediction she made in the opening chapter. In the first few pages, when the narrator is supposedly telling readers what will happen to Joe and Violet after Dorcas's death, she sees a bleak picture, as they re-establish another triangle substituting Felice for Dorcas. According to the narrator, only one thing changes: "What turned out different was who shot whom" (6). So we read the entire novel waiting for a second shooting that never happens. Instead, by the end of the novel, Joe and Violet have worked through their problems, and the narrator comes to understand her own fallibility:

I was sure one would kill the other. I waited for it so I could describe it. I was so sure it would happen. That the past was an abused record with no choice but to repeat itself at the crack and no power on earth could lift the arm that held the needle. I was so sure, and they danced and walked all over me. Busy, they were, busy being original, complicated, changeable— human, I guess you'd say, while I was the predictable one, confused in my solitude into arrogance, thinking my space, my view was the only one that was or that mattered. (220)

The narrator sees the limits of her earlier attempts to narrate the past: she has been an overly confident historian, focusing so concertedly on the big picture and its predictable patterns that she has forgotten to take into consideration human agency and the mystery of individual lives. The narrator's confession is a key moment in the novel. Elsewhere Morrison links the ability to learn from one's mistakes to jazz as a genre: "In a performance you make mistakes, and you don't have the luxury of revision that a writer has; you have to make something out of a mistake, and if you do it well enough it will take you to another place where you never would have gone had you not made that error. So, you have to be able to risk making that error in performance" ("Art of Fiction" 116–117). The narrator not only risks making mistakes, but she integrates those mistakes into the performance of her role as narrator.

Joe too takes such a risk when he reaches out of his loneliness to speak to Dorcas, but rather than trying to move on to a new place, he tries to reenact the past by conflating Dorcas and Wild. Trying to touch Wild/Dorcas, Joe shoots his lover: "I had the gun but it was not the gun—it was my hand I wanted to touch you with" (130–131). The narrator thinks that the appearance of Felice at the end of the novel will also lead to a scene of dangerous reenactment, hence her prediction in the opening chapter. This prediction, significantly, does not hold true: despite the fact that Felice was not only Dorcas's best friend, but resembles Dorcas so remarkably that Violet at first mistakes Felice for the dead woman, Violet, Joe, and Felice do not reenact the lover's triangle that previously led to tragedy. They instead make possible a future for themselves. Though Felice initially comes to the Traces' apartment to get some help in recovering the opal ring from her mother that she had lent to Dorcas and to tell Joe not to be so broken up about Dorcas, this passing encounter turns into a promising relationship as they reconstitute the black family: Felice gains surrogate parents in Violet and Joe,

whom she can talk to and learn from; Violet gets a surrogate daughter to receive some of her hard-earned pearls of wisdom and affection; Joe is reborn as father and lover, able to leave behind his
unbearable sadness when Felice passes on Dorcas's final words:
" 'There's only one apple. . . . Just one. Tell Joe' " (213).

Morrison's novel emphasizes the role of narration in achieving
this bond. By talking about their individual lives and pasts, Felice,
Joe, and Violet heal themselves through a collective and reciprocal
effort to face, tell, and renegotiate what has happened to them.
Watching their felicitous companionship, the narrator learns that a
past of trauma, pain, and unfulfilled longing does not have to continue on into the present or the future—if one can arrive at a narrative
that will enable reflection and renegotiation. This point is critical for
Morrison's efforts to reconstruct African-American history. Through
the use of a self-reflexive narrator, who can provide commentary on
the usefulness of certain kinds of narratives, and through the intricate retelling of past events, *Jazz* emphasizes that history is first of
all a story—a set of stories African Americans need to tell and retell
in order to create the foundation for a livable life and a viable future.
By insisting on the narrative and fictive—the storytelling—aspects of
history, Morrison's novels align themselves with current trends in the
postmodern novel, a genre so obsessed with history that theorist
Linda Hutcheon defines postmodernism as "historiographic metafiction." While the historical content of novels like *Beloved* and *Jazz*
should be taken seriously, it also seems clear that Morrison strategically emphasizes narrative patterns in her novels that work against
the construction of a new, monolithic black history. *Jazz*, for instance, does not attempt to present one clear picture of the Harlem
Renaissance or the Jazz Age from a black perspective, but self-
consciously re-presents the past in order to emphasize that historical understanding must be dynamic and constantly reworked if it is
to be useful.

Nowhere is this more clear than in the final paragraphs of the
novel. The narrator, who has been observing the newly found tenderness Joe and Violet have for each other, begins to meditate on
love and intimacy. She confesses, "I envy them their *public* love"
(229; emphasis added). The odd choice of "public" to modify "love"
might recall the words of Baby Suggs in the Clearing in *Beloved*,
urging her audience of black people to love themselves, to love their
own bodies and flesh (88). This collective act of self-love cannot be
sustained in *Beloved*, for Baby Suggs is shattered after whitefolks
enter her yard and precipitate Sethe's fatal embrace of her baby.

Neither could this self-love be sustained in the literary movement of the Harlem Renaissance, as analyses such as Baker's and Huggins's suggest. *Jazz*, however, as a historical novel, revisits these past traumas and refigures them, closing with an articulation of the kind of public or collective self-love these other texts long for:

I myself have only known it in secret, shared it in secret and longed, aw longed to show it—to be able to say out loud what they have no need to say at all: *That I have loved only you, surrendered my whole self reckless to you and nobody else. That I want you to love me back and show it to me. That I love the way you hold me, how close you let me be to you. I like your fingers on and on, lifting, turning. I have watched your face for a long time now, and missed your eyes when you went away from me. Talking to you and hearing you answer—that's the kick.* (229)

This passage evokes the intimacy, the connection through communication, the joining together that the narrator has just observed between Joe, Violet, and Felice.

It also surprisingly suggests a new "identity" for the narrator of *Jazz*: the book itself, talking to the reader, describing a reading experience that is intimate, passionate, and dynamic.[16] Reminiscent of "the talking book" that Gates discusses in *The Signifying Monkey*, the self-reflexivity of postmodern fiction, and the nonlinear design of *The Black Book*, the narrator as the book itself invites the reader to participate in the construction of the story: "If I were able I'd say it. Say make me, remake me. You are free to do it and I am free to let you because look, look. Look where your hands are. Now" (229). Books literally do not speak to readers, and paradoxically, the narrator manages to say what she has just said she is not able to; somewhere in the course of the novel, the typical story, the typical history has gotten off track. In this dazzling puzzle, though, lies an insight that has repercussions for Morrison's historical reconstruction—(black) history books have no life, no meaning, unless they engage readers and compel them to "make" and "remake" the story in order to locate something useful for living today and tomorrow.

This does not mean, though, that anything goes: just as the improvisational sections of a jazz piece must make recognizable reference to a previous phrase if listeners are to perceive the passage as improvisation and not as something entirely new, so too would playing fast and loose with the details make Morrison's historical novel illegible as history. Morrison's emphasis on the mutual and collective construction of the story is not an invitation to radical historical relativism,[17] but an insistence on a necessary, collective support for counternarratives in order for them to become something other than marginalized or alternative or muted perspectives. In the ending paragraphs of *Jazz*, as in the concept of rememory so central to *Beloved*, Morrison claims the power of engaging and compelling narratives and stories to contest and displace disabling hegemonic narratives in a culture's memory. In essence, *Jazz* repairs the dislocations and traumas of the past for African Americans so stunningly portrayed in Morrison's novels by beginning a communal, collective project, the ongoing reconstruction of a genuinely useful African-American history.

NOTES

[1]*Beloved* and *Jazz* are two volumes of a planned historical trilogy; Morrison is currently at work on the third novel of this group, which is tentatively titled *Paradise*.

[2]In 1974, Morrison wrote two important essays on *The Black Book*, in which she discusses her ideas on what constitutes genuine and useful black history; see "Behind the Making of *The Black Book*" and "Rediscovering Black History." I explore these essays in detail in the chapter on Morrison in my book manuscript.

[3]See page 208 of Morrison and Naylor's interview for Morrison's remarks about putting the two stories in the same novel. Although Morrison would eventually decide to tell the stories in separate novels, it is clear that strong connections—in terms of theme, image, and purpose—link *Beloved* to *Jazz*. Some of the most significant intratextual connections include "Sth," the voiced syllable that begins *Jazz* and is explained in *Beloved* as one of "the interior sounds a woman makes when she believes she is alone and unobserved at her work" (172). In addition, the word "trace" and the idea of going "wild" so important to *Jazz* are also first encountered in *Beloved* as undercurrents to the main narrative stream (see 222, 275 for "trace"; 149 on Sethe's wildness). In her 1995 interview with *Belle Lettres*, Morrison even goes so far as to draw strong links between Wild and Beloved, hinting that perhaps Wild *is* Beloved ("Toni Morrison" 43).

[4]Melissa Walker, like I do, finds this passage suggestive of Morrison's treatment of history in *Beloved* (see 38–39), but as this essay will make clear, we take quite different positions on the relation of private lives and public history in Morrison's work. Walker, it seems to me, overemphasizes "Morrison's rigorous adherence to the historical facts of the African-American experience" (9), especially when she argues that *Beloved* creates "characters whose lives are so intertwined with the exigencies of history that the most private acts and thoughts derive from public policy" (33).

[5]See the description of this significant moment in Nathan Huggins's important study, 55–56.

[6]Gilbert Osofsky emphasizes this fact: "*Prior to World War I*, the neighborhood was already the 'largest colony of colored people, in similar limits, in the world'—and it continued to expand. By 1920 the section of Harlem bordered approximately by One Hundred and Thirtieth Street on the south, One Hundred and Forty-fifth Street on the north and west of Fifth to Eighth Avenue was.predominately Negro—

and inhabited by some 73,000 people" (122–123). He also observes that Harlem was unique among the various urban areas blacks migrated to not only because of its population numbers but also because it was a genteel, elegant place to live. Unlike the slumlike areas blacks were relegated to in other cities, Harlem was the "ideal place" to live in New York (111). No doubt these physical surroundings helped to foster the feeling of black pride and historical momentousness that came to be associated with the Harlem Renaissance.

[7]In 1969, a landmark exhibit designed to increase public awareness of the history of Harlem opened at the Metropolitan Museum of Art in New York. Titled "Harlem on My Mind," this exhibit sparked controversy and thus huge crowds of people: "During the first week and a half it was open, over seventy-seven thousand visitors saw 'Harlem On My Mind,'" and "[e]very day that the museum was open, long lines of museum-goers of all races stretched down Fifth Avenue" (Birt 64). It also marked the rediscovery of James Van Der Zee, who was living in impoverished conditions when Reginald McGhee, following up on a lead about a photographer who had had a well-known studio in Harlem, tracked him down. Van Der Zee became the single largest contributor to the exhibit, and the showing of his remarkable photographs of Harlem at that exhibit launched a belated integration of his work into the history of photography (see Birt 62).

Morrison's novel contributes to this reawakened historical consciousness of Harlem (and, indirectly, of Van Der Zee), begun by scholars like Osofsky and Huggins, and made popular by exhibits like "Harlem on My Mind." This effort continues in a recent burst of scholarship on Harlem, the Renaissance, and various exhibits of artwork from the period, including a national tour of Jacob Lawrence's *Migration* series in 1995.

[8]In "Rootedness: The Ancestor as Foundation" (1984), Morrison remarks, "[N]ice things don't always happen to the totally self-reliant if there is no conscious historical connection" (344)—a comment that anticipates the emphasis of her recent historical novels. A strong connection between claiming one's heritage/history and realizing self-identity for black women is made in Missy Dehn Kubitschek's analysis of contemporary black women's novels, which includes a discussion of Morrison.

[9]Farah J. Griffin sees *Jazz* as "a portrait of a people in the midst of self-creation, a document of what they created and what they lost along the way" (197); her chapter on Morrison's novel incisively analyzes "the negative and positive consequences of migration" presented in *Jazz*.

[10]Consider the literal wounds that black women, especially mothers, bear in *Beloved*: Sethe learns to identify her mother by the mark under her breast, "a circle and a cross burnt right in the skin" (61); Sethe is marked by the "tree" schoolteacher's whippings have written on her back; Beloved bears the scar of Sethe's cut; even Nan is distinguished by having one "good arm" and "the stump of the other" (63).

[11]In his essay on *Beloved*, James Berger discusses the Moynihan Report in much greater detail than I do here. Although I agree with his argument that *Beloved* critiques the discourse and practices of white liberalism, I would not argue, as he implicitly does, that a central purpose of Morrison's novel is to address the inadequacies of various white-dominant political theories. Morrison has said she thinks of a black audience when she is writing, and wouldn't such a critique be old news to her primary audience? Denise Heinze briefly discusses various sociological

studies of black families, including Moynihan's, and analyzes the portrayal of black families in all of Morrison's novels in chapter 2 of her book, titled "Distant Mothers and Incomprehensible Fathers."

[12]The reference to Bluebird Records is anachronistic in Morrison's novel: *Jazz* is set in 1926, but Bluebird Records was not founded until 1933 in Chicago. To become overly concerned about this detail, however, would be to miss the larger implications of Morrison's reference.

[13]In her *Paris Review* interview, Morrison employs this same terminology while discussing the novel: "It's important not to have a totalizing view. In American literature we [African Americans] have been so totalized—as though there is only one version. We are not one indistinguishable block of people who always behave the same way" ("Art of Fiction" 117).

[14]I am aware that my reference to the narrator as a "she" is problematic. Even though Morrison does not offer any clear indications of the gender of this narrator, I am persuaded by Eusebio Rodrigues's connection of the epigraph from the *Nag Hammadi*, which features a female goddess, to the narrator's identity, and by the empathy the narrator has for especially the black women in the novel. Craig Werner also offers a fascinating reading of Morrison's epigraph as invoking the voice of "a visionary African woman" (302).

[15]Golden Gray is the beautiful—light-skinned—baby boy that True Belle fed Violet stories of while she was growing up. Golden Gray brings the very pregnant Wild to Hunters Hunter's cabin, and so he is present at Joe's birth. Morrison's readers are able to put Violet's and Joe's stories together in this way, but we have no indication in the novel that they are aware of this amazing coincidence.

[16]In her *Belle Lettres* interview, Morrison, perhaps anticipating the difficulties readers would have with the ending paragraphs, offers a direct explanation of the narrative voice: "The voice is the voice of a talking book. . . . This is a love song of a book talking to the reader" ("Toni Morrison" 42).

[17]The treatment of history as story in the postmodern novel has often been criticized for sealing off any consideration of the historical real. In his fine essay on *Beloved*, however, Rafael Pérez-Torres suggests that Morrison's postmodernism results not in a flight away from history, but in a complicated return to reference.

WORKS CITED

Baker, Houston, A., Jr. *Workings of the Spirit: The Poetics of Afro-American Women's Writing*. Chicago: U of Chicago P, 1991.

Berger, James. "Ghosts of Liberalism: Morrison's *Beloved* and the Moynihan Report." *PMLA* 111 (1996): 408–420.

Birt, Rodger C. "A Life in American Photography." *VanDerZee, Photographer, 1886–1983*. New York: Henry Abrams, with the National Portrait Gallery of the Smithsonian Institution, 1993. 26–73.

Elkins, Stanley M. *Slavery: A Problem in American Institutional Life*. Chicago: U of Chicago P, 1959.

Gates, Henry Louis, Jr. Rev. of *Jazz*, by Toni Morrison. *Toni Morrison: Critical Perspectives Past and Present*. Ed. Henry Louis Gates, Jr., and K. A. Appiah. New York: Amistad, 1993. 52–55.

——. *The Signifying Monkey: A Theory of African-American Literary Criticism*. New York: Oxford UP, 1988.

Griffin, Farah J. *"Who Set You Flowin'?": The African-American Migration Narrative*. New York: Oxford UP, 1995.

Harris, Middleton, et al., eds. *The Black Book*. New York: Random House, 1974.

Heinze, Denise. *The Dilemma of "Double-Consciousness": Toni Morrison's Novels*. Athens: U of Georgia P, 1993.

Huggins, Nathan I. *Harlem Renaissance*. New York: Oxford UP, 1971.

Hutcheon, Linda. *The Politics of Postmodernism*. New York: Routledge, 1989.

Kubitschek, Missy Dehn. *Claiming the Heritage: African-American Women Novelists and History*. Jackson: UP of Mississippi, 1991.

Morrison, Toni. "Behind the Making of *The Black Book*." *Black World* Feb. 1974: 86–90.

——. *Beloved*. New York: Knopf, 1987.

——. Foreword. Van Der Zee, Dodson, Billops n. pag.

——. "Interview with Toni Morrison." With Ntozake Shange. *American Rag* Nov. 1978: 48–52.

——. *Jazz*. New York: Knopf, 1992.

——. "Memory, Creation, and Writing." *Thought* 59 (1984): 385–390.

——. "Rediscovering Black History." *New York Times Magazine* 11 Aug. 1974: 14–24.

——. "Rootedness: The Ancestor as Foundation." *Black Women Writers, 1950–1980: A Critical Evaluation*. Ed. Mari Evans. New York: Doubleday-Anchor, 1984. 339–345.

——. "The Site of Memory." *Inventing the Truth: The Art and Craft of Memoir*. Ed. William Zinsser. Boston: Houghton Mifflin, 1987. 101–124.

——. "Toni Morrison." With Angels Carabi. *Belle Lettres* 10.2 (1995): 40–43.

——. "Toni Morrison: The Art of Fiction." With Elissa Schappell and Claudia Brodsky Lacour. *Paris Review* 128 (1993): 83–125.

Morrison, Toni, and Gloria Naylor. "A Conversation." 1985. *Conversations with Toni Morrison*. Ed. Danille Taylor-Guthrie. Jackson: UP of Mississippi, 1994. 188–217.

Moynihan, Daniel Patrick. *The Negro Family: The Case for National Action*. 1965. *The Moynihan Report and the Politics of Controversy*. Ed. Lee Rainwater and William L. Yancey. Cambridge: MIT P, 1967. 39–124.

Osofsky, Gilbert. *Harlem: The Making of a Ghetto*. New York: Harper and Row, 1966.

Pérez-Torres, Rafael. "Knitting and Knotting the Narrative Thread—*Beloved* as Postmodern Novel." *Modern Fiction Studies* 39 (1993): 689–707. Reprinted in this volume.

Rodrigues, Eusebio. "Experiencing *Jazz*." *Modern Fiction Studies* 39 (1993): 733–754. Reprinted in this volume.

Van Der Zee, James (photography), Owen Dodson (poetry), and Camille Billops (text). *The Harlem Book of the Dead*. Dobbs Ferry, NY: Morgan and Morgan, 1978.

Walker, Melissa. *Down from the Mountaintop: Black Women's Novels in the Wake of the Civil Rights Movement, 1966–1989*. New Haven: Yale UP, 1991.

Werner, Craig H. *Playing the Changes: From Afro-Modernism to the Jazz Impulse*. Urbana: U of Illinois P, 1994.

Wofford, Chloe Ardelia [Toni Morrison]. "Virginia Woolf's and William Faulkner's Treatment of the Alienated." Masters Thesis. Cornell U, 1955.

part four

READERLY AND WRITERLY PERSPECTIVES

TOWARD A RHETORICAL READER-RESPONSE CRITICISM: THE DIFFICULT, THE STUBBORN, AND THE ENDING OF *BELOVED*

James Phelan

> The imagination that produces work which bears and invites rereadings, which motions to future readings as well as contemporary ones, implies a sharable world and an endlessly flexible language. Readers and writers both struggle to interpret and perform within a common language sharable imaginative worlds.
> —Toni Morrison, *Playing in the Dark*

1. READING *BELOVED*

I AM IN *BELOVED* AND *BELOVED* IS IN ME.

Like Stamp Paid, I enter without knocking. For days I live at 124. I become Sethe. Paul D. Denver. Amy Denver; Baby Suggs; Stamp Paid. The days are intense, difficult, exhausting, rewarding. I reach to understand. Stretching, straining, marveling, I perform Morrison's world.

But *Beloved* also eludes me. Like Stamp Paid on the threshold of 124, I cannot enter. Parts of Morrison's world won't let mé in. Especially Beloved herself and the narrative's last two pages. *Who, what is Beloved? Yes, Sethe's murdered daughter. And—or?—a survivor of the Middle Passage.* Labels, not understanding. And why the cryptic ending? Why move away from the intimate scene between Sethe and Paul D to declare "this is not a story to pass on"?

Another label for Beloved—from the litcrit drawer: oppositional character. Spiteful ghost, manipulating lover, selfish sister, all-consuming daughter. But also innocent—and representative—victim. Where is the integration—or the reason for no integration? A label for the ending: confrontational. But why this prose: "In the place where long grass opens, the girl who waited to be loved and cry shame erupts into her separate parts, to make it easy for the chewing laughter to swallow her all away"?

These questions, I see, are interconnected—answer one and other answers will follow—but something, someone blocks my way. *Morrison? Me? My race? Gender? Something I have locked away in a tobacco tin inside my heart? Some other ignorance or insensitivity? All of these?*

Oppositional character, confrontational ending indeed.

There is a loneliness that reads.

2. READING, RESPONSE, AND INTERPRETATION

Other critics of *Beloved* both relieve and exacerbate the loneliness, especially in relation to Beloved. In particular, Elizabeth House, Judith Wilt, Barbara Rigney, Deborah Horvitz, Jean Wyatt, and Ashraf H. A. Rushdy offer excellent insights about Beloved, perceptions about her or her monologue that substantially advance my efforts to share Morrison's world.[1] At the same time, their work paradoxically increases my loneliness because Beloved still seems to elude explanation and a gap remains between response and interpretation. Beloved is a survivor of the Middle Passage and of a white man found dead in his cabin around the time she shows up at 124 (House). She is both Sethe's murdered daughter and her murdered African mother (Wyatt), a specific character in a specific family and a representative of all the middle passage women (Rigney), "and also all Black women in America trying to trace their ancestry back to the mother on the ship attached to them" (Horvitz 157). She is a figure filled with the psychokinetic energy of the others, who then use that energy to act out their needs and desires (Wilt). She is the incarnation of Sethe's guilt (Rushdy). Because the novel supports—indeed, insists on—all these not entirely compatible accounts, it prevents us from resting with any one and makes the struggle to "perform" her part of Morrison's world extraordinarily demanding. Moreover, adding the possibilities together gives us something less than the sum of the parts: Beloved dissolves into multiple fragments.

This gap between the experience of reading Beloved and the explanations offered by its interpreters is, in one respect, par for practical criticism's course. Despite the significant work done in reader-response theory in the last twenty-five years, including such useful recent books as those by Iser, Rabinowitz, Steig, Crosman, and Flynn and Schweickart, most interpretive practice remains unaffected by this work, rarely taking its starting point from the critic's response.[2] Perhaps the most dramatic example of this general critical habit of separating the experience of reading from the act of interpretation occurs in Robert Scholes's widely read Textual Power. Scholes proposes a progression from reading to interpretation to criticism but does not build the act of interpretation on the act of reading. For Scholes, to read is to see (the world of the text) but to interpret is to thematize, and to thematize is to divide the text into a series of repetitions and oppositions and to link these repetitions and oppositions to cultural codes. By locating the fundamental interpretive move in the division of the text into binary categories rather than in either the reader's seeing or a sequence of responses to that seeing, Scholes effects a divorce between reading and interpretation.[3]

I would like to take a closer look at the activities of reading and interpretation in order to explore further the relations and gaps between them and to highlight significant features of our conventional behavior as practical critics. Reading is the act of taking in, responding, and seeking to make sense of the text, as we follow its sequence from beginning to end. In reading, we are, strikingly, both passive and active, as the text acts upon us and we act upon it; the text calls upon—and we respond with—our cognitive, emotive, psychological, social, and ethical selves (though of course different texts will engage some of these selves more fully than others). When I speak of "experiencing the text," I refer to this two-sided, multidimensional, multileveled activity. Furthermore, because reading is active as well as passive, the shape it takes for any one text will depend on many things, including our individual subjectivities and the assumptions about reading that we bring to the text. That is, although reading is the activity set in motion by our primary encounter with the text, that activity, like interpretation, is not pure, innocent, or unmediated, but influenced by who we are, our training as readers, how we are positioned socially and culturally, and other traits and dispositions we bring to the act.

Interpretation is the act of formulating a cognitive understanding of the text. The sense-making that we do as part of reading is one kind of interpretation, and, thus, strictly speaking, reading and interpretation are so closely related that they are not wholly separable. In standard academic interpretation (hereafter SAI), however, this act of formulating a cognitive understanding is systematized and presented in formal, often highly abstract language—and in that systematizing a gap frequently develops between critics' reading experiences and their interpretations. To expand upon this point, I turn to a more detailed look at SAI.

To do SAI is to explain as coherently and comprehensively as possible the how and why of a text's signification. Because SAI has as its goal cognitive explanation, it involves a kind of translation. The text's language is viewed as that which is in need of explanation; the interpreter provides some other context and some other language—in effect, a code—to achieve that explanation.[4] In SAI, the key move in developing the explanatory code is abstraction from the details of the text. My claim about the gap between reading and SAI is that academic interpreters typically do not attend to the multileveled act of reading when they perform this abstraction.

I hasten to add that I consider this situation neither a scandal nor a surprise. Because the numbers and kinds of possible translation are potentially infinite (though at any given juncture in the history of criticism only a finite number will be practiced[5]), there is no *necessary* connection between reading and the endpoint of any one interpretation, and the last thing I want to do is to try to legislate one. Indeed, much of the current valuable work in cultural studies and the New Historicism depends on the interpreter doing such things as finding points of contact between literary and other cultural representations—activities that often appear unconnected to the interpreter's reading experience.[6]

Nevertheless, I believe that our conventional habits leave largely undeveloped one very rich kind of interpretive practice, one that I will call rhetorical reader-response. This practice takes from rhetorical theory the assumption that the text is a sharable medium of a multileveled communication between author and reader, and from reader-response theory the strategy of taking the reader's experience of the text as the starting point for interpretation. Its effort is to link response to interpretation by seeking textual sources for individual responses, while also acknowledging that the construal of those textual sources is influenced by the reader's subjectivity. In other words, in its way of linking reading to interpretation, rhetorical reader-response maintains both that the text constructs the reader and that the reader constructs the text, with the result that it does not believe that there is always a clear, sharply defined border between what is sharable and what is personal in reading and interpretation. Furthermore, even as the approach starts with response, it does not regard that response as something fixed beyond question but rather as something that may change and develop in the very effort to link reading and interpretation.[7] All this helps clarify the claims I want to make for what follows: when I speak of the experience of reading *Beloved* here, I am referring to my experience. Nevertheless, I will try to focus on elements of my experience that I take to be not idiosyncratic but sharable. Moreover, in this essay I am not primarily concerned with trying to specify the boundary between textual and personal sources of experience. Instead, I want to explore further the typical gap between reading and SAI in order to reconsider SAI's treatment of textual recalcitrance, a reconsideration that in turn will reveal the desires driving SAI—and both of these explorations will have significant consequences for the claims I want to make about *Beloved* and about rhetorical reader-response criticism.

3. THE DIFFICULT, THE STUBBORN, AND INTERPRETIVE DESIRE

One of the challenges and pleasures of interpretation is finding the "right translation," uncovering a code that allows us to claim cognitive understanding of the text, to hear the "click" of the numerous signals of the text rearranging themselves into our new system of intelligibility. Virtually all texts, to one degree or another, present some obstacles to the interpreter, some material that initially seems resistant to whatever translation schema the interpreter is employing. We academic interpreters naturally gravitate toward recalcitrant material, but we typically assume that all recalcitrance can yield to understanding, even if all that is finally revealed is the inevitability of recalcitrance.[8] Indeed this desire for and faith in explanation is the enabling assumption of some of our best criticism. But by always assuming that everything can be explained, we overlook the possibility that sometimes recalcitrance may not be overcome—that is, may not be overcome without some sacrifice of explanatory power. Saying that Beloved is this and this and this and that and that and that without attending to the difficulty of integrating all those identities explains Beloved in one way, but it does not explain what it is like to read and respond to her in the novel. Reading *Beloved* leads me to propose a distinction between two kinds of obstacles to understanding that result in two kinds of reading experience: The *difficult* is recalcitrance that yields to our explanatory efforts, while the *stubborn* is recalcitrance that will not yield.[9]

The first chapter of Morrison's narrative offers an encounter with the difficult. Morrison herself has offered a response-based account of her strategy, saying that she wanted her readers to experience "the compelling confusion of being there as they [the characters] are; suddenly, without comfort or succor from the 'author,' with only imagination, intelligence, and necessity available for the journey" ("Unspeakable Things" 33). Morrison's technique does, indeed, induce a "compelling confusion," one that envelops all the characters and even the setting. Questions about Sethe, Denver, Baby Suggs, the ghost, and Paul D, about their pasts, their presents, and their futures, pile up with each new sentence. Yet, with some work, including re-reading, and some patience, this confusion yields to understanding, and we can see how Morrison uses this difficulty to influence our entrance into her "imaginative world." In making us feel off-balance, she highlights many of that world's particular ground rules, including some that not all of her readers will share: in this world, ghosts are not only present but taken for granted; in this world, the past coexists with the present.

As I've already suggested, I believe that Beloved herself is a paradigm case of the stubborn. Despite the best efforts of many careful readers, her character escapes any comprehensive, coherent account. No matter how we arrange or rearrange the information about Beloved, there is always something that does not fit with the experience of everything else. We can solve the problem by following Deborah Ayer Sitter's advice to "regard Beloved as a function rather than a person" (29), advice which in effect says "change your assumptions and your expectations; stop trying to read about a person here and recognize that you are reading about a synthetic construct that Morrison can maneuver as she sees fit." But finally, following this advice seems to require neglecting the way Morrison cues us to read Beloved as both a function and a person. When we read, say, about Paul D's encounter with her in the cold house, we experience him first struggling against and then consenting not just to a function but also to a person—however enigmatic.

In the brief discussion of *Beloved*'s first chapter as an instance of the difficult, I have followed Morrison's lead and suggested some positive role, some functionality for that experience. I want to claim a similar functionality for the stubborn, a claim that highlights its paradoxical nature. On the one hand, I am identifying the stubborn as that which resists explanation; on the other, in claiming that it has a positive functionality, I am suggesting that it can yield to one kind of explanation, thereby apparently containing and confining it—and so collapsing it back into the difficult. I will say more about this paradox after trying to clarify the claim about functionality by distinguishing the stubborn and the difficult from a third kind of recalcitrance, one that lacks a positive functionality, the *erroneous*.

Again *Beloved* furnishes an example. Despite Morrison's careful planning of so much of the book, she indicates, in the first chapter, two conflicting dates for the narrative's present time action: 1873 and 1881.[10] I see no way of resolving this conflict, and apart from specious generalizations about Morrison dramatizing the difficulty of reconstructing history, I cannot find any account of its functionality.[11] The conflict is an instance of the erroneous, a small distraction (if noticed at all) that has no positive contribution to make and no functionality within Morrison's narrative. By contrast, the stubborn is an experienced recalcitrance whose very resistance to explanation contributes significantly to the experience of the larger narrative. In other words, although it cannot itself be fully comprehended, we may be able to comprehend its effects. Indeed, when the reader encounters the stubborn, the interpretive task shifts from explicating it to explaining the purpose of its recalcitrance.

Articulating the distinction between the difficult and the stubborn invites reflection on SAI's underlying desire for mastery—and articulating the paradox of the stubborn invites similar reflection about the desire of a rhetorical reader-response criticism. Whatever we do with texts, however much we admire their power, and however much we pay lip service to their inexhaustibility, the act of interpretation rests upon a desire to make texts yield up their secrets, to take possession of them. This desire to possess, as I said above, often leads to brilliant interpretive insights, but it also blinds interpretation to its own hubris. Introducing the category of the stubborn into rhetorical reader-response makes possible a recognition of that hubris. The paradox of the stubborn, however, also allows for the repression of that recognition: if we get caught up in explaining the stubborn's functionality, we can erase its elusiveness and turn its stubbornness into the Truth of the text, which we once again possess.

Letting the stubborn remain stubborn means that we accept the possibility that "the struggle to interpret and perform" a sharable world (Morrison, *Playing* xii) is one we cannot entirely win. In this light, the paradox of the stubborn can be seen as its simultaneous effect of enriching that struggle and preventing it from being completely successful.[12]

4.   ENCOUNTERING THE STUBBORN: READING/INTERPRETING *BELOVED*

A baby ghost. A spiteful, venomous baby ghost. No, a "sad" ghost (8). Or a "lonely and rebuked" one (13)? Still, a powerful baby ghost, who can make the whole house pitch. A tired breathing.

These multiple signifiers attach to Beloved and haunt or brood over her later bodily incarnation(s).

An innocent, needy twenty-year old. In need of a mother. With no wrinkles. Who comes when Sethe's water breaks. Who calls herself Beloved. Who has a scar on her neck. Who can't walk but picks up a chair single-handed. Denver's guess about her identity is also mine. But what does Beloved want? None of the previous associations seems exactly apt—she is not spiteful or venomous or powerful and, after a while, not tired. *Self-absorbed and Sethe-obsessed. Thirsty—for motherlove. "Tell me your diamonds" (58).* Her appearance is disruptive—Sethe, Denver, and Paul were moving toward some harmony—and exciting. What mysteries does she contain?

Puzzling conversation with Denver. Cross-purpose communications?

"Why you call yourself Beloved?"
. . . "In the dark my name is Beloved."
. . . "What's it like over there, where you were before? Can you tell me?"
"Dark. . . . I'm small in that place."
. . . "Tell me, how did you get here?"
"I wait; then I got on the bridge. I stay there in the dark, in the daytime, in the dark, in the daytime. It was a long time." (75)

Return from the underworld? Survival of the Middle Passage? There is a difference but what is it? As the mystery deepens, my attachment grows.

Return of the spiteful. Why strangle Sethe? Revenge? Seems more like jealousy: Sethe is thinking that she is glad to have Paul D. A warning delivered? So obscurely? But is Beloved the strangler?

She denies it when Denver asks her why, but acts guilty. Still, she claims, "I kissed her neck. I didn't choke it. The circle of iron choked it" *(101). ok, Sethe as slave. But Sethe never wore the literal iron. Is Beloved a seer then? A haunting, strangely frightening prophet.*

The Ghost of Sex. Moving Paul D. Against his conscious will. Finally coming to him in the cold house. "You have to touch me. On the inside part. And you have to call me my name" *(117). Motivation? Yes, separate Paul D from Sethe. But there's more. She wants him for herself. Why? To be Sethe's rival? Electra? And why does she have power over Paul D?* Wilt says that Beloved acts out the other characters' psychic needs; suggests Denver's desire to separate Paul and Sethe, and Paul D's need to break the lock on his tobacco tin. *Suggestive, but not finally satisfying. Beloved loses her identity in this view. Perhaps the sexual battle is the flip side of their battle when she was a ghost? And now she wins? But why can she break apart Paul D's tobacco tin when his loving Sethe hasn't yet done that? Emotions mingle here: touched by her vulnerability, haunted by her power, scared and relieved for Paul D.*

More puzzles. Beloved knows one white man. *Perhaps she is not the crawling-already? baby returned.* Beloved disappears when she accompanies Denver to the cold house. *She must be a returned ghost.* Beloved curls up in the dark and points to a face Denver can't see—"her face" which is then "Me. It's me" (124). *A middle passage ghost?* Beloved "knows" that she could wake up and find herself in pieces. *More conflicting feelings: tenderness, fear, and always the mystery.*

Sethe comes to believe that Beloved is her daughter come back to her.

Beloved never tells her story the way Denver tells hers or Sethe and Paul D rememory theirs. And Morrison, who employs a remarkably protean narrator, never offers an inside view of Beloved—until the monologue. House and Horvitz each explicate its cryptic discourse admirably. The central story it tells is that of a small girl and her mother being forced to travel on a very crowded slave ship. The girl keeps looking for her mother's face, but she loses it when the mother jumps into the sea. She is eventually put with a man who "hurts where I sleep," but she escapes from there and comes out of the blue water to see "the face that left me"— Sethe's (212, 213). As House says, the monologue supports the view that what we have been reading is a complicated case of mistaken identities. Beloved is not Denver's sister and Sethe's daughter, but a survivor of the middle passage. And as Morrison says, the desires of this independent survivor and those of Sethe and Denver meet. Perhaps stubbornness is only difficulty.

Doesn't work. Why privilege the monologue over everything else? Though things like the white man get explained (or more accurately, now have possible explanations), much is still left unexplained: the strangling, the moving of Paul D, the disappearance. Furthermore, so much of the experience of the previous twenty-one chapters depends on the *possibility* that Beloved is Sethe's daughter, that transforming the stubbornness into difficulty denies the experience.

BETTER TO THINK OF THE MONOLOGUE AS A COUNTER TO THE POWERFUL RESPONSES TO BELOVED AS DAUGHTER AND SISTER IN DENVER'S AND SETHE'S MONOLOGUES. MONOLOGUE DEEPENS STUBBORNNESS RATHER THAN TRANSFORMS IT. NOW MOVED INSIDE BELOVED'S FEAR AND CONFUSION AND PAIN—ATTACHMENT AND SYMPATHY INCREASE EVEN AS THE MYSTERY DOES.

The stubbornness persists as Beloved fades into the background and Denver moves up front. *Who is this character draining Sethe of her life?* Rushdy says the incarnation of Sethe's guilt. *Makes good sense of some things—Sethe on a hopeless quest of expiation. But Beloved-as-Guilt-Incarnate denies the experience of her monologue and simplifies the complex dynamics between Beloved, Sethe, and Denver. But her childlike selfishness complicates feelings further— understandable yet dangerous; I fear for Sethe: Beloved is too much with her. And me?*

The strange disappearance. How? Where? Is she pregnant?
Who is she in the last two pages?

5.   FROM ENCOUNTER TO FORMAL INTERPRETATION: THE ENDING OF *BELOVED*

After concluding the penultimate chapter with an intimate scene of hope and reconciliation between Sethe and Paul D, the narrator suddenly swerves to a very different spatial, temporal, and emotional stance, one that puts considerable distance between that intimate scene and the concerns of the final two pages. In them, the narrator writes a kind of elegy for Beloved that also subtly calls attention to some larger claims that Morrison herself wants to make for her narrative. The effects of attending to Beloved as stubborn are inseparable from the development of these claims as we seek to interpret the difficulties of this chapter. After the opening paragraph which effectively breaks the mood of the previous scene by discussing different kinds of loneliness (Sethe's loneliness that "can be rocked," and Paul D and Beloved's loneliness that "roams" [274]), the narrator turns her full attention to Beloved.

Everybody knew what she was called, but nobody anywhere knew her name. Disremembered and unaccounted for, she cannot be lost because no one is looking for her, and even if they were, how can they call her if they don't know her name. (274)

These sentences complicate our relation to Beloved and to the larger narrative, because they emphasize her stubbornness, and they begin to introduce the paradox of the reading/writing situation as well as to split the awareness of the authorial and narrative audiences.[13] The characters may forget Beloved, but we do not. Indeed, the narrator's insistence on bringing her back into the narrative and calling her "disremembered" paradoxically emphasizes that she is not entirely forgotten, not entirely disremembered. We cannot, however, escape the assertion of the first sentence. And since we do not know her name, we do not know her origin—and do not, cannot fully know her. The two sentences together deepen the paradox of reading Beloved: unlike the others who knew her name, we do not dismember her by "disremembering" her, but we also do not really know this woman we are remembering.

The shift to the present tense in the second sentence further complicates the reading situation. On the very first page of the narrative, the narrator has made us aware that she and her audience are contemporaries, that we exist together in a present distant from the time of the action. "In fact," she says, "Ohio had been calling itself a state *only* seventy years" (3; emphasis added). Only from a temporal vantage point of considerably later than 1873 would the narrator use that *only*. By employing the present tense here and not clearly indicating that it is the historical present, the narrator subtly includes her contemporary audience among those who are not looking for Beloved. But this very inclusion foregrounds the split between the narrative and the authorial audiences. As members of the narrative audience, we may at one level be among those who are not seeking Beloved, but at another level, by the very act of taking in the narrator's words, we are seeking her and remembering her. As members of the authorial audience, we can initially exempt ourselves from any implication in the "disremembering" or the looking because we know that Beloved is a fictional character rather than a historical person. By using the narrator to call attention to the split between audiences, Morrison is beginning to move toward some larger claims about the *kind* of story she has been telling.

Although she has claim, she is not claimed. In the place where the long grass opens, the girl who waited to be loved and cry shame erupts into her separate parts, to make it easy for the chewing laughter to swallow her all away. (274)

Again the present tense signals our inclusion. Beloved has claim on our attention, our knowledge. But her stubbornness means that she cannot be contained by our knowledge. The first sentence also conveys an implied challenge to the authorial audience. Will we claim, if not her reality, her story—with all its stubbornness? This question becomes more urgent as the narrator picks up numerous threads from Beloved's monologue—the long grass where Beloved first lost her African mother, her fear of breaking into pieces and being chewed and swallowed—and interweaves them in a metaphorical description of her erasure from history. As the narrator turns elegiac for Beloved here, Morrison also begins to draw upon the stubbornness of the character and the complex emotions the narrative has evoked to proliferate her signification and make a claim about her significance. The erasure of Beloved from history is the erasure of the small African child who lost her mother in the long grass, as well as the African American who feared she would fall apart when she lost her tooth, as well as all the slave women she comes to represent.

It was not a story to pass on. (274)

The bald statement, after white space, and with the vague "It" disrupts our reading because it is so apparently self-contradictory. Hasn't the narrator just "passed on" the story, and haven't we just spent an enormous amount of emotional energy reading it? Of course one way to naturalize the sentence is to stay in the narrative audience and read it as the indirect discourse of Beloved's community, to interpret it as their response to her appearance and disappearance. But because the white space encourages our attributing the vision and voice of the sentence to the narrator, we become aware of additional readings, even in the narrative audience. "It was not *a story* to pass on" and "it was not a story *to pass on*"—in the sense of "to pass by"—but it was something else, *a reality to be confronted.* Sethe and Denver were not able to read the story of Beloved's possible other identity. Beloved was never able to recognize the difference of Sethe's story from her African mother's. Only we have seen the irreconcilable stories and the character who cannot be contained by either; only we have felt the full range of emotions generated by her narrative. Will we adopt the attitude expressed in the indirect discourse and find the stubbornness of Beloved's character a reason not to pass on her story? Or will we accept the challenge of confronting its multiple, stubbornly shifting realities?[14]

There is yet another layer here, one that we may see more clearly in the light of both the paradox of stubbornness and the underlying desire of interpretation for mastery. In focusing so far on the productive functionality of Beloved's stubbornness, I have in a sense been making that stubbornness the key to the ending—and by extension to Morrison's narrative. I have, in other words, been turning the stubborn into the difficult—and exhibiting once again the power of interpretation's desire for mastery and possession. But even as "It was not a story to pass on" challenges the authorial audience to confront the multiple realities of Beloved, it also challenges our ability to share those realities. More particularly, I must ask how much I, as a privileged, white, male reader, see and fail to see, share and fail to share in Morrison's vision of the horrors of the middle passage, of slavery, of the intensity and desperation of Sethe's—and Margaret Garner's—motherlove. To presume mastery here would be to flaunt my hubris.

They forgot her like a bad dream. After they made up their tales, shaped and decorated them, those that saw her that day on the porch quickly and deliberately forgot her. It took longer for those who had spoken to her, lived with her, fallen in love with her, to forget, until they realized they couldn't remember or repeat a single thing she said, and began to believe that, other than what they themselves were thinking, she hadn't said anything at all. So, in the end, they forgot her too. Remembering seemed unwise. . . .

It was not a story to pass on. (274-275)

Morrison continues to implicate her audience in the narrator's statements and to press her challenge about what we will do with our reading of Beloved's story. Beloved is a painful memory even for those who knew her, because she reminds everyone of the depths of pain they endured in slavery. A white reader like myself may try to escape the pain—and any responsibility—by confessing, as I just did, the limits of his understanding. But this passage blocks that move. In reading this narrative, we—white readers, all readers—have, in a sense, lived with Beloved. Will we forget her because it is unwise to remember, unwise because remembering may entail some responsibility to her memory? At this juncture, the repetition of "It was not a story to pass on" continues the challenge in the same vein: to pass on this story is to be unwise because the story is too disturbing and too unsettling, has depths of pain that may never be plumbed. The implication about the cowardice of turning one's back is clear.

So they forgot her. Like an unpleasant dream during a troubling sleep. Occasionally, however, the rustle of a skirt hushes when they wake, and the knuckles brushing a cheek in sleep seem to belong to the sleeper. . . . They can touch it [an old photograph] if they like, but don't, because they know things will never be the same if they do.
This is not a story to pass on. (275)

The ending takes a significant turn at "however." They may forget/repress—we may forget/repress—but Beloved is not thereby erased from history. She lives on in some way. Furthermore, once we acknowledge her presence in history "things will never be the same." By having the narrator shift from "It was" to "This is" not a story to pass on, Morrison addresses the authorial audience most directly. Furthermore, the sentence is now loaded with almost as many meanings as Beloved, and it has its force precisely because Beloved has been so loaded with meanings. This is not just a story to tell for amusement; this is not a story to pass by; this is not a story to tell lightly because once you tell it things will never be the same. But this is also not a story that you will ever fully comprehend.

At this point, then, Morrison has gradually built up to some very significant claims for *Beloved*. Morrison has transformed the historical event that provided the germ of the narrative, Margaret Garner's killing her child in 1855 and expressing serenity afterwards, into an emotionally powerful fiction; in this conclusion, however, she is challenging us to treat the narrative as a species of history. In insisting on Beloved's enduring presence and the power of her story, Morrison is drawing upon the representative quality of all the possibilities that Beloved has come to stand for and be associated with: all the daughters and all the families whose lives were twisted by "the men without skin"; all those who lived under slavery and who lived with its legacy even after it was outlawed; indeed, the "sixty million and more" who died on the slave ships and to whom Morrison dedicates the book. At the same time, by concentrating the power of all these possibilities within the single character, Morrison is pointing to the depths of each: we can name the multiplicity, but we cannot claim to know it in the sense of mastering it.

By and by all trace is gone, and what is forgotten is not only the footprints but the water too and what is down there. The rest is weather. Not the breath of the disremembered and unaccounted for, but wind in the eaves, or spring ice thawing

**too quickly. Just weather. Certainly no clamor for a kiss.
Beloved. (275)**

These last two segments of the narrative complete it in an appropriately powerful way. Remaining in the present tense, the narrator details the final disappearance of Beloved and then employs the negatives to suggest her ineradicable presence beneath all denials of her. And more than that, to suggest her need to "be loved." Then finally, the narrator utters her name. The functions of this signifier are now manifold. In the immediate context, "Beloved" signals the return of the repressed. Not just ineradicably there underneath our history, she—and all those she stands for—are now produced for our contemplation and are what this narrative leaves us with. Unable to do justice to all the complex realities signified by "Beloved," we nevertheless end our reading by attending to them. Moreover, this narrative, which takes its title from this word, stands as testimony to the presence and the complexity of those realities.

At the same time, the word breaks the pattern of repetitions. "It was not a story to pass on." "It was not a story to pass on." "This is not a story to pass on." "Beloved." The eruption of the word itself exemplifies the point: not a story to pass on, but a person whose multiplicity transcends any story that can be told about her. And here the importance of the fiction comes back: her story stands in for the millions and millions of other slaves, whose lives and deaths, though not passed on in story, are just as deep, just as emotionally wrenching, just as important—and just as stubborn— as hers.

The pattern also makes "Beloved" available to be read not just as the narrator's final word but also as Morrison's final address to her readers. Just as the preacher at Beloved's funeral began by addressing his audience, "Dearly beloved," so Morrison ends by addressing us as "Beloved." The intratextual link makes it a gesture of affection and a reminder of the challenge: we are beloved, not yet Dearly Beloved. This reminder of the character's naming effectively blocks any impulse to romanticize the character even as we keep her story alive: the reminder calls back what Sethe did to get the name on the tombstone and, indeed, calls back the knowledge that "Beloved" is the tombstone marker itself. Furthermore, this reminder once again blocks any impulse to master the stubbornness of her character by pointing to the gaps that keep her from yielding to our understanding and then, by extension, to all the history that we have lost, especially to that of the sixty million and more whose names we do not know. "Everybody knew what she was called, but nobody anywhere knew her name" (274).

6.   RECURSIVENESS AND THE LIMITS OF INTERPRETATION

Beloved still eludes me, but I feel that I see more of her. I still cannot—and do not want to—transform Beloved's stubbornness into a difficulty to solve, but I comprehend some of the reasons for that stubbornness. Furthermore, just as the effort to attend to the stubborn has helped root interpretation in the experience of reading, so too has interpretation allowed for a clarification, an enrichment of that reading experience. Within this rhetorical reader-response approach, reading and interpretation, like thinking and writing, can be endlessly recursive, each one opening up the possibility of revision in what the other has just done.

Perhaps more significantly, the stubborn helps reveal the limitations of interpretation's desire for mastery, helps remind us that the effort to perform an author's world does not always have to result in a virtuoso performance for the interpretation to be valuable and enlightening. In the spirit of that recognition, I offer the conclusions of this essay not as fixed, frozen, and beyond question but as working hypotheses about complex matters. To claim any more would be to exhibit a decidedly unproductive personal stubbornness.[15]

NOTES

[1]Morrison's novel, in the short time since its publication, has already attracted a significant number of very fine interpretive essays. In addition to the essays that I draw upon here because they most directly address the question of Beloved's identity, see also Schapiro, Holloway, Finney, Henderson, and the five essays published together in the Autumn 1992 issue of *African American Review* by Sale, Demetrakopoulos, Page, Sitter, and Bell.

[2]None of the numerous essays on *Beloved* I have read shows any significant debt to reader-response theory. One of the very attractive features of Steig's fine book is how tightly he connects the experience of reading and the act of interpretation. Rabinowitz, as his title suggests, is primarily interested in the conventions that influence the experience of reading. Crosman is concerned with the different frames that we can bring to the act of interpretation. The contributors to Flynn and Schweickart's collection offer a variety of perspectives on the difference gender makes in reading.

[3]That Scholes's book won the NCTE's David Russell Award I would like to read as a sign of both its excellence and a wide acceptance of its views. In his more recent *Protocols of Reading*, Scholes redescribes interpretation as having both centripetal (in toward the text and its intentionality) and centrifugal movements (out

toward the reader and her subjectivity); in making the space for the centrifugal, he allows more play for the reader's response, yet stops far short of locating interpretation in experience. For a fuller discussion of the model Scholes sets forth in *Textual Power*, including some reservations about its heavy reliance on repetitions and oppositions, see my *Reading People, Reading Plots*.

[4]The typical code consists of (1) categories that organize the numerous signals in the language of the text into fewer, more general units; and (2) rules for combining the categories. Sometimes the categories are provided by the text (that is, "rememory" or "claiming one's freedom" or "circling" in *Beloved*); sometimes they are provided by an interpretive system the critic brings to all texts (that is, object relations; gender and power; dialogism); and sometimes they are provided by some combination of text and interpretive system (call and response; maternity and slavery). The critic then employs the rules for combining the categories and seeks to develop a coherent and comprehensive account of how the text's language (or at least some significant subset of that language) can be understood as signifying a particular set of meanings. Standard accounts of interpretive adequacy, such as those in Booth and Hirsch, usually include a criterion of "precision" or "correspondence" in addition to comprehensiveness and coherence. I do not include it here because, unlike them, I am not trying to establish the philosophical grounds of interpretive adequacy but to describe what practical critics generally do under the umbrella of interpretation. For the same reason, I will not try to sort out—and create a hierarchy among—different notions of comprehensiveness, coherence, or precision. For a fuller description of interpretation along the lines I've sketched here, see Steven Mailloux's essay on the term in Lentricchia and McLaughlin.

[5]Stanley Fish, among others, has of course argued that at any one time the institution of criticism will sanction only a limited number of translation schemes (or in Fish's language, interpretive communities). Fish's point here, whatever reservations one might have about his larger account of the profession (see Battersby), is descriptively accurate. My point is that interpretation is potentially, not actually, infinite.

[6]I recognize that this statement is open to the objection that such critics, having been trained in a certain way, are in fact basing their interpretations on their reading responses, that, for example, they read with a knowledge of the cultural networks they trace in their interpretations and so respond accordingly. Objection sustained—and indeed, I have tried to account for this possibility in my description of reading. But my point here is that the ground of the appeal in, say, Stephen Greenblatt's interpretation of *King Lear* in *Shakespearean Negotiations*, is not at all to the act of reading or viewing the play, but rather on his work of contextualizing and analogizing. His claim is not at all about what it is like to view this play, but very much about what the play can be said to mean in its cultural moment. I admire his work, but want to ask a different question: what happens when we ground our interpretations in the act of reading?

[7]The approach I am advocating here has links with the reader-response criticism of Iser and Rosenblatt and with the rhetorical poetics associated with Chicago School criticism. But I am more interested in the affective dimensions of reading than Iser or Rosenblatt, and I depart from the Chicago School's treatment of the reader as, ultimately, a property of the text.

[8]For a lively argument that recalcitrance itself is the basis of literary form and quality, see Wright. I find much of Wright's argument to be appealing but stop short of accepting his strongest claims, which seem to make recalcitrance not just a means but also the purpose of literary form.

[9]The category of the stubborn clearly has some affinities with the deconstructive notion of unreadability, especially as it has been developed by Paul de Man's rigorous analyses. But I take the concept of the stubborn in a direction different from the one he takes the notion of unreadability. Where his rhetorical concerns focus on the figures of the text, mine move to questions of author-reader relations. Where his unreadability leads to the *mise en abyme*, my stubbornness leads to a paradoxical functionality within a larger system of what can be read (as I try to demonstrate below).

[10]The fourth sentence reads, "For years each put up with the spite in his own way, but by 1873 Sethe and her daughter Denver were its only victims" (3), suggesting 1873 as the present. Then in dating the departures of Howard and Buglar from 124, the narrator says that "Ohio had been calling itself a state only seventy years when first one brother and then the next stuffed quilt packing into his hat, snatched up his shoes, and crept away from the lively spite the house felt for them" (3). Since Ohio became a state in 1803, this sentence puts their departure in 1873, which could still fit with that fourth sentence. On the next page, the narrator says first that "Baby Suggs died shortly after the brothers left" and then that Denver "was ten and still mad at Baby Suggs for dying" (4). So Denver appears to have been born in 1863. Later in the chapter, in present time, Sethe says to Paul D that Baby Suggs has been dead "Eight years now. Almost nine," which suddenly jumps the present action to 1881. That would fit with our learning that Denver is eighteen, but of course later we learn that Denver was born in 1855 during Sethe's escape from Sweet Home, so the present action must be occurring in 1873. And indeed, after the first chapter all the signals point to 1873-74 as the time of the narrative's present action.

[11]Later on Morrison gives inconsistent evidence about how long Sethe was at 124 before schoolteacher arrives: sometimes she says three weeks, other times four. Since these dates often come through a character's stream of consciousness, I believe that this inconsistency can be read as functional in its demonstration of the interaction of history and memory.

[12]Introducing this distinction between the difficult and the stubborn, or, more precisely, introducing a category called "the stubborn" (the difficult has long been our stock in trade) is of course not without its own potential problems. One critic's example of stubbornness will be another's instance of mild difficulty. The category of the stubborn could easily become a wastebasket into which tired critics—or those facing deadlines—toss their recalcitrant data. But the abuse of a thing is no argument against it. Like all interpretive hypotheses, claims about the stubborn will be subject to the scrutiny of other interpreters; those that wither under such scrutiny will turn out to be, well, not so stubborn after all. Furthermore, given the pride of place currently accorded to the ability to produce innovative close readings, I doubt that critics will rush to proclaim any given textual phenomenon as an instance of the stubborn. The risks of being wrong are too great. If another critic shows that what I take to be the stubborn is actually the difficult, then I am in the embarrassing position of having to admit that I have not read closely enough. I am less worried about the possible abuses of the concept than I am hopeful about its potential to advance the cause of tightening the connections between the experience of reading and the activity of interpretation.

[13]I borrow Rabinowitz's helpful distinction here: the narrative audience is the narrator's implied addressee, and the authorial audience is the author's ideal audience. The key difference between these two audiences at this juncture of *Beloved* is that the narrative audience believes in the reality of the character and events while the authorial audience knows that it is reading fiction. See "Truth in Fiction."

[14]For a related account of the sentence, "It was not a story to pass on," one that emphasizes Morrison's ambivalence about narrative, see Homans. Indeed, though developed independently and ultimately concerned with different issues—Homans investigates Morrison's relation to traditional narrative structures that white feminists have found to be patriarchal—my discussion of the ending has many similarities with hers.

[15]And here I would like to thank the many readers who have already contributed to the development of my ideas, especially the Faculty Novel Group in the Ohio State University English Department; the participants in my informal seminar; and Elizabeth Patnoe, Peter J. Rabinowitz, James Battersby, and Peggy Phelan.

WORKS CITED

Battersby, James L. "Relativism, Rationality, and Professionalism." *PMLA* 107 (1992): 51-64.

Bell, Bernard W. "*Beloved*: A Womanist Neo-Slave Narrative; or Multivocal Remembrances of Things Past." *African American Review* 26 (1992): 7-15.

Booth, Wayne C. *The Company We Keep*. Berkeley: U of California P, 1988.

———. *Critical Understanding: The Powers and Limits of Pluralism*. Chicago: U of Chicago P, 1979.

Crosman, Inge. *A Poetics of Reading*. Princeton: Princeton UP, 1989.

de Man, Paul. *Allegories of Reading*. New Haven: Yale UP, 1979.

Demetrakopoulos, Stephanie A. "Maternal Bonds as Devourers of Women's Individuation in Toni Morrison's *Beloved*." *African American Review* 26 (1992): 51-59.

Finney, Brian. "Temporal Defamiliarization in Toni Morrison's *Beloved*." *Obsidian II* 5 (1990): 20-36.

Fish, Stanley. *Is There a Text in This Class?* Cambridge: Harvard UP, 1980.

Flynn, Elizabeth, and Patrocinio Schweickart, eds. *Gender and Reading*. Baltimore: Johns Hopkins UP, 1986.

Greenblatt, Stephen. *Shakespearean Negotiations*. Berkeley: U of California P, 1988.

Henderson, Mae G. "Toni Morrison's *Beloved*: Re-Membering the Body as Historical Text." *Comparative American Identities: Race, Sex, and Nationality in the Modern Text*. Ed. Hortense J. Spillers. New York: Routledge, 1991. 62-86.

Hirsch, E. D., Jr. *Validity in Interpretation*. New Haven: Yale UP, 1967.

Holloway, Karla. "*Beloved*: A Spiritual." *Callaloo* 13 (1990): 516-525.

Homans, Margaret. "Feminist Fictions and Feminist Theories of Narrative." *Narrative* 2 (1994): 3-16.

Horvitz, Deborah. "Nameless Ghosts: Possession and Depossession in *Beloved*." *Studies in American Fiction* 17 (1989): 157-167.

House, Elizabeth. "Toni Morrison's Ghost: The Beloved Who Is Not Beloved." *Studies in American Fiction* 18 (1990): 17-26.

Iser, Wolfgang. *The Act of Reading*. Baltimore: Johns Hopkins UP, 1978.

Mailloux, Stephen. "Interpretation." *Critical Terms for Literary Study*. Ed. Frank Lentricchia and Thomas MacLaughlin. Chicago: U of Chicago P, 1990. 121-134.

Morrison, Toni. *Beloved*. New York: Knopf, 1987.

_____. *Playing in the Dark: Whiteness and the Literary Imagination*. Cambridge: Harvard UP, 1992.

_____. "Unspeakable Things Unspoken: The Afro-American Presence in American Literature." *Michigan Quarterly Review* 28 (1989): 1-34.

Page, Philip. "Circularity in Toni Morrison's *Beloved*." *African American Review* 26 (1992): 31-39.

Phelan, James. *Reading People, Reading Plots: Character, Progression, and the Interpretation of Narrative*. Chicago: U of Chicago P, 1989.

Rabinowitz, Peter J. *Before Reading: Narrative Conventions and the Politics of Interpretation*. Ithaca: Cornell UP, 1987.

_____. "Truth in Fiction: A Re-Examination of Audiences." *Critical Inquiry* 4 (1976): 121-141.

Rigney, Barbara. *The Voices of Toni Morrison*. Columbus: Ohio State UP, 1991.

Rosenblatt, Louise. *The Reader, the Text, the Poem*. Carbondale: Southern Illinois UP, 1978.

Rushdy, Ashraf H. A. "Daughters Signifyin(g) History: The Example of Toni Morrison's *Beloved*." *American Literature* 64 (1992): 567-597.

Sale, Maggie. "Call and Response as Critical Method: African-American Oral Traditions and *Beloved*." *African American Review* 26 (1992): 41-50.

Schapiro, Barbara. "The Bonds of Love and the Boundaries of Self in Toni Morrison's *Beloved*." *Contemporary Literature* 32 (1991): 194-210.

Scholes, Robert. *Protocols of Reading*. New Haven: Yale UP, 1989.

_____. *Textual Power*. New Haven: Yale UP, 1985.

Sitter, Deborah Ayer. "The Making of a Man: Dialogic Meaning in *Beloved*." *African American Review* 26 (1992): 17-29.

Steig, Michael. *Stories of Reading*. Baltimore: Johns Hopkins UP, 1989.

Wilt, Judith. *Abortion, Choice, and Contemporary Fiction*. Chicago: U of Chicago P, 1989.

Wright, Austin. *Recalcitrance, Faulkner, and the Professors*. Iowa City: U of Iowa P, 1989.

Wyatt, Jean. "Giving Body to the Word: The Maternal Symbolic in Toni Morrison's *Beloved*." *PMLA* 108 (1993): 474-488.

EXPERIENCING *JAZZ*

Eusebio L. Rodrigues

1.

WE MAY AS WELL ENTER THE NOVEL BY WAY of the one word title, *Jazz*, a stop consonant and a flatted monosyllable that extends into a voiced double sibilant. Like the muted soundsplash of a brush against a snare drum. "Sth, I know that woman," a woman's voice cautions in a whisper, then it suddenly drops us, without warning, into a confusing world.

The confusion arises from the speed of the telling. Fragments of information rush along unconnectedly. A woman and a flock of birds; a man both sad and happy; he has shot an eighteen-year-old girl; Violet (the voice drops briefly, between commas, to touch on the woman's name) cuts up the girl's dead face at a funeral, then hurries back to her apartment where she sets the flock free "to freeze or fly" (an unusual yoking of verbs and choices); one is a parrot that says, "I love you."

The voice, a written voice, hurtles along offering no explanations, dropping more bits of information that stubbornly refuse to come together and make sense: that the man, Joe Trace, is Violet's husband, that Violet is fifty and skinny, that the dead girl had a creamy face, that the girl has an aunt, that there's an upstairs neighbor, Malvonne. We read on impatiently, wanting to interrupt and ask questions, but this voice is in a reckless hurry to tell everything at once without stopping. It throws in additional information, about spring, about another girl, another threesome. It slows down at last, a little out of breath, hinting at some kind of mystery at the end: "What turned out different was who shot whom" (6). We read on, on, bewildered but intrigued, looking at the words, listening to their rhythm, their rhythms, seeking desperately to discover the meanings of the text. Halfway through the novel we pause to take stock, to put things together, to get our bearings.

A visual examination of the layout of *Jazz* reveals that it has no numbered chapters and no chapter titles to act as guides. The text has been cut into unnumbered unequal sections, ten of them, divided by blank pages that compel even the fast page turner to slow down. Each section is further cut into a number of unequal subsections: the first (1-21) has three subsections separated by two-line gaps; the last (219-229), seven.

Here is a musical score that has to be made to spring into audial life, into sound and rhythm and beat. The inner ear listens to what one reads, and the words begin to take wing, to leap into sound:

> Blues man. Black and bluesman. Blacktherefore blue man.
> Everybody knows your name.
> Where-did-she-go-and-why man. So-lonesome-I-could-die man.
> Everybody knows your name. (119)

A six string guitar at play. The first line sounds three chords, the tonic, the subdominant, and the dominant, combinations of "blues" and "black" and "man." Words are made to merge, like notes, to create run-on sounds. The third line continues the run-ons, the finger style playing of the individual notes of two chords that echo, and rhyme, and connect "why" and "die" but leave the connection a mystery ("man" here is not a word but an expression, an afternote). Line four is a repeat of line two ("Everybody knows your name"), and both act as chordal closures.[1] The text, vibrant with sound and rhythm, invites us, we slowly realize, to set aside Cartesian logic in order to enter a magic world that cries out for deeper modes of knowing. We flip back to pages that had sounded intriguing, but we did not know why.

Dorcas' aunt listens to the maddening new sounds that spring out of Harlem and hit her below the sash, as she puts it. A "dirty, get-on-down" music (58), a "juke joint, barrel hooch, tonk house, music" (59) that compelled hips and feet to move, a music that infuriated her "for doing what it did and did and did to her and everybody else she knew or knew about" (59). The harsh blare of the consonants, the staccato generated by the commas that insist on hesitations needed to accelerate the beat, the deliberate use of alliteration and of words repeated to speed tempo—all come together to recreate the impact of jazz.

Eighteen-year-old Dorcas, lying in bed, listens to the same intoxicating music that courses through and is part of her being:

> tickled and happy knowing that there was no place to be where somewhere, close by, somebody was not licking his licorice stick, tickling the ivories, beating his skins, blowing off his horn while a knowing woman sang ain't nobody going to keep me down you got the right key baby but the wrong keyhole you got to get it bring it and put it right here, or else. (60)

This time Toni Morrison seeks to create the very rhythms of jazz, a very specific sexual term in its origins, according to James Baldwin, as in "*jazz me, baby*" (*The Price* 650). Sexual metaphors, charged with energy, leap into life. Language is made to syncopate, the printed words loosen up and begin to move, the syntax turns liquid and flows. It is not just the jargon—licorice stick for clarinet, ivories for the piano, skins for drums—but the sounds of jazz that arise from the text and hit the ear.

The syllables "ick" and "ing" act in counterpoint. The "ick," first sounded in "t*ick*led," continues to sound, like a pair of drumsticks clicking, in l*ick*ing, l*ick*orice, st*ick*, t*ick*ing, making the submerged sexual innuendoes sound loud and clear. The participial "-ing" (set up by the first "knowing") is repeated to maintain a continuous flow of movement: licking, tickling, beating, blowing, knowing, going. Internal echo-rhymes ("where," "somewhere") and balanced repetition ("somewhere," "somebody") quicken the tempo. The tiny riff ("where somewhere, close by, somebody") with its deliberate commas, placed to compel the voice to pause, enacts a slow shimmy. The three song titles, unpunctuated, are made to run on together so that the sexual vibes, released by a "knowing" woman, are light and easy before they develop a pronounced sexual beat ("you got to get it bring it and put it right here").[2] The whole passage ends with a period that is no period, for the voice does not drop but continues to sound. "Or else" is indefinite, incomplete, it is a warning, or else a promise. It resonates, and how does one punctuate a resonance?

That the whole of *Jazz* resonates becomes clear only after we slowly discover how to respond to its rhythms. Then sentences sing, then adjectives turn into breathless run-ons. Dorcas has a "cream-at-the-top-of-the-milkpail" face (12). Violet lies under a quilt made of "no-question-about-it" satin (224). Harlem, in New York, in 1926, is a Jordan, a City of promise that the narrator trumpets forth with joy: "Here comes the new. Look out. There goes the sad stuff. The bad stuff. The things-nobody-could-help stuff" (7). Violet imagines Joe Trace and Dorcas listening to music, the girl's hand under the table, "drumming out the rhythm on the inside of his thigh, his thigh, his thigh, thigh, thigh" (95).

In *Jazz* Morrison transposes into another medium the music that sprang out of her people and expressed their joys, their sorrows, their beliefs, their psyche. This music—spirituals, blues, ragtime, jazz—has spread throughout the world in our time, and is no longer uniquely or exclusively African American. There's need now, suggests Morrison, to make fiction do what the music used to do, tell the whole wide world the ongoing story of her people. In *Beloved* she used the blues mode of fiction to conjure up and exorcise, to expiate and to pass on, the "disremembered" dark world of slaves and of slavery.[3] *Jazz* dramatizes what happened to those born after Emancipation who migrated from the rural South to the industrial cities of the North to seek both refuge and a new way of life. To transform what happened into a magical performance staged for an audience of readers Morrison had to invent (in its Latin meaning) a language and discover a new form.

She had gradually (by writing the first four novels) to make the language she inherited her very own, then transform it (in *Beloved* and in *Jazz*) into a powerful instrument that could play her music. In this, she is like Louis Armstrong, who played a number of instruments, including the cornet, before he discovered the tonal range of the trumpet (after "West End Blues"), an instrument he made his very own, according to Graham Collier, "by incorporating all manner of vibratos, glissandos, growls, shakes and gradations of tone into his technique" (10).

The range of my language determines the range of my world, says Wittgenstein. By the time she came to the writing of *Jazz*, Morrison had created a medium for herself that had a tonal stretch and an intrinsic musicality. She made the black vernacular blend harmoniously with standard English so that we do not sense awkward or obvious shifts of key. She combed out the vernacular; she purified the dialect of the tribe.[4] Words of all kinds flow smoothly along.

Black idiom does not call attention to itself, nor is the language surface disturbed by heavy abstract Latinate words. The basic voice used in *Jazz* is warm and human, reassuring, a voice of quiet authority in command of itself.

That's the kind of voice that issues out of the audible text, Morrison's tape recording of *Jazz*.[5] Very like the voice of Ma Rainey or of Bessie Smith singing the blues on early records. The words that pour out sound rich and mellow, with a lilt all their own and a steady speed. Toni Morrison's voice has a low but dynamic register. No dramatic changes of tempo occur, but there are subtle modulations and variations especially when it presents dialogue. During the exchanges between Alice Manfred and Violet (79-87, 109-114) tonal inflections—pauses, voice drops, punctuations of silence—communicate why and how the two women feel drawn to each other. Towards the end, when Felice and Violet and Joe Trace talk and offer dramatic revelations (198-216), the black vernacular with its flicks of irony, its touches of humor, its use of understatement (and quite purged of phonetic dross), comes alive and resonant.

Morrison uses many strategies to make the visual, as opposed to the audible, text resound. Her aim was, as she has said in several of her interviews, "to . . . remove the print-quality of language to put back the oral quality, where intonation, volume, gesture are all there" ("Toni Morrison," Tate 126). She wanted "to make the story appear oral, meandering, effortless, spoken" ("Rootedness" 341). She wanted to "make a truly aural novel" ("Toni Morrison," Ruas 233). The reader has to actively participate in the process of musicalizing the text before it will yield up all its meanings.

Often she uses the rhetorical device of repetition to intensify the beat in order to deepen meaning. A deceptively simple two-part statement about the Beast that "slaughtered children because it yearned to be slaughtered children" (78) has to be eye-read first, then ear-read with care. For the beat falls on the first "slaughtered" (a verb) and not on the second (an adjective) where it shifts to "children." Eight-year-old Dorcas must have seen the flames of the house in which her mother was burned alive to a crisp. But, the narrator says, "she *never said. Never said* anything about it. She went to two funerals in five days, and *never said* a word" (57; italics mine). The repetition does not merely generate the rhythm of pause and emphasis and release, it calls attention to and dramatizes the psychic wound that festers silently in the eighteen-year-old Dorcas.

Morrison generally abides by the conventions of print and rarely uses typography to convey signals to her readers. In *Jazz* only once does she juxtapose capitals, an exclamation mark, and italics to call for an increase in volume: "NO! *that* Violet is not somebody walking round town" (95). The expression, *"that* Violet," is used nineteen times in one section (89-114) to indicate a Violet powerfully affected and changed by the city. What Morrison uses as a major device is punctuation. Not of the modern kind, not one that is merely correct and grammatical, not one that aims at logic, clarity and directness of meaning. The punctuation in *Jazz* is rhythmical. It transforms the text into a musical score, it compels the use of both eye and ear; what it generates is a cadence that makes meanings vibrate. Morrison's use of the art of pointing (that's what punctuation is) enables the listening reader to descend into a deeper mode of knowing. What appears on the surface to be just the story of a sordid affair— a fifty-three-year-old man deceives his wife of thirty-three years to have a fling with an eighteen-year-old girl who soon deserts him before he shoots her at a house rent party—turns into a delicate exploration of the mystery of love.

Punctuation and repetition combine to set in motion rhythms that amplify the significance of this story. "Abandoned" by their mothers, Joe and Dorcas feel drawn to each other because of the "inside nothing" within them, a nothing that only they can fill for each other. A paragraph dramatizes the genesis of Dorcas' "inside nothing":

Maybe her nothing was worse since she knew her mother, and had even been slapped in the face by her for some sass she could not remember. But she did remember, and told him so, about the slap across her face, the pop and sting of it and how it burned. How it burned, she told him. And of all the slaps she got, that one was the one she remembered best because it was the last. She leaned out the window of her best girlfriend's house because the shouts were not part of what she was dreaming. They were outside her head, across the street. Like the running. Everybody running. For water? Buckets? The fire engine, polished and poised in another part of town? There was no getting in that house where her clothespin dolls lay in a row. In a cigar box. But she tried anyway to get them. Barefoot, in the dress she had slept in, she ran to get them, and yelled to her mother that the box of dolls, the box of dolls was up there on the dresser can we get them? Mama? (38)

This deceptively simple paragraph both conceals and reveals Morrison's superb skill as a writer. The opening sentence pours out of the narrator, easy and casual, the colloquial "sass" folding into the language flow. Four interconnected words send forth vibrations. The first two, "nothing" and "mother," stir up a double sense of loss,

Dorcas' and Joe's; the other two, "slapped" and "remember," take us into Dorcas' nothingness. What Dorcas remembers is not her mother but the slap, the last slap she got from her mother, the slap that "burned" (this verb quivers with meanings). What Dorcas really remembers and misses intensely is her dead mother's caring love. Rhythmic phrasing transforms the slap into a form of love. Words ("slap," "remember," "told") and phrases ("how it burned") are not just repeated but made to flow across sentences, like musical slurs across bars, to create continuity. Commas and periods carefully placed after the words repeated ("remember," "burned") make for subtle variations of rising and falling pitch.

The shifts in rhythm parallel the shifts in narration. The narrator of the first sentence steps aside. The second sentence, and the third, and the fourth, are channeled through the eighteen-year-old Dorcas who tells her lover about her recall of the last slap. Then the narrative becomes a torrent of sensations and feelings and detail that pours out of the eight-year-old Dorcas, who relives the incident that caused her psychic wound. The pace quickens, the tempo now increases. There are syntactic breaks, fragments and repetition across fragments ("Like the running. Everybody running"). Question marks signal the bewilderment of the eight-year-old who is frantic about her beloved clothespin dolls. Details—the bare feet, the dress, the cigar box, the dresser—make the scene vividly real, while the information about the gleaming fire engine, ready in whitetown but deliberately not dispatched, provides a political dimension of which the little girl is unaware. What she knows is that her box of dolls is in the burning house. In a state of panic she runs and screams, screams to her mother to get the dolls on the dresser. At the end the eight-year-old just screams. For her mother. We do not know what happens, nor do we need to know. The last word ("Mama?") with its question mark is more than a child's scream, it is eighteen-year-old Dorcas' intolerable cry of remembered anguish, it is a question that soars straight up despairingly into the sky, resounding silence the answer.

2.

Jazz is made up of a number of such rhythmic paragraphs, subsections and sections that together compose a musical score. The novel has a loose fluid non-Aristotelian experimental form. Not the tight, climactic, Freytag-pyramid structure of conventional fiction, but the form of a jazz piece.[6] Toni Morrison oralizes print. She also uses her language instrument to try out some daring modes and techniques of play and to create the informal, improvisatory patterning of jazz.

The visual layout—the lack of rigid chapter divisions, the unnumbered sections with blank pages in between, the unequal subsections separated by two-line gaps—appears to dissolve as word sounds begin to move. Toni Morrison produces a textual continuum by using transitional slurs and glides across sections. "In a *hat* in the morning" ends one section; "the *hat* pushed back on her forehead. . ." the next section begins (87, 89; italics mine). "Pain" opens another section, picking up the last wordsound, "pain," of the previous section (216, 219). Two words "spring" and "city" act as a *glissando* causing two sections to slide together (114, 117). "But where is *she?*", at the end of a section, is a dramatic question about Wild, the mother whom Joe hunts for in Vienna for the last time in 1906; the answer, two blank pages later, "there she is," opens the next section and refers, strangely, not to Wild but to Dorcas in 1926 in the City (184, 187).

Such carry-overs make for rhythmic flow. Unlike the clearly demarcated movements of a symphony, the sections of *Jazz* never come to a complete stop. Like nonstop sequences during a jam session, they keep moving restlessly on and on giving the text a jazz feel. For Morrison tries to approximate not only the sounds of jazz but also the patterning. The first few pages, like a twelve-bar jazz "tune" or set melody, tell in summary the whole story of Violet and Joe and Dorcas, a story repeated and modulated at the end by that of Violet and Joe and Felice, Dorcas' friend, "another true-as-life Dorcas" (197), as the narrator informs us. In between the beginning and the end are amplifications, with improvisations, variations and solo statements, a virtuoso display of jazz play. Morrison wants her fiction "to recreate play and arbitrariness in the way narrative events unfold" ("Memory" 388). *Jazz* is a shimmering network of characters and of strands of action.

The characters are cross-connected in strange ways. Joe's Dorcas (whose biblical name means "gazelle") is a city version and a repeat of the deer-eyed Wild, the mother who orphaned her newly born baby, never looked at it, or held it in her arms (170). Young Joe hunted for a mother he never could find, and then discovers there-she-is Dorcas in the City in 1926. His Violet helped Joe escape the emptiness within himself in 1893, when he fell out of a walnut tree into her life. By marrying Violet, Joe rescued her from the dark memory of her mother, Rose Dear, who had flung herself into a well in 1892.

These story strands do not assume a plot pattern. Nor do they build to a climax or climb steadily to a crescendo. The narrative sets its own pace and meanders along through place and time, shifting between the City and the country, presenting freeflowing associated events in the lives of Joe and Violet and Dorcas, wandering off at times to relate the experiences of their friends and relations. And so we get to know a whole cast of tangential characters and events seemingly unconnected. We are told what happened to Joe and Violet before the move to the City in 1906. Orphan Joe's story is connected with that of Hunters Hunter, who was present when Wild gave birth to Joe and, as a father figure, taught him hunting skills and shaped his sensibility, especially his protective regard for women.

We also come to know in some detail the story of Hunters Hunter who, as a boy, was briefly involved with a rich landowner's daughter, Vera Louise Gray. The strange by-product of their sexual escapades would have been just a "mortification" to be disposed of (178), had the baby not had radiantly golden skin and, later, gray eyes. Golden Gray was raised and spoiled by his mother in Baltimore, helped by her servant, True Belle, Violet's grandmother, who also adored the little boy with his golden curls.

At eighteen, told by his mother that his father was "a black-skinned nigger" (145), in despair perhaps at the paradox of being a white black, then told what he has to do by True Belle, Golden Gray journeys to Vienna to discover and, perhaps, to kill his father. On the way he encounters Wild and, fascinated by her, she "of luminous eyes and lips to break your heart" (155), forgets his mission of vengeance and disappears with her into the woods, after assisting at the birth of Joe. The strange story of Joe, the strange attendants at his strange birth and his unsuccessful quest for his mother, reads like a primitive folk tale with mythic overtones.

More down to earth is the interconnected story of Violet and her family, a tragic story of poverty and dispossession, with an absent father (involved in some way with the Virginia Readjusters, but of no real help to his own family) and a mother who commits suicide. It is the grandmother, True Belle, a former slave, who rescues the family from despair and teaches them the lessons of laughter and survival. She is what Morrison has termed the "advising, benevolent, protective, wise Black ancestor" ("City Limits" 39), the tribal mother in whom rests the wisdom of the race, the savior figure who propels Violet to Palestine where she meets Joe and acquires inner strength and confidence.

These intertwined strands of stories seem to lead nowhere and appear to lack coherence and pattern. Of all the characters, only Joe and Violet migrate to the City where they are involved with Malvonne, the Traces's upstairs neighbor from whom Joe rents a room for his meetings with Dorcas, and with Alice Manfred, Dorcas' aunt, who brought the eight-year-old orphan from riot-torn East St. Louis to live with her in Harlem. The other stories are incomplete. Some characters disappear. We never know what happens to Hunters Hunter—neither does Joe. Nor is the mystery of Wild and of Golden Gray ever solved. We never see them again. What we are left with is what Joe sees in 1906: a cave, sunlit and set in a rock formation above a flowing river named Treason by white folks, and unmistakable signs of domesticity and peace within (184). But where is *she*, Joe's question, triggers other questions never answered: what? who? why?

Why? we too ask. Why the strange patterning, the crazy chronology, why not focus on the story of Joe and Violet and Dorcas? Answers suggest themselves. More than just a story of three individuals, the novel, a continuation of *Beloved*, jazzifies the history of a people. Morrison extends the range of her fictional world by giving us rapid and vivid glimpses of their life in the rural South after emancipation.

The stories of Joe and Violet are set against the bleak conditions in the South at the time: segregation, the exploitation of labor by white landowners, the miserable wages paid, brutal eviction from lands and houses, the injustices and deceptions practiced on people deliberately kept illiterate. This sociopolitical context is not just background detail presented in the detached language of sociology. It is brought to dynamic life by breaking up chronology (so that time-fragments can be moved and can be kept moving) and by using light irony and wry humor to undercut the pain.

Morrison appropriates the blues mode to distance and so to intensify and refine the suffering in order to strip it of sentimentality. Four years after the dispossession, in 1892, the narrator twice tells us, Rose Dear jumped in the well and missed all the fun (99, 102). In 1901 Joe and Violet were evicted from a piece of land they had bought, but Joe does not complain, only stating, "'Like a fool I thought they'd let me keep it. They ran us off with two slips of paper I never saw nor signed'" (126). The technique is like that used in a Louis Armstrong jazz piece: "What did I do," he asks, "what did

I do, to be so black and blue?'', playing on words lightly, uncomplainingly, repeating them softly. "My only sin," he sings, "is in my skin," the echo-rhyme giving the words an ironic edge. His raspy growl with its tonal spread (on the words "do" and "black"), the accompanying groundbeat, both intensify and deepen what he means.

The rhythm changes for the presentation of the race riots of the time, but the technique does not. Facts are set down coldly, matter-of-factly, the voice never raised. Over two hundred dead in East St. Louis, the narrator tells us and then adds a deadly aside: "So many whites killed the papers would not print the number" (57). Dorcas' father is "pulled off a streetcar and stomped to death," her mother "burned crispy" (57). Joe does not elaborate on the 1917 summer riots of New York when he was almost burned alive. There were four-day hangings in Rocky Mount, the narrator tells us. But it wasn't messy at all, no, an orderly decorum was maintained: "the men on Tuesday, the women two days later" (101). A young tenor is tied to a log and castrated. The narrator focuses not on visual horror but on the grandmother, "refusing to give up his waste-filled trousers, washing them over and over although the stain had disappeared at the third rinse" (101). The obvious is never stated: that the act of repeated washing is the grandmother's way of expressing her helpless inexpressible grief. Distancing intensifies horror.

One of the ways of escape from the horror and the suffering in the South was to go north. The rhythm changes once again to present the theme of migration, of people on the move, on the go. It has a quick beat that accelerates to capture the excitement, the anxieties laced with hope, the joy and the abandon of a million people entering a land where the cities of the North dissolve into one big City, Harlem.[7] Trains carry them there, and Morrison's phrasing enacts both the rhythm of the wheels and the cascading swirl of sensations and feelings just before entry:

When the train trembled approaching the water surrounding the City, they thought it was like them: nervous at having got there at last, but terrified of what was on the other side. Eager, a little scared, they did not even nap during the fourteen hours of a ride smoother than a rocking cradle. The quick darkness in the carriage cars when they shot through a tunnel made them wonder if maybe there was a wall ahead to crash into or a cliff hanging over nothing. The train shivered with them at the thought but went on and sure enough there was ground up ahead and the trembling became the dancing under their feet. Joe stood up, his fingers clutching the baggage rack above his head. He felt the dancing better that way, and told Violet to do the same. (30)

The ten participial "-ing"s create a sensation of continuous speed; the anapestic beat is unmistakable, and nonstop like the rhythm of a train; commas, found at the beginning of the passage and reintroduced towards the end, enact the hesitations of the people, the slowdown of the train; the train itself, with its trembling and dancing carriage cars, comes alive, like the trembling (with fear and anxiety) and the dancing (with joy) people it carries along.

The jazz sequence (30-34) celebrates the frenzy of a flood of people seeking a promised haven they now can see: "The wave of black people running from want and violence crested in the 1870s; the '80s; the '90s but was a steady stream in 1906 when Joe and Violet joined it" (33). Morrison and her language turn into a one-woman band to convey the frantic search for the City of refuge. The ensemble turns a roll-call of city names into music and plays repetitions and modulations of the groundbeat: the mad rush of people escaping from "Springfield Ohio, Springfield Indiana, Greensburg Indiana, Wilmington Delaware, New Orleans Louisiana" (33), moving "west to Kansas City or Oklahoma; north to Chicago or Bloomington Indiana" (98), shuttling between cities, traveling "from Georgia to Illinois, to the City, back to Georgia, out to San Diego" (32), finally surrendering themselves to the City.

Then Morrison's solo comes through loud, clear, and unique, distinctly her own, telling the story of two to represent a million, singing the experiences of Joe and Violet as they "train-dance" into the big City (36): "They weren't even there yet and already the City was speaking to them. They were dancing. And like a million others, chests pounding, tracks controlling their feet, they stared out the windows for first sight of the City that danced with them, proving already how much it loved them. Like a million more they could hardly wait to get there and love it back" (32).

3.

This sequence initiates the setting up of the novel's major theme: the impact of their most recent move on the psyche of a people. The earlier "move," over two hundred years ago, had taken place on black slaveships from a land beyond the sea.[8] This time the journey, from the rural South—which for many of the uprooted had begun to feel like home (111)—to the industrial North, from country to city, was not as traumatic but was profound. It changed them.

In order to record and present this continuing process of change in fictional form, Morrison had to use unusual narrative strategies.

A totally objective narrator would have been too distant, too impersonal; an ordinary first-person one too involved, too limited, to understand the tribulations of a people. Morrison makes use of a number of voices and tellers. These voices blend and change, then shift into viewpoints that switch (at times in the same paragraph) and slide, then become voices again. The process of thinking turns into a point of view, then changes into a voice. A mysterious "I" enters and speaks for a while, turns objective, disappears, and re-enters again and again. We have to be alert at all times, the ear at the ready, to pick up and put together the "arrangement" of echoes of sound and meaning that these connected voices release. Morrison adapts the oral/musical mode of storytelling that relies on listening and memory.

Section four (89-114), which revolves around the activities of Violet, illustrates this mode vividly. It is late March 1926, and we enter a drugstore (Duggie's) with Violet. The narrator takes us into a Violet aware of another Violet, "*that* Violet," within her. The angles of the telling keep shifting constantly, shuttling between the Violet that was, in the country, and the Violet that is, the one whose psyche has been deformed by her twenty years in the City, so that people call her "Violent." At times Violet recalls the past briefly, she talks with Alice Manfred, at times she uses the first person (97); at other times the strange narrator slips into an "I," quite unobtrusively (101). We move back and forth in time (between 1888 and 1926) and in place (from Vesper County, Virginia, to the City), coming to know almost the whole story of Violet, bits and pieces of which we had been told in the first three sections.

We come to know details about Dorcas' funeral, about Violet's first meeting with Joe, about Rose Dear's suicide. We are now aware of the reasons behind Violet's "public craziness" (22), of the forces in her that made her pick up (not steal) the baby with the "honey-sweet, butter-colored face" (19) so that people thought she was crazy. And of the two hungers in her: the unfulfilled "mother-hunger" (108)—she and Joe didn't want babies at first; she had three miscarriages; later she sleeps with a doll in her arms—and the stories True Belle had fed Violet about the golden-skinned baby that made her yearn to be "White. Light. Young again" (208),[9] as she later confesses to Alice. Amid the whirl of detail a truth hits Violet about Joe and about herself: "Standing in the cane, he was trying to catch a girl he was yet to see, but his heart knew all about, and me, holding on to him but wishing he was the golden boy I never saw either. Which means from the very beginning I was a substitute and so was he" (97). We easily make the cross-connections: that Joe's heart drew him inevitably, via Wild, to Dorcas, and that for Violet, Joe was a substitute for Golden Gray. Perhaps Violet will be able to solve the "mystery of love" (5).

We are given more hints about the mystery. Morrison offers three sections that take us into the inner beings of three major characters, Joe, Dorcas and Felice. She does not use the Joycean stream-of-consciousness, perhaps because she wants to do more, penetrate below consciousness into the psyche. She makes use of the first-person talking voice, a voice that talks not to someone else but to one's unpolluted self. Joe talks to himself and, towards the end of his section, to Dorcas, his other self. His section, placed in quotation marks (121-135), compels us to realize how the city has changed him.

In the country, hunting in vain for Wild, having tracked her down to an isolated rock formation above a river teeming with fish, aware of the music of her unseen presence everywhere around, Joe had first whispered a loud plea to her to say something, to give him a sign, at least to show him a hand. What he got was a nothing (which lodged within him) and a resounding silence. Then desperate when four redwings (a sure sign of Wild's presence) "shot" up out of the base of a strange white-oak tree (it was entwined in its own roots as though nourishing and protecting itself), Joe had "shot" at it with an unloaded shotgun, discharging his anger harmlessly. In the City, hunting for Dorcas, who has abandoned him, Joe is driven by his hunter self to shoot her using a silencer: "But if the trail speaks, no matter what's in the way, you can find yourself in a crowded room aiming a bullet at her heart, never mind it's the heart you can't live without" (130).

Dorcas too is driven by forces the City unleashes in her. Lacking the sustenance provided by nature and by the country, cut off suddenly from her mother's nurturing love, strictly disciplined by her terrified aunt, Dorcas is a rebel, a wild creature of the City who takes in the intoxicating words of that "knowing" woman: you got to get it bring it and put it right here or else (60). Her talk to her self, just after she is shot, compresses all we need to know: "They need me to say his name so they can go after him. Take away his sample case with Rochelle and Bernadine and Faye inside. I know his name but Mama won't tell. The world rocked from a stick beneath my hand, Felice. There in that room with the ice sign in the window" (193). A dying girl talking urgently to her inner self, and to Felice, her other self, telling what she now knows about her self. Joe's sample case with its Cleopatra products dissolves into the cigar box with the clothespin dolls she had loved. The room with the ominous iceman's sign in the window becomes not just a place for assignation but one where human love, noble and pure, and almost cosmic ("the world rocked"), and warmly sexual ("a stick beneath my hand") also fleetingly manifests itself. Her love is so generous and self-sacrificial that she allows herself to bleed to death rather than reveal his name for the police to find him.[10] "Mama won't tell," she says, using a vibrant word that refers beyond herself to the primal source out of which all love springs.

The story of Dorcas reveals the tremendous impact the City makes on the young and the defenseless. It deludes them into believing that they are free to do what they want and get away with it. They do not realize the insidious "plans" of the well laid-out streets of the City that makes people do what it wants. The intoxicating rhythms of its music with its jazz beat never stop, they urge everyone every day to "come and do wrong" (67). City life is essentially street life (120). Country images, when used for city life, become charged with irony. Young men are sheiks "radiant and brutal" (120) or else "roosters" that never pursue but lie in wait for the "chicks" to pass by and find them. Country tracks for hunting become city trails as Joe discovers. The City pumps desire (34) and transforms love into a soaring "love appetite" (67). Only a nameless parrot in a cage can utter an "I love you" in the City.

Even the older women are affected by the City. Some await the arrival of "Imminent Demise" (56) or the coming of the God of Wrath. The call-and-response give-and-take of church preaching generates a jazz patterning with words repeated, questions asked, answers given:

He was not just on His way, coming, coming to right the wrongs done to them, He was here. Already. See? See? What the world had done to them it was now doing to itself. Did the world mess over them? Yes but look where the mess originated. Were they berated and cursed? Oh yes but look how the world cursed and berated itself. Were the women fondled in kitchens and the back of stores? Uh huh. (77-78)

Questions trigger staccato responses like "yes" qualified by a "but" and confirmed by an "uh huh." Lacking a wise ancestor, some turn for support to "leagues, clubs, societies, sisterhoods" (78). Others turn wild, for there's no helping hand to rely on. They arm themselves with "folded blades, packets of lye, shards of glass taped to their hands" (78) in order to attack, and to defend themselves from attack.

4.

Morrison had to create a special narrator who could survey and present the City's far-ranging impact and also maintain the jazz pace of the story. Not one who was objective (too cold, human involvement was essential), not one who was omniscient (that kind wouldn't be dramatic and couldn't produce tempo), not one of the characters (that kind would limit story range). She made use of an overarching narrator who could be both detached and involved and, perhaps, unlike the other voices and tellers, attempt to understand the significance of the story of a people, the meaning of their history.

"Sth," this narrator begins, using a cautionary female whisper. We read on wanting to discover to whom this first-person voice belongs. Our first clue is a tantalizing proclamation: "I'm crazy about this City" (7). Almost immediately the mystery deepens, for we are offered a series of strange statements:

I haven't got any muscles, so I can't really be expected to defend myself. But I do know how to take precaution. Mostly it's making sure no one knows all there is to know about me. Second, I watch everything and everyone and try to figure out their plans, their reasonings, long before they do. You have to understand what it's like, taking on a big city: I'm exposed to all sorts of ignorance and criminality. Still, this is the only life for me. (8)

Patiently we play detective, note the clues, make deductions about this narrator who tries to be self-effacing, never intrusive. No muscles: a disembodied voice perhaps, the voice of the City. It uses city idiom; its language is simple and colloquial, but not quite clear. What does it mean to take on a city, why is this the only life? I watch everything and everyone, it says. Perhaps this "I" is an all-seeing eye, all-piercing too, one that can penetrate human motives and plans. We think suddenly of the myths of Plato and of the *Bhagavad Gita*.

And then of the epigraph of *Jazz* which we had bypassed:

I am the name of the sound
    and the sound of the name.
I am the sign of the letter
    and the designation of the division.

        "Thunder, Perfect Mind,"
        The Nag Hammadi

"Thunder," a short tractate in the Nag Hammadi collection, is a revelation discourse uttered by a goddess figure whose name is

Thunder, which in Greek is feminine. Thunder is the way in which Zeus *tonans* makes his presence known on earth, a heavenly voice. In this tractate, according to Douglas M. Parrott, "Thunder is allegorized as Perfect Mind, meaning the extension of the divine into the world" (296). That it is the thunder goddess who narrates the story becomes clear at last in the first paragraph of the final section of *Jazz*, where the words "thunder" and "storm," the phrase "I the eye of the storm," and the statement "I break lives to prove I can mend them back again" are heard (219).

A strange narrator this, this female immanence of the divine, perplexing, full of contradictions, a narrator that changes as her story moves on. By the time the end draws near, she has lost the city confidence she had in herself and in her telling. At first she claims to be "curious, inventive and well-informed" (137). But then she accuses herself of being careless, stupid and unreliable (160). She bewails her racially determined mistake about Golden Gray's motive: not out of revenge related to skin color does he drive to Vienna, but because of his desperate need for a father figure and for authentic being (159). The narrator-deity hastens to mend matters. What she does is unclear: she uses her powers to invoke the spirit of love that rises mysteriously out of a well (surely the one into which Rose Dear flung herself)[11] and enters Golden Gray's being. That's why, perhaps, he and Wild go away together.

Despite all her powers, this female deity cannot really penetrate human hearts and understand what being human means. She is surprised at the way the story of Violet and Joe and Dorcas/Felice ends, for she had overestimated the powerful impact of the City and underestimated the human resilience that enables a whole people to believe they will overcome. She had expected that "one would kill the other" (220). Instead Violet and Joe come together and heal each other. Felice heals Joe by telling him that Dorcas loved him at the end, that she let herself die for his sake. Unlike Dorcas who allowed the City to shape her, Felice, urged on by the changed Violet, will not allow the world to change her self, but will make up her own world. And will be happy, as her name suggests.

At the end it is spring, a time of awakening. We now know the many implications of the question that had sounded simple at the beginning: "who shot whom" (6). We know, even though City people think that the threesome on Lenox Avenue is "scandalizing" (6), that all three have somehow managed to put their lives together. Even the invisible narrator, who has watched human beings love and heal each other, changes, released from her long isolation after she is touched (in more ways than one) by Wild's eyes and her hug, and her hand—Wild's mysterious way of showing love, perhaps (221).

Jazz doesn't solve but does celebrate instead the mystery of human love. Of human life, too. It asks questions, not cosmic questions like *unde malum*, but questions about the presence of evil in the city streets. The story of Joe and Dorcas is associated with the Garden of Eden and the apple.[12] Human beings (as Morrison's other novels, especially *Tar Baby*, imply) have to move out of Paradise to enjoy the fruit of knowledge and to experience love and pleasure and pain. After twenty years in the City, fifty-three-year-old Joe has not lost his country innocence and is still a sixteen-year-old "kid" (121), until he meets Dorcas. Through Felice, Dorcas sends Joe a cryptic message, "There's only one apple. . . . Just one" (213). The message confirms Joe's interpretation of the Eden story: "I told you again that you were the reason Adam ate the apple and its core. That when he left Eden, he left a rich man. Not only did he have Eve, but he had the taste of the first apple in the world in his mouth for the rest of his life" (133).

Violet, at fifty, aware that the place of shade without trees awaits her (110), sighs out her disappointment with life. It is Alice Manfred who tells her what to do: don't just accept life, but "make it, make it" in this world (113). Through what happened to Dorcas, Alice was taught "just how small and quick this little bitty life is" (113) and that it doesn't help to live in fear. She turns into the city version of True Belle, who taught Violet and her family how to survive, with the truth that laughter is more serious than tears.

Dorcas' "Mama?," hurled up into the overarching sky, is a question that has no answer. It is a personal cry of anguish, a cry for help. It is also the cry of a whole people seeking a way out of suffering and injustice and despair. No answers are provided. Help is perhaps possible, suggested by the word "hand," which people seek, and offer, and sometimes find, and by "love," which can rise up like a Rose Dear smile out of a dark well, and which never really dies, even in the City. And also by jazz and the blues, music that quickens the sad bird Violet bought for Joe and for their apartment, a music that can render a people's pain and so transmute and transcend it.

What all this leads to is a question not to be asked. Like jazz, *Jazz* hits us below the Cartesian belt and offers us a powerful experience that does not insist on definite meanings. Hunters Hunter stops speculating about his encounters with the mysterious Wild:

"there's no gain fathoming more" (166).[13] *Jazz* does not offer us any solutions, or even a resolution.

Like Louis Armstrong's classic "West End Blues" (1928), the novel ends with a closing ensemble of interludes and breaks and brief solos. Played in a low register, at a slow blues tempo, the seven subsections (219-229) use stretched blue notes to restate and to purify earlier experiences of joy and pain. We catch, as in a break, a glimpse of fifty-eight-year-old Alice Manfred, who has gone back to Springfield, where she has "someone who can provide the necessary things for the night" (222). We see Felice walking with slow confidence on the City streets. A musical interlude gently evokes the memory of Violet, in 1906, in the country, tired and asleep after a day's hard work, laughing and happy as she lies dreaming, with Joe watching over her protectively. Another interlude: Joe and Violet, together again, walk the streets of the City together, or lie in bed together under a satin quilt as memories filter through to them:

> Lying next to her, his head turned toward the window, he sees through the glass darkness taking the shape of a shoulder with a thin line of blood. Slowly, slowly it forms itself into a bird with a blade of red on the wing. Meanwhile Violet rests her hand on his chest as though it were the sunlit rim of a well and down there somebody is gathering gifts (lead pencils, Bull Durham, Jap Rose Soap) to distribute to them all. (224-225)

Darkness dissolves as we listen to this slow soft music that, like Joe's two-colored eyes, like Joe himself, is both sad and happy, a music of sibilants. The bloodred streak on Dorcas' shoulder turns into one of Wild's escort of redwings, while sunlight rims Rose Dear's well for Violet and a phantom father returns bearing small tokens of love (101).

The lead player then begins an improvisatory solo (226-228) using a moderate tempo. The words and notes and sounds stir our musical memories, for we have heard them all before: click and clicking, tap and snap and snapping fingers, shade and crevices, wells and the world, and golden hair, and hand. We now know better than to try to figure out what the solo means. What we experience is language trying to become music as it tries to capture the flow of human time.

At the very end the narrator-goddess, awakened by the mysterious power of human love, acutely conscious now of the "division" of the divine she had mentioned in the epigraph, intensely aware of her own aloneness and of her need for a hand and for a healing of division, utters a loud silent plea that is almost human: "If I were able I'd say it. Say make me, remake me. You are free to do it and I am free to let you because look, look. Look where your hands are. Now'' (229).[14]

NOTES

[1]The ear immediately picks up the aural counter-echo of a James Baldwin title, *Nobody Knows My Name.*

[2]Lawrence W. Levine (277) quotes lines from *Bessie Smith: Empty Bed Blues* (Columbia Records, G 30450), where Bessie lays down an ultimatum to her man: "He's got to get it, bring it, and put it right here / O' else he's gonna keep it out there."

[3]See my "The Telling of *Beloved.*"

[4]I borrow Dante's term from *De Vulgari Eloquentia* (Ed. Schapiro) and T. S. Eliot's line from *Four Quartets.*

[5]Morrison read and recorded *Jazz* (abridged by Trebbe Johnson) on two cassettes (total playing time: 3 hours) for Random House AudioBooks.

[6]Walter Ong, in *Orality and Literacy,* refers to the well-known Freytag's pyramid, an upward slope, followed by a downward slope. He also writes about oral patterning, stating that "an oral culture has no experience of a lengthy, epic-size or novel-size climactic linear plot. It cannot organize even shorter narrative in the studious, relentless climactic way that readers of literature for the past 200 years have learned more and more to expect—and, in recent decades, self-consciously to depreciate" (142-143).

[7]There are over 80 references in the novel to Harlem, which is always the City, with a capital C.

[8]Morrison smuggles in a reference to the earlier "move" in *Jazz.* Watching Alice Manfred ironing, Violet is reminded of True Belle, who always used to do the "yoke" last. At one moment Alice forgets to lift the iron off the board, and both women see their slave past in the scorch mark: "the black and smoking ship burned clear through the yoke" (113). The middle passage reverberates in this line.

[9] A faint echo of Pecola's yearning in *The Bluest Eye.*

[10]*The Harlem Book of the Dead* has, next to the photograph of a dead girl, the photographer's version of what happened to her (Van Der Zee 84):

> She was the one I think was shot by her sweetheart at a party with a noiseless gun. She complained of being sick at the party and friends said, "Well, why don't you lay down?" and they taken her in the room and laid her down. After they undressed her and loosened her clothes, they saw the blood on her dress. They asked her about it and she said, "I'll tell you tomorrow, yes, I'll tell you tomorrow." She was just trying to give him a chance to get away. For the picture, I placed the flowers on her chest.

Owen Dodson, the poet, composed a "Dorcas" poem for the book (52):

> *They lean over me and say:*
> *"Who deathed you who,*
> *who, who, who, who. . . .*
> *I whisper: "Tell you presently. . .*

> *Shortly . . . this evening. . . .*
> *Tomorrow. . .''*
> *Tomorrow is here*
> *And you out there safe.*
> *I'm safe in here, Tootsie.*

[11]Rose Dear, with her leftover smiles (161), is not just a suicide. She turns into an embodiment of "some brief benevolent love" (161) that rises out of the darkness of the well to influence others. She does not "abandon" her children, for she loves them very much. She waits for four long years after the arrival of True Belle, and only after she knows they will be looked after does she surrender to her despair.

[12]References to the Biblical story can be found on the following pages: Eve (133), apple (34, 40, 133, 134, 213), core (63, 133, 134), Eden (133, 180), Paradise (63), snake (76).

[13]We cannot violate the mystery that is Wild but can, perhaps, offer some tentative thoughts: that she is associated with a Kali-like "mother" nature; that she voices a music kin to the one the world makes which has no words (177); that she seeks refuge from modern man and his violence; that she is, according to Joe, everywhere and nowhere, like the memory of Dorcas for Violet (179, 28).

[14]My deep thanks to my colleagues Patricia O'Connor, Keith Fort, and Ray Reno for ear-reading this piece with great care (in both senses). I also thank Terence McPartland who transferred *Jazz* into the "word cruncher" set up.

WORKS CITED

Armstrong, Louis. "Black and Blue." *Satch Plays Fats*. Columbia, CL 708, 1955.

——. "West End Blues." *West End Blues*. OK 8597, 1928.

Baldwin, James. *Nobody Knows My Name*. New York: Dial, 1961.

——. *The Price of the Ticket*. New York: St. Martin's/Marek, 1961.

Collier, Graham. *Jazz*. London: Cambridge UP, 1975.

Eliot, T[homas]. S[tearns]. *Four Quartets*. New York: Harcourt, Brace, 1943.

Levine, Lawrence W. *Black Culture and Black Consciousness*. New York: Oxford UP, 1977.

Morrison, Toni. *Beloved*. New York: Knopf, 1987.

——. *The Bluest Eye*. New York: Washington Square P, 1970.

——. "City Limits, Village Values: Concepts of the Neighborhood in Black Fiction." *Literature and the Urban Experience*. Ed. Michael C. Jaye and Ann Chalmers Watts. New Brunswick: Rutgers UP, 1981. 35-43.

——. *Jazz*. New York: Knopf, 1992.

——. *Jazz*. New York: Random House AudioBooks, 1992.

——. "Memory, Creation, and Writing." *Thought* 59 (1984): 385-390.

——. "Rootedness: The Ancestor as Foundation." *Black Women Writers (1950-1980)*. Ed. Mari Evans. London: Pluto, 1985. 339-345.

——. *Tar Baby*. New York: Knopf, 1981.

——. "Toni Morrison." Interview with Claudia Tate. *Black Women Writers at Work*. Ed. Claudia Tate. New York: Continuum, 1983. 117-131.

——. "Toni Morrison." Interview with Charles Ruas. *Conversations with American Writers*. Ed. Charles Ruas. New York: Knopf, 1985. 215-243.

Ong, Walter. *Orality and Literacy*. New York: Methuen, 1982.

Parrott, Douglas M., ed. *Nag Hammadi Library in English*. Introd. and trans. George W. Macrae. Gen. ed. James M. Robinson. San Francisco: Harper and Row, 1988.

Rodrigues, Eusebio L. "The Telling of *Beloved*." *Journal of Narrative Technique* 21.2 (1991): 153-169.

Shapiro, Marianne, ed. *De Vulgari Eloquentia: Dante's Book of Exile*. Lincoln: U of Nebraska P, 1990.

Van Der Zee, James, Owen Dodson, and Camille Billops. *The Harlem Book of the Dead*. Foreword by Toni Morrison. Dobbs Ferry: Morgan and Morgan, 1978.

NOBEL LECTURE 1993

Toni Morrison

"Once upon a time there was an old woman. Blind but wise." Or was it an old man? A guru, perhaps. Or a griot soothing restless children. I have heard this story, or one exactly like it, in the lore of several cultures.

"Once upon a time there was an old woman. Blind. Wise."

In the version I know the woman is the daughter of slaves, black, American, and lives alone in a small house outside of town. Her reputation for wisdom is without peer and without question. Among her people she is both the law and its transgression. The honor she is paid and the awe in which she is held reach beyond her neighborhood to places far away, to the city where the intelligence of rural prophets is the source of much amusement.

One day the woman is visited by some young people who seem to be bent on disproving her clairvoyance and showing her up for the fraud they believe she is. Their plan is simple: they enter her house and ask the one question the answer to which rides solely on her difference from them, a difference they regard as a profound disability: her blindness. They stand before her, and one of them says, "Old woman, I hold in my hand a bird. Tell me whether it is living or dead."

She does not answer, and the question is repeated. "Is the bird I am holding living or dead?"

Still she doesn't answer. She is blind and cannot see her visitors, let alone what is in their hands. She does not know their color, gender, or homeland. She only knows their motive.

The old woman's silence is so long, the young people have trouble holding their laughter.

Finally she speaks and her voice is soft but stern. "I don't know," she says. "I don't know whether the bird you are holding is dead or alive, but what I do know is that it is in your hands. It is in your hands."

Her answer can be taken to mean: if it is dead, you have either found it that way or you have killed it. If it is alive, you can still kill it. Whether it is to stay alive, it is your decision. Whatever the case, it is your responsibility.

For parading their power and her helplessness, the young visitors are reprimanded, told they are responsible not only for the act of mockery but also for the small bundle of life sacrificed to achieve its aims. The blind woman shifts attention away from assertions of power to the instrument through which that power is exercised.

Speculation on what (other than its own frail body) that bird-in-the-hand might signify has always been attractive to me, but especially so now, thinking, as I have been, about the work I do that has brought me to this company. So I choose to read the bird as language and the woman as a practiced writer. She is worried about how the language she dreams in, given to her at birth, is handled, put into service, even withheld from her for certain nefarious purposes. Being a writer, she thinks of language partly as a system, partly as a living thing over which one has control, but mostly as agency—as an act with consequences. So the question the children put to her—"Is it living or dead?"—is not unreal because she thinks of language as susceptible to death, erasure, certainly imperiled and salvageable only by an effort of the will. She believes that if the bird in the hands of her visitors is dead, the custodians are responsible for the corpse. For her a dead language is not only one no longer spoken or written; it is unyielding language content to admire its own paralysis. Like statist language, censored and censoring. Ruthless in its policing duties, it has no desire or purpose other than maintaining the free range of its own narcotic narcissism, its own exclusivity and dominance. However moribund, it is not without effect, for it actively thwarts the intellect, stalls conscience, suppresses human potential. Unreceptive to interrogation, it cannot form or tolerate new ideas, shape other thoughts, tell another story, fill baffling silences. Official language smitheryed to sanction ignorance and preserve privilege is a suit of armor, polished to shocking glitter, a husk from which the knight departed long ago. Yet there it is: dumb, predatory, sentimental. Exciting reverence in school-children, providing shelter for despots, summoning false memories of stability, harmony among the public.

She is convinced that when language dies, out of carelessness, disuse, and absence of esteem, indifference or killed by fiat, not only she herself but all users and makers are accountable for its demise. In her country children have bitten their tongues off and use bullets instead to iterate the voice of speechlessness, of disabled and disabling language, of language adults have abandoned altogether as a device for grappling with meaning, providing guidance, or expressing love. But she knows tongue-suicide is not only the choice of children. It is common among the infantile heads of state and power merchants whose evacuated language leaves them with no access to what is left of their human instincts, for they speak only to those who obey, or in order to force obedience.

The systematic looting of language can be recognized by the tendency of its users to forgo its nuanced, complex, midwifery properties for menace and subjugation. Oppressive language does more than represent violence; it is violence; does more than represent the limits of knowledge; it limits knowledge. Whether it is obscuring state language or the faux-language of mindless media; whether it is the proud but calcified language of the academy or the commodity-driven language of science; whether it is the malign language of law-without-ethics, or language designed for the estrangement of minorities, hiding its racist plunder in its literary cheek—it must be rejected, altered, and exposed. It is the language that drinks blood, laps vulnerabilities, tucks its fascist boots under crinolines of respectability and patriotism as it moves relentlessly toward the bottom line and the bottomed-out mind. Sexist language, racist language, theistic language—all are typical of the policing languages of mastery, and cannot, do not permit new knowledge or encourage the mutual exchange of ideas.

The old woman is keenly aware that no intellectual mercenary, no insatiable dictator, no paid-for politician or demagogue, no counterfeit journalist would be persuaded by her thoughts. There is and will be rousing language to keep citizens armed and arming, slaughtered and slaughtering in the malls, courthouses, post offices, playgrounds, bedrooms, and boulevards; stirring, memorializing language to mask the pity and waste of needless death. There will be more diplomatic language to countenance rape, torture, assassination. There is and will be more seductive, mutant language designed to throttle women, to pack their throats like paté-producing geese with their own unsayable, transgressive words; there will be more of the language of surveillance disguised as research; of politics and history calculated to render the suffering of millions mute; of language glamorized to thrill the dissatisfied and bereft into assaulting their neighbors; arrogant, pseudoempirical language crafted to lock creative people into cages of inferiority and hopelessness.

Underneath the eloquence, the glamour, the scholarly associations, however stirring or seductive, the heart of such language is languishing, or perhaps not beating at all—if the bird is already dead.

She has thought about what could have been the intellectual history of any discipline if it had not insisted upon, or been forced into, the waste of time and life that rationalizations for and representations of dominance required—lethal discourses of exclusion blocking access to cognition for both the excluder and the excluded.

The conventional wisdom of the Tower of Babel story is that the collapse was a misfortune. That it was the distraction, or the weight of many languages that precipitated the tower's failed architecture. That one monolithic language would have expedited the building and heaven would have been reached. Whose heaven, she wonders? And what kind? Perhaps the achievement of Paradise was premature, a little hasty, if no one could take the time to understand other languages, other views, other narratives. Had they, the heaven they imagined might have been found at their feet. Complicated, demanding, yes, but a view of heaven as life, not heaven as postlife.

She would not want to leave her young visitors with the impression that language should be forced to stay alive merely to be. The vitality of language lies in its ability to limn the actual, imagined, and possible lives of its speakers, readers, writers. Although its poise is sometimes in displacing experience, it is not a substitute for it. It arcs toward the place where meaning may lie. When a President of the United States thought about the graveyard his country had become and said "The world will little note nor long remember what we say here. But it will never forget what they did here," his simple words were exhilarating in their life-sustaining properties because they refused to encapsulate the reality of 600,000 dead men in a cataclysmic race war. Refusing to monumentalize, disdaining the "final word," the precise "summing up," acknowledging their "poor power to add or detract," his words signal deference to the uncapturability of the life it mourns. It is the deference that moves her, that recognition that language can never live up to life once and for all. Nor should it. Language can never "pin down" slavery, genocide, war. Nor should it yearn for the arrogance to be able to do so. Its force, its felicity is in its reach toward the ineffable.

Be it grand or slender, burrowing, blasting, or refusing to sanctify, whether it laughs out loud or is a cry without an alphabet, the choice word, the chosen silence, unmolested language surges toward knowledge, not its destruction. But who does not know of literature banned because it is interrogative, discredited because it is critical, erased because alternate? And how many are outraged by the thought of a self-ravaged tongue?

Word-work is sublime, she thinks, because it is generative; it makes meaning that secures our difference, our human difference—the way in which we are like no other life.

We die. That may be the meaning of life. But we do language. That may be the measure of our lives.

"Once upon a time . . . ," visitors ask an old woman a question. Who are they, these children? What did they make of that encounter? What did they hear in those final words: "The bird is in your hands"? A sentence that gestures toward possibility or one that drops a latch? Perhaps what the children heard was "It's not my problem. I am old, female, black, blind. What wisdom I have now is in knowing I cannot help you. The future of language is yours."

They stand there. Suppose nothing was in their hands? Suppose the visit was only a ruse, a trick to get to be spoken to, taken seriously as they have not been before? A chance to interrupt, to violate the adult world, its miasma of discourse about them, for them, but never to them? Urgent questions are at stake, including the one they have asked: "Is the bird we hold living or dead?" Perhaps the question meant: "Could someone tell us what is life? What is death?" No trick at all; no silliness. A straightforward question worthy of the attention of a wise one. An old one. And if the old and wise who have lived life and faced death cannot describe either, who can?

But she does not; she keeps her secret, her good opinion of herself, her gnomic pronouncements, her art without commitment. She keeps her distance, enforces it, and retreats into the singularity of isolation, in sophisticated, privileged space.

Nothing, no word follows her declarations of transfer. That silence is deep, deeper than the meaning available in the words she has spoken. It shivers, this silence, and the children, annoyed, fill it with language invented on the spot.

"Is there no speech," they ask her, "no words you can give us that help us break through your dossier of failures? Through the education you have just given us that is no education at all because we are paying close attention to what you have done as well as to what you have said? To the barrier you have erected between generosity and wisdom?

"We have no bird in our hands, living or dead. We have only you and our important question. Is the nothing in our hands something you could not bear to contemplate, to even guess? Don't you remember being young when language was magic without meaning? When what you could say, could not mean? When the invisible was what imagination strove to see? When questions and demands for answers burned so brightly you trembled with fury at not knowing?

"Do we have to begin consciousness with a battle heroines and heroes like you have already fought and lost, leaving us with nothing in our hands except what you have imagined is there? Your answer is artful, but its artiness embarrasses us and ought to embarrass you. Your answer is indecent in its self-congratulation. A made-for-television script that makes no sense if there is nothing in our hands.

"Why didn't you reach out, touch us with your soft fingers, delay the sound bite, the lesson, until you knew who we were? Did you so despise our trick, our modus operandi, you could not see that we were baffled about how to get your attention? We are young. Unripe. We have heard all our short lives that we have to be responsible. What could that possibly mean in the catastrophe this world has become, where, as a poet said, 'nothing needs to be exposed since it is already barefaced.'? Our inheritance is an affront. You want us to have your old, blank eyes and see only cruelty and mediocrity. Do you think we are stupid enough to perjure ourselves again and again with the fiction of nationhood? How dare you talk to us of duty when we stand waist deep in the toxin of your past?

"You trivialize us and trivialize the bird that is not in our hands. Is there no context for our lives? No song, no literature, no poem full of vitamins, no history connected to experience that you can pass along to help us start strong? You are an adult. The old one, the wise one. Stop thinking about saving your face. Think of our lives and tell us your particularized world. Make up a story. Narrative is radical, creating us at the very moment it is being created. We will not blame you if your reach exceeds your grasp, if love so ignites your words they go down in flames and nothing is left but their scald. Or if, with the reticence of a surgeon's hands, your words suture only the places where blood might flow. We know you can never do it properly—once and for all. Passion is never enough; neither is skill. But try. For our sake and yours, forget your name in the street; tell us what the world has been to you in the dark places and in the light. Don't tell us what to believe, what to fear. Show us belief's wide skirt and the stitch that unravels fear's caul. You, old woman, blessed with blindness, can speak the language that tells us what only language can: how to see without pictures. Language alone protects us from the scariness of things with no names. Language alone is meditation.

"Tell us what it is to be a woman so that we may know what it is to be a man. What moves at the margin. What it is to have no home on this place. To be set adrift from the one you knew. What it is to live at the edge of towns that cannot bear your company.

"Tell us about ships turned away from shorelines at Easter, placenta in a field. Tell us about a wagonload of slaves, how they sang so softly their breath was indistinguishable from the falling snow. How they knew from the hunch of the nearest shoulder that the next stop would be their last. How, with hands prayered in their sex they thought of heat, then suns. Lifting their faces as though it was there for the taking. Turning as though there for the taking. They stop at an inn. The driver and his mate go in with the lamp, leaving them humming in the dark. The horse's void steams into the snow beneath its hooves, and its hiss and melt is the envy of the freezing slaves.

"The inn door opens: a girl and a boy step away from its light. They climb into the wagon bed. The boy will have a gun in three years, but now he carries a lamp and a jug of warm cider. They pass it from mouth to mouth. The girl offers bread, pieces of meat, and something more: a glance into the eyes of the one she serves. One helping for each man, two for each woman. And a look. They look back. The next stop will be their last. But not this one. This one is warmed."

It's quiet again when the children finish speaking, until the woman breaks into the silence.

"Finally," she says, "I trust you now. I trust you with the bird that is not in your hands because you have truly caught it. Look. How lovely it is, this thing we have done—together."

Stockholm, 8 December 1993

selected bibliography

WORKS BY TONI MORRISON

Novels

The Bluest Eye. New York: Holt, Rinehart, and Winston, 1970.
Sula. New York: Knopf, 1973.
Song of Solomon. New York: Knopf, 1977.
Tar Baby. New York: Knopf, 1981.
Beloved. New York: Knopf, 1987.
Jazz. New York: Knopf, 1992.

Other Fiction

"Recitatif." Short story. *Confirmation: An Anthology of African American Women*. Ed. Amiri Baraka and Amina Baraka. New York: Quill, 1983. 243–261.
Dreaming Emmett. Play. Performed 4 Jan. 1986 by the Capital Repertory Theater in Albany, New York.

Edited Collections

The Black Book. Comp. Middleton Harris, et al. New York: Random House, 1974.
Race-ing Justice, En-Gendering Power: Essays on Anita Hill, Clarence Thomas, and the Construction of Social Reality. Ed. Toni Morrison. New York: Pantheon, 1992.
Birth of a Nation'hood: Gaze, Script, and Spectacle in the O.J. Simpson Case. Ed. Toni Morrison and Claudia Brodsky Lacour. New York: Pantheon, 1997.

Essays and Reviews

"To Be a Black Woman." Rev. of *Portraits in Fact and Fiction*, ed.
Mel Watkins and Jay David. *New York Times Book Review* 28
March 1971: 8.

"What the Black Woman Thinks about Women's Lib." *New York
Times Magazine* 22 Aug. 1971: 14–15, 63–66.

"Behind the Making of *The Black Book*." *Black World* Feb. 1974:
86–90.

"Rediscovering Black History." *New York Times Magazine* 11 Aug.
1974: 14–24.

"Reading." *Mademoiselle* May 1975: 14.

"A Slow Walk of Trees (as Grandmother Would Say) Hopeless (as
Grandfather Would Say)." *New York Times Magazine* 4 July
1976: 104–105, 150–164.

Foreword. *The Harlem Book of the Dead*. By James Van Der Zee,
Owen Dodson, and Camille Billops. Dobbs Ferry, NY: Morgan
and Morgan, 1978. N. pag.

"Cinderella's Stepsisters." *Ms.* Sept. 1979: 41–42.

"City Limits, Village Values: Concepts of the Neighborhood in Black
Fiction." *Literature and the Urban Experience*. Ed. Michael C.
Jaye and Ann Chalmers Watts. New Brunswick: Rutgers UP,
1981. 35–43.

"Writers Together." Address given at the American Writers' Congress, 9 Oct. 1981. *Nation* 24 Oct. 1981: 396–397, 412.

"Memory, Creation, and Writing." *Thought* Dec. 1984: 385–390.

"Rootedness: The Ancestor as Foundation." *Black Women Writers
(1950–1980): A Critical Evaluation*. Ed. Mari Evans. Garden
City, NY: Anchor-Doubleday, 1984. 339–345.

"A Knowing So Deep." *Essence* May 1985: 230.

"Faulkner and Women." *Faulkner and Women: Faulkner and Yok-
napatawpha*. Ed. Doreen Fowler and Ann J. Abadie. Jackson:
UP of Mississippi, 1986. 295–302.

"The Site of Memory." *Inventing the Truth: The Art and Craft of
Memoir*. Ed. William Zinnser. Boston: Houghton Mifflin, 1987.
101–124.

"Unspeakable Things Unspoken: The Afro-American Presence in
American Literature." *Michigan Quarterly Review* 28 (1989): 1–
34.

Playing in the Dark: Whiteness and the Literary Imagination. Cambridge: Harvard UP, 1992.

"Introduction: Friday on the Potomac." *Race-ing Justice, En-*

gendering Power: Essays on Anita Hill, Clarence Thomas, and the Construction of Social Reality. Ed. Toni Morrison. New York: Pantheon, 1992. vii-xxx.

"Nobel Lecture 1993." *World Literature Today* 68 (1994): 5–8.

"On the Backs of Blacks." *Arguing Immigration: The Debate Over the Changing Face of America*. Ed. Nicolaus Mills. New York: Simon and Schuster, 1994. 97–100.

"The Official Story: Dead Man Golfing." *Birth of a Nation'hood: Gaze, Script, and Spectacle in the O. J. Simpson Trial*. New York: Pantheon, 1997. vii–xxviii.

Interviews and Profiles

"I Will Always Be a Writer." With Jessica Harris. *Essence* Dec. 1976: 54, 56, 90–92.

Toni Morrison: Profile of a Writer. Prod. and dir. Alan Benson. Ed. Melvyn Bragg. Videocassette. London Weekend Television, 1987.

Toni Morrison. Part 3 of *In Black and White: Six Profiles of African American Writers*. Dir. Matteo Bellinelli. Prod. RTSI-Swiss Television. Videocassette. California Newsreel, 1992.

"Living Memory: A Meeting with Toni Morrison." With Paul Gilroy. *Small Acts: Thoughts on the Politics of Black Cultures*. London: Serpent's Tail, 1993. 175–182.

"Toni Morrison: The Art of Fiction." With Elissa Schappell and Claudia Brodsky Lacour. *Paris Review* 128 (1993): 83–125.

Conversations with Toni Morrison. Ed. Danille Taylor-Guthrie. Jackson: UP of Mississippi, 1994.

"Interview with Toni Morrison." With Cecil Brown. *Massachusetts Review* 36 (1995): 455–473.

"Toni Morrison." With Angels Carabi. *Belle Lettres* 10.2 (1995): 40–43.

WORKS ABOUT TONI MORRISON

Books on Morrison

Bjork, Patrick Bryce. *The Novels of Toni Morrison: The Search for Self and Place Within the Community*. New York: Peter Lang, 1992.

Bloom, Harold, ed. *Toni Morrison*. New York: Chelsea House, 1990.

Butler-Evans, Elliott. *Race, Gender, And Desire: Narrative Strategies in the Fiction of Toni Cade Bambara, Toni Morrison, and Alice Walker*. Philadelphia: Temple UP, 1989.

Carmean, Karen. *Toni Morrison's World of Fiction*. Troy, NY: Whitston, 1993.

Coser, Stelamaris. *Bridging the Americas: The Literature of Paule Marshall, Toni Morrison, and Gayl Jones*. Philadelphia: Temple UP, 1995.

Furman, Jan. *Toni Morrison's Fiction*. Columbia: U of South Carolina P, 1996.

Gates, Henry Louis, Jr., and K. A. Appiah, eds. *Toni Morrison: Critical Perspectives Past and Present*. New York: Amistad, 1993.

Harding, Wendy, and Jacky Martin. *A World of Difference: An Inter-Cultural Study of Toni Morrison's Novels*. Westport, CT: Greenwood, 1994.

Harris, Trudier. *Fiction and Folklore: The Novels of Toni Morrison*. Knoxville: U of Tennessee P, 1991.

Heinze, Denise. *The Dilemma of "Double-Consciousness": Toni Morrison's Novels*. Athens: U of Georgia P, 1993.

Holloway, Karla F. C., and Stephanie A. Demetrakopoulos. *New Dimensions of Spirituality: A Biracial and Bicultural Reading of the Novels of Toni Morrison*. New York: Greenwood, 1987.

Jones, Bessie W., and Audrey L. Vinson. *The World of Toni Morrison: Explorations in Literary Criticism*. Dubuque, IA: Kendall-Hunt, 1985.

Kolmerten, Carol A., Stephen M. Ross, and Judith Bryant Wittenberg, eds. *Unflinching Gaze: Morrison and Faulkner Re-Envisioned*. Jackson: UP of Mississippi, 1997.

Mbalia, Doreatha Drummond. *Toni Morrison's Developing Class Consciousness*. Selinsgrove, PA: Susquehanna UP, 1991.

McKay, Nellie Y., ed. *Critical Essays on Toni Morrison*. Boston: Hall, 1988.

Mobley, Marilyn Sanders. *Folk Roots and Mythic Wings in Sarah Orne Jewett and Toni Morrison: The Cultural Function of Narrative*. Baton Rouge: Louisiana State UP, 1991.

Otten, Terry. *The Crime of Innocence in the Fiction of Toni Morrison*. Columbia: U of Missouri P, 1989.

Page, Philip. *Dangerous Freedom: Fusion and Fragmentation in Toni Morrison's Novels*. Jackson: UP of Mississippi, 1995.

Peach, Linden. *Toni Morrison*. New York: St. Martin's, 1995.

Rice, Herbert W. *Toni Morrison and the American Tradition: A Rhetorical Reading*. New York: Peter Lang, 1996.

Rigney, Barbara. *The Voices of Toni Morrison*. Columbus: Ohio State UP, 1991.

Samuels, Wilfred D., and Clenora Hudson-Weems. *Toni Morrison*. Boston: Twayne, 1990.

Smith, Jeanne R. *Writing Tricksters: Mythic Gambols in American Ethnic Literature*. Berkeley: U of California P, 1997.

Smith, Valerie, ed. *New Essays on* Song of Solomon. New York: Cambridge UP, 1995.

Weinstein, Philip M. *What Else but Love?: The Ordeal of Race in Faulkner and Morrison*. New York: Columbia UP, 1996.

Books That Include Morrison

Awkward, Michael. *Inspiriting Influences: Tradition, Revision, and Afro-American Women's Novels*. New York: Columbia UP, 1991.

——. *Negotiating Difference: Race, Gender, and the Politics of Positionality*. Chicago: U of Chicago P, 1995.

Baker, Houston A., Jr., with Elizabeth Alexander and Patricia Redmond. *Workings of the Spirit: The Poetics of Afro-American Women's Writing*. Chicago: U of Chicago P, 1991.

Barksdale, Richard K. *Praisesong of Survival: Lectures and Essays, 1957–89*. Urbana: U of Illinois P, 1992.

Bell, Bernard W. *The Afro-American Novel and its Tradition*. Amherst: U of Massachusetts P, 1987.

Braxton, Joanne M., and Andrée Nicola McLaughlin, eds. *Wild Women in the Whirlwind: Afra-American Culture and the Contemporary Literary Renaissance*. New Brunswick: Rutgers UP, 1990.

Budick, Emily Miller. *Engendering Romance: Women Writers and the Hawthorne Tradition, 1850–1990*. New Haven: Yale UP, 1994.

Byerman, Keith E. *Fingering the Jagged Grain: Tradition and Form in Recent Black Fiction*. Athens: U of Georgia P, 1985.

Campbell, Jane. *Mythic Black Fiction: The Transformation of History*. Knoxville: U of Tennessee P, 1986.

Christian, Barbara T. *Black Feminist Criticism*. New York: Pergamon, 1985.

——. *Black Women Novelists: The Development of a Tradition, 1892–1976*. Westport, CT: Greenwood, 1980.

Cooey, Paula M. *Religious Imagination and the Body: A Feminist Analysis*. New York: Oxford UP, 1994.

Cornell, Drucilla. *Beyond Accommodation: Ethical Feminism, Deconstruction, and the Law*. New York: Routledge, 1991.

Daly, Brenda O., and Maureen T. Reddy, eds. *Narrating Mothers: Theorizing Maternal Subjectivities*. Knoxville: U of Tennessee P, 1991.

de Weever, Jacqueline. *Mythmaking and Metaphor in Black Women's Fiction*. New York: St. Martin's, 1992.

Dixon, Melvin. *Ride Out the Wilderness: Geography and Identity in Afro-American Literature*. Urbana: U of Illinois P, 1987.

Dubey, Madhu. *Black Women Novelists and the Nationalist Aesthetic*. Bloomington: Indiana UP, 1994.

Evans, Mari, ed. *Black Women Writers (1950–1980): A Critical Evaluation*. Garden City, NY: Anchor-Doubleday, 1984.

Freeman, Barbara C. *The Feminine Sublime: Gender and Excess in Women's Fiction*. Berkeley: U of California P, 1995.

Gallop, Jane. *Around 1981: Academic Feminist Literary Theory*. New York: Routledge, 1992.

Gilroy, Paul. *The Black Atlantic: Modernity and Double Consciousness*. Cambridge: Harvard UP, 1993.

Griffin, Farah Jasmine. *"Who Set You Flowin'?": The African-American Migration Narrative*. New York: Oxford UP, 1995.

Hernton, Calvin. *The Sexual Mountain and Black Women Writers*. New York: Anchor-Doubleday, 1987.

Hirsch, Marianne. *The Mother/Daughter Plot: Narrative, Psychoanalysis, Feminism*. Bloomington: Indiana UP, 1989.

Holloway, Karla F. C. *Moorings and Metaphors: Figures of Culture and Gender in Black Women's Literature*. New Brunswick: Rutgers UP, 1992.

Hubbard, Dolan. *The Sermon and the African American Literary Imagination*. Columbia: U of Missouri P, 1994.

Jones, Gayl. *Liberating Voices: Oral Tradition in African American Literature*. Cambridge: Harvard UP, 1991.

Kubitschek, Missy Dehn. *Claiming the Heritage: African-American Women Novelists and History*. Jackson: UP of Mississippi, 1991.

Ledbetter, Mark. *Victims and the Postmodern Narrative, or Doing Violence to the Body: An Ethic of Reading and Writing*. New York: St. Martin's, 1995.

McDowell, Deborah E. *"The Changing Same": Black Women's Literature, Criticism, and Theory*. Bloomington: Indiana UP, 1995.

Pryse, Marjorie, and Hortense J. Spillers, eds. *Conjuring: Black Women, Fiction and Literary Tradition*. Bloomington: Indiana UP, 1985.

Rubenstein, Roberta. *Boundaries of the Self: Gender, Culture, Fiction*. Urbana: U of Illinois P, 1987.

Schapiro, Barbara A. *Literature and the Representational Self*. New York: New York UP, 1994.

Scruggs, Charles. *Sweet Home: Invisible Cities in the Afro-American Novel*. Baltimore: Johns Hopkins UP, 1993.

Singh, Amritjit, Joseph T. Skerrett, and Robert E. Hogan, eds. *Memory, Narrative, and Identity: New Essays in Ethnic American Literature*. Boston: Northeastern UP, 1994.

Smith, Valerie. *Self-Discovery and Authority in Afro-American Narrative*. Cambridge: Harvard UP, 1987.

Spillers, Hortense J., ed. *Comparative American Identities: Race, Sex, and Nationality in the Modern Text*. New York: Routledge, 1991.

Wade-Gayles, Gloria. *No Crystal Stair: Visions of Race and Sex in Black Women's Fiction*. New York: Pilgrim P, 1984.

Walker, Melissa. *Down from the Mountaintop: Black Women's Novels in the Wake of the Civil Rights Movement, 1966–1989*. New Haven: Yale UP, 1991.

Wall, Cheryl A., ed. *Changing Our Own Words: Essays on Criticism, Theory, and Writing by Black Women*. New Brunswick: Rutgers UP, 1989.

Wallace, Michele. *Invisibility Blues: From Pop to Theory*. New York: Verso, 1990.

Werner, Craig H. *Playing the Changes: From Afro-Modernism to the Jazz Impulse*. Urbana: U of Illinois P, 1994.

Wilentz, Gay. *Binding Cultures: Black Women Writers in Africa and the Diaspora*. Bloomington: Indiana UP, 1992.

Willis, Susan. *Specifying: Black Women Writing the American Experience*. Madison: U of Wisconsin P, 1987.

Winsbro, Bonnie C. *Supernatural Forces: Belief, Difference, and Power in Contemporary Works by Ethnic Women*. Amherst: U of Massachusetts P, 1993.

Wisker, Gina, ed. *Black Women's Writing*. New York: St. Martin's, 1993.

Selected Articles

Askeland, Lori. "Remodeling the Model Home in *Uncle Tom's Cabin* and *Beloved*." *American Literature* 64 (1992): 785–805.

Babbitt, Susan E. "Identity, Knowledge, and Toni Morrison's *Beloved*: Questions about Understanding Racism." *Hypatia* 9.3 (1994): 1–18.

Badt, Karin L. "The Roots of the Body in Toni Morrison: A *Mater* of 'Ancient Properties.'" *African American Review* 29 (1995): 567–577.

Bell, Bernard W. "*Beloved*: A Womanist Neo-Slave Narrative; or Multivocal Remembrances of Things Past." *African American Review* 26 (1992): 7–15.

Berger, James. "Ghosts of Liberalism: Morrison's *Beloved* and the Moynihan Report." *PMLA* 111 (1996): 408–420.

Boudreau, Kristin. "Pain and the Unmaking of Self in Toni Morrison's *Beloved*." *Contemporary Literature* 36 (1995): 447–465.

Bowers, Susan. "*Beloved* and the New Apocalypse." *Journal of Ethnic Studies* 18.1 (1990): 59–77.

Branch, Eleanor. "Through the Maze of the Oedipal: Milkman's Search for Self in *Song of Solomon*." *Literature and Psychology* 41.1–2 (1995): 52–84.

Brenkman, John. "Politics and Form in *Song of Solomon*." *Social Text* 39 (1994): 57–82.

Butler-Evans, Elliott. "The Politics of Carnival and Heteroglossia in Toni Morrison's *Song of Solomon* and Ralph Ellison's *Invisible Man*: Dialogic Criticism and African American Literature." *The Ethnic Canon: Histories, Institutions, and Interventions*. Ed. David Palumbo-Liu. Minneapolis: U of Minnesota P, 1995. 117–139.

Christian, Barbara. "Fixing Methodologies: *Beloved*." *Cultural Critique* 24 (1993): 5–15.

Cormier-Hamilton, Patrice. "Black Naturalism and Toni Morrison: The Journey Away from Self-Love in *The Bluest Eye*." *MELUS* 19.4 (1994): 109–127.

Dittmar, Linda. "'Will the Circle Be Unbroken?' The Politics of Form in *The Bluest Eye*." *Novel* 23 (1990): 137–155.

Duvall, John N. "Doe Hunting and Masculinity: *Song of Solomon* and *Go Down, Moses*." *Arizona Quarterly* 47.1 (1991): 95–115.

Farrell, Susan. "'Who'd He Leave Behind?': Gender and History in Toni Morrison's *Song of Solomon*." *Bucknell Review* 39.1 (1995): 131–150.

Goldman, Anne E. "'I Made the Ink': (Literary) Production and Reproduction in *Dessa Rose* and *Beloved*." *Feminist Studies* 16 (1990): 313–330.

Hardack, Richard. "'A Music Seeking its Words': Double-Timing and Double-Consciousness in Toni Morrison's *Jazz*." *Black Warrior Review* 19.2 (1993): 151–171. Rpt. in *Callaloo* 18 (1995): 451–471.

Holloway, Karla F. C. "*Beloved*: A Spiritual." *Callaloo* 13 (1990): 516–525.

Keenan, Sally. "'Four Hundred Years of Silence': Myth, History, and Motherhood in Toni Morrison's *Beloved*." *Recasting the World:*

Writing after Colonialism. Ed. Jonathan White. Baltimore: Johns Hopkins UP, 1993. 45–81.

Kuenz, Jane. "*The Bluest Eye*: Notes on History, Community, and Black Female Subjectivity." *African American Review* 27 (1993): 421–431.

Lewis, Charles. "The Ironic Romance of New Historicism: *The Scarlet Letter* and *Beloved* Standing in Side by Side." *Arizona Quarterly* 51.1 (1995): 32–60.

Liscio, Lorraine. "*Beloved*'s Narrative: Writing Mother's Milk." *Tulsa Studies in Women's Literature* 11 (1992): 31–46.

Middleton, Joyce Irene. "Orality, Literacy, and Memory in Toni Morrison's *Song of Solomon*." *College English* 55 (1993): 64–75.

Moglen, Helene. "Redeeming History: Toni Morrison's *Beloved*." *Cultural Critique* 24 (1993): 17–40.

Mohanty, Satya P. "The Epistemic Status of Cultural Identity: On *Beloved* and the Postcolonial Condition." *Cultural Critique* 24 (1993): 41–80.

Paquet, Sandra Pouchet. "The Ancestor as Foundation in *Their Eyes Were Watching God* and *Tar Baby*." *Callaloo* 13 (1990): 499–515.

Rimmon-Kenan, Shlomith. "Narration, Doubt, Retrieval: Toni Morrison's *Beloved*." *Narrative* 4 (1996): 109–123.

Rody, Caroline. "Toni Morrison's *Beloved*: History, 'Rememory,' and a 'Clamor for a Kiss.'" *American Literary History* 7 (1995): 92–119.

Rushdy, Ashraf H. A. "Daughters Signifyin(g) History: The Example of Toni Morrison's *Beloved*." *American Literature* 46 (1992): 567–597.

Sale, Maggie. "Call and Response as Critical Method: African-American Oral Traditions and *Beloved*." *African American Review* 26 (1992): 41–50.

Sitter, Deborah Ayer. "The Making of a Man: Dialogic Meaning in *Beloved*." *African American Review* 26 (1992): 17–29.

Stockton, Kathryn Bond. "Heaven's Bottom: Anal Economics and the Critical Debasement of Freud in Toni Morrison's *Sula*." *Cultural Critique* 24 (1993): 81–118.

Stryz, Jan. "The Other Ghost in *Beloved*: The Spectre of *The Scarlet Letter*." *Genre* 24 (1991): 417–434.

Trace, Jacqueline. "Dark Goddesses: Black Feminist Theology in Morrison's *Beloved*." *Obsidian II* 6.3 (1991): 14–30.

Travis, Molly Abel. "*Beloved* and *Middle Passage*: Race, Narrative, and the Critic's Essentialism." *Narrative* 2 (1994): 179–200.

Walther, Malin LaVon. "Toni Morrison's *Tar Baby*: Re-Figuring the

Colonizer's Aesthetics." *Cross-Cultural Performances: Differ-ences in Women's Re-Visions of Shakespeare*. Ed. Marianne Novy. Urbana: U of Illinois P, 1993. 137–149.

Wolff, Cynthia Griffin. " 'Margaret Garner': A Cincinnati Story." *Mas-sachusetts Review* 32 (1991): 417–440.

Wong, Shelley. "Transgression as Poesis in *The Bluest Eye*." *Call-aloo* 13 (1990): 471–481.

Wyatt, Jean. "Giving Body to the Word: The Maternal Symbolic in Toni Morrison's *Beloved*." *PMLA* 108 (1993): 474–488.

Bibliographies

Alexander, Harriet S. "Toni Morrison: An Annotated Bibliography of Critical Articles and Essays, 1975–1984." *CLA Journal* 33 (1989): 81–93.

Fikes, Robert, Jr. "Echoes from Small Town Ohio: A Toni Morrison Bibliography." *Obsidian* 5.1–2 (1979): 142–148.

Folsom, Tonya. "Toni Morrison Bibliography: 1990–1993." *Toni Morrison Society Newsletter* 1.1 (1994): 8–11.

Middleton, David L. *Toni Morrison: An Annotated Bibliography*. New York: Garland, 1987.

contributors

Barbara T. Christian is Professor of African American Studies at the University of California, Berkeley, where she helped found the doctoral program in African Diasporic Studies. She is the author of *Black Women Novelists: The Development of a Tradition* (1980), which won the Before Columbus Foundation American Book Award in 1983, and of *Black Feminist Criticism* (1985); she has also edited a casebook on Alice Walker's "Everyday Use" (1994). Her essays on African American women writers and African American literature and theory have appeared in such journals as *Women's Studies*, *Cultural Critique*, *Callaloo*, the *Journal of Ethnic Studies*, *NWSA Journal*, and *Feminist Studies*. Most recently she has served as the contemporary editor of the first *Norton Anthology of African American Literature* (1996) and has coedited a collection titled *Female Subjects in Black and White: Psychoanalysis, Race, and Feminism* (1997) with Elizabeth Abel and Helene Moglen.

Marianne DeKoven, Professor of English and Director of the Institute for Research on Women at Rutgers University, is the author of *A Different Language: Gertrude Stein's Experimental Writing* (1983) and *Rich and Strange: Gender, History, Modernism* (1991). She has published essays on Stein, Joyce, crime fiction, modernism, and other theoretical topics in *Contemporary Literature*, *Women's Studies*, *ELH*, *New Literary History*, *Studies in the Literary Imagination*, and *LIT*. Her essay on Morrison and Doctorow comes from her current project: a book on the sixties and the transition to postmodernism.

Dwight A. McBride, a University of California President's Postdoctoral Fellow in the UCLA Department of English, recently completed a dissertation titled "Impossible Witnesses: Restrictive and Resistive Discourses on Nineteenth Century Slavery and Abolitionism." He will join the University of Pittsburgh as an Assistant Professor of English in the fall of 1997.

Patricia McKee's essay on *Sula* comes from her current research interest: a book on spatial conceptions of race and gender in James, Faulkner, and Morrison. Professor of English at Dartmouth College, she has published *Heroic Commitment in Richardson, Eliot, and James* (1986) and *Public and Private Experience in the British Novel* (forthcoming) as well as essays on William Faulkner and Henry James.

Richard C. Moreland, Associate Professor of English and Director of Graduate Studies at Louisiana State University, is the author of *Faulkner and Modernism: Rereading and Rewriting* (1990). His essay for this collection is part of a book-length study of cross-cultural encounters in Twain, Eliot, Ellison, and Morrison.

Rafael Pérez-Torres is the author of *Movements in Chicano Poetry—Against Myths, Against Margins* (1995) as well as essays on multiculturalism and postmodernism, Chicano identity, John Rechy, and Morrison. Associate Professor of Chicano Studies at University of California, Santa Barbara, he is currently at work on a book manuscript that examines the influence *mestizaje* and racial politics have had on Chicano cultural production.

Nancy J. Peterson, Assistant Professor of English and American Studies at Purdue University and assistant editor of *Modern Fiction Studies*, has published essays on Louise Erdrich and Margaret Atwood. Her essay for this collection comes from a book she is completing on contemporary North American women writers and the crisis in historical memory.

James Phelan, Professor of English and Chair of the English Department at Ohio State University, is currently working on a study of narrative dynamics that focuses on *Beloved* and J. M. Coetzee's *Waiting for the Barbarians*. He is the author of *Narrative as Rhetoric: Technique, Audiences, Ethics, Ideology* (1996), *Beyond the Tenure Track* (1991), *Reading People, Reading Plots* (1989), and *Worlds from Words* (1981). He has also edited or coedited several books on narrative theory and is the editor of *Narrative*, the journal of the Society for the Study of Narrative Literature.

Eusebio L. Rodrigues has published a book-length study of Saul Bellow, *Quest for the Human: An Exploration of Saul Bellow's Fiction* (1981), as well as articles on Morrison, William Faulkner, William Gass, Graham Greene, and E. M. Forster. Professor of English at Georgetown University, he is completing a historical novel set in sixteenth-century India titled *Love and Samsara*.

Judylyn S. Ryan, Assistant Professor of English, teaches African diaspora literatures at Rutgers University and has published several articles on Morrison. She is currently at work on a book manuscript, *Foundation of Ancient Power: Spirituality and/as Ideology in Black Women's Fiction and Film*, begun during her postdoctoral fellowship year in the Women's Studies in Religion Program at Harvard Divinity School.

Caroline M. Woidat earned her Ph.D. in English at Vanderbilt University, where she completed a dissertation entitled "The Indian in the Mirror: White Women Writers and the Native American Other." Currently a lecturer in English at SUNY-Geneseo, she teaches courses in Native American literature and poetry writing.

Library of Congress Cataloging-in-Publication Data

Toni Morrison : critical and theoretical approaches / edited by
    Nancy J. Peterson.
        p.   cm. — (A Modern fiction studies book)
    Includes bibliographical references and index.
    ISBN 0-8018-5701-5 (acid-free paper). — ISBN 0-8018-5702-3
    (pbk. : acid-free paper)
    1. Morrison, Toni—Criticism and interpretation.   2. Women and
literature—United States—History—20th century.   3. Afro-
American women in literature.   4. Afro-Americans in literature.
I. Peterson, Nancy J.   II. Series.
PS3563.08749Z898 1997
813'.43—dc21   97-13838
                                                                          CIP

Toni Morrison.

10/98

$48.50

DATE